DR. RON & MARSHA HARVELL

WATCHMAN
on the
WALL

DAILY DEVOTIONS FOR
PRAYING GOD'S WORD
OVER THOSE YOU LOVE

The WATCHMAN *on the* WALL

Daily Devotions for Praying God's Word Over Those You Love

DISCLAIMER: These devotions are reflections of personal faith as they relate to contemporary events and do not represent the views of the Department of Defense or the United States Air Force.

Printed in the USA

Cover Design & Layout by Wendy K. Walters | www.wendykwalters.com

ISBN (Hardcase): 978-0-9916104-3-3

ISBN (Paperback): 978-0-9916104-4-0

ISBN (Kindle): 978-0-9916104-5-7

ISBN (eBook): 978-0-9916104-6-4

Library of Congress Control Number: 2014951174

Published By

Xaris Publications
Amarillo, Texas

To Contact the Authors:

www.GodsGreaterGrace.com

DEDICATION

To our mamas,
Jean Mills and Gloria Harvell

You have unceasingly prayed for us
even before God formed us in your wombs.
Our establishment in the LORD's plans
is His answer to your prayers.
Thank you for faithfully, prayerfully watching over us.

"True prayer is measured by weight, not by length. A single groan before God may have more fullness of prayer in it than a fine oration of great length."

—C. H. SPURGEON

CONTENTS

INTRODUCTION

by Marsha Harvell

Pick up your Bible. You are holding in your hand the greatest prayer book ever written. It contains everything you would ever want or need to pray for someone.

For the next 366 days, you are going to mine the Word of God for treasure verses you can pray for yourself and others. You will be able to say the words confidently because they will be the very Words of God that contain God's will. By the end of the year, you will be in the holy habit of finding Bible verses to pray, so for the rest of your life, you can constantly pray God's Words back to Him.

Prayer is a gift and a privilege from the LORD. It is amazing the God of all creation not only gives you permission to talk to Him but desires to converse with you, to be in intimate nonstop communication with you. Proverbs 3:32 says the LORD is intimate with the upright. *Intimate* in this verse carries within its meaning the idea of sitting on a couch with a friend and engaging in rich personal conversation. God is drawing you into that kind of relationship with Him.

God is also calling you to be a prayer warrior for the sake of others. Isaiah 62:6-7 says God has appointed watchmen who all day and all night never keep silent. They keep talking and talking to God about Jerusalem. They remind God of His promises, of His good Word, of His good name. They refuse to back down or take a break, and they do not give God rest. These watchmen are tirelessly determined to pray until God does what He promised to do, and that is to establish Jerusalem and make her a praise in the earth.

The LORD is an establisher. *Establish* is a powerful word. It means to make stable and constant, to be firm and fastened, to be settled and secure, to be directed and fixed aright, to be enduring and steadfast.

In the Bible, Jerusalem is not the only thing God has or will establish. Others are:

- The earth—Psalm 119:90; Jeremiah 33:2; Isaiah 45:18
- The mountains—Psalm 65:6
- The heavens—Proverbs 3:19; 8:27
- Equity—Psalm 99:4
- His faithfulness—Psalm 89:2
- His throne and sovereignty—Psalm 103:19
- The steps of a good man— Psalm 37:23; 40:2; 119:133; Proverbs 16:9
- The children and descendants of the LORD's servants—Psalm 102:28
- The work of your hands—Psalm 90:17
- The making and fashioning (establishing) of you—Psalm 119:73
- A steadfast spirit in you—Psalm 51:10
- Your ways—Psalm 119:5
- Your plans—Proverbs 16:3
- You in righteousness—Isaiah 54:14
- You in truth—2 Peter 1:12
- Your heart without blame in holiness— 1 Thessalonians 3:11-13
- Your calling to His eternal glory in Christ— 1 Peter 5:8-11

God wants to establish you and those you love. God invites you to be part of the establishment by praying for those He is establishing. Who in your life does God need to make stable and steadfast in righteousness, truth, and holiness? Do you love that person enough to pray for them until God establishes them and makes them a praise in the earth?

Picture the watchmen on the walls as they keep watch over Jerusalem. The watchmen can see what is going on inside the city, and they can see approaching enemies. From their position on the walls, they are literally praying over Jerusalem.

Their prayers offer protection to the inhabitants of the city. Like shepherds keeping watch over their flock by night (Luke 2:8), pray over those you love and picture the protective hand of God covering them in answer to your prayers.

I began praying Bible verses over my family when our children were babies. Everyday I would pray at least one verse over them. One of the verses I have prayed hundreds of times is: "I am confident of this very thing, that He who began a good work in you will perfect it until the day of Christ Jesus" (Philippians 1:6).

My husband and I have been married for 30 years; our children love the LORD and are married to spouses who love Jesus. They have children who are being raised to love and serve God faithfully. God is being true to His Word and perfecting His work in my family.

It is a privilege to be a watchman on the wall for my husband, children, and grandchildren. It is a joy to see God fulfilling His promises. However, beware it is not an easy job to be a watchman. There have been seasons in my family's life when all I could do was hunker down in the Word of God and pray, pray, pray for God to change situations and people's thoughts, hearts, and attitudes. Everything around me was screaming, "This is going to turn out bad!" God taught me how to read and pray His Word in faith over the situation. He taught me how to pray without ceasing, how to pray believing God's will would be done, how to pray until God was glorified.

I am challenging you to ask God for whom He has appointed you to be a faithful, prayerful watchman. Are you willing to take no rest for yourself and give God no rest until He establishes that person? If you are willing to be a watchman on the wall, let's get started. You are about to live an amazing year with the LORD that will have eternal impact on you and those you love.

As you begin this journey as a faithful, prayerful watchman, I pray Ephesians 3:14-21 over you.

For this reason I bow my knees before the Father,
from whom every family in heaven and on earth derives its name,
that He would grant you, according to the riches of His glory, to be
strengthened with power through His Spirit in your inner man,
so that Christ may dwell in your hearts through faith;
and that you, being rooted and grounded in love,
may be able to comprehend with all the saints what is
the breadth and length and height and depth,
and to know the love of Christ which surpasses knowledge,
that you may be filled up to all the fullness of God.
Now to Him who is able to do far more abundantly
beyond all that we ask or think,
according to the power that works within us,
to Him be the glory in the church and in Christ
Jesus to all generations forever and ever.
Amen~

HELPFUL HINTS FOR USING THE WATCHMAN ON THE WALL

by Dr. Ron Harvell

I have a few words of encouragement and helpful habits to offer you as you pray. Each devotion in *The Watchman on the Wall* begins with a chapter from the Bible to be read. For the devotional and prayer to be fully understood, it is important to read the entire Bible chapter. If you read all of the suggested chapters, you will read nearly 1/3 of the Bible in a year. With a few exceptions, the devotions flow directly through entire books of the Bible.

Start your day by reading and praying God's Word. This will tune your spiritual ears to hear the LORD say to you, "This is the way; walk in it" (Isaiah 30:21). Having your "connect with God time" only at night is like a violinist tuning their violin after the concert is over. *The Watchman on the Wall* is a good devotion book to use in the mornings or throughout the day as you walk with the LORD.

The Watchman on the Wall is also a good Bible study and prayer guide to use for family devotions or other group gatherings. Praying with friends and family can bring tremendous joy as you see those you are praying for changed by God! The daily prayers are easily modified to 'we' and 'us' in place of '_____and me.'

A Charge to Men

Men, take the lead in being a watchman on the wall praying for your family. I have witnessed the value of sentries on the walls in Afghanistan and Iraq. They are literally protecting those who live within the walls. Evil is real. And God is greater than evil. Most of you would physically die to protect your families from an outside intruder. I want to challenge you to die to yourself and your work for a few minutes of each day to pray for God's blessings on those you love. You can use this book to stand in the gap for them (Ezekiel

22:30). If you are married, consider asking your wife to be a faithful, prayerful watchman with you. What a powerful team you will be! If she is asking you to read and use *The Watchman on the Wall*, then take your place on the wall with her and lead your family in prayer.

Stand firm! Stay faithful! See the Glory of the LORD as He answers your prayers!

On your walls, O Jerusalem,
I have appointed watchmen;
All day and all night they
will never keep silent.
You who remind the LORD,
take no rest for yourselves;
And give Him no rest
until He establishes
And makes Jerusalem a
praise in the earth.
ISAIAH 62:6-7, NASB

JANUARY 1

Please read Isaiah 62.

Meditate on verses 6-7.

> *On your walls, O Jerusalem, I have appointed watchmen;*
> *all day and all night they will never keep silent.*
> *You who remind the LORD, take no rest for yourselves,*
> *and give Him no rest until He establishes*
> *and makes Jerusalem a praise in the earth.*

Isaiah 62 is for prayer warriors. It is God's will for people to be established, settled, stable, and steadfast in Him. God wants faithful watchmen who will remind Him of that truth day and night. God declared in Ezekiel 22:30-31, "I searched for a man among them who would build up the wall and stand in the gap before Me for the land, so that I would not destroy it, but I found no one. Thus I have poured out My indignation on them; I have consumed them with the fire of My wrath; their way I have brought upon their heads."

Do your prayers make a difference in the lives of those you love? God says they do. In fact, He wants you to constantly remind Him about those you want Him to establish, and He is not pleased when no one is willing to be that watchman for others. Do not grow weary and lose heart. It is God's will for your family to be established in Him. It is God's will for you to pray it into reality.

Pray Isaiah 62:6-7 over yourself and those for whom you stand guard as a faithful, prayerful watchman, inserting their name in the blank.

> *"LORD, You have appointed me*
> *a watchman on the wall of* Todd Hall.
> *All day and all night I will not keep silent.*
> *I will remind You, LORD,*
> *and I will take no rest for myself,*
> *and I will give You no rest*
> *until You establish and make them a praise in the earth.*
> *Because of Your name, Jesus~"*

Please read Colossians 3. *— Discussed, in context of slavery. To pray a debt.*

Meditate on verse 16a.

Let the Word of Christ richly dwell within you.

Colossians 3 is rich with verses to pray over your family. As you learn how to let the Word of Christ live in you, try to memorize a short verse or phrase from the Bible, meditate on it, praying it over yourself and others all day long. For example: "Let the Word of Christ richly dwell within my family; let the Word of Christ richly dwell within my family..." The more you do this, the more God's Word will be dwelling within you. As needs arise, you will already have a verse hidden in your heart that will come to mind to pray immediately over that specific person and situation.

Pray Colossians 3:15-16 over yourself and those for whom you stand guard as a faithful, prayerful watchman (Isaiah 62:6-7).

"Let the peace of Christ rule in __Todd__ *and my heart.*
Let us be thankful.
Let the Word of Christ richly dwell within us with all wisdom,
teaching and admonishing one another
with psalms and hymns and spiritual songs,
singing with thankfulness in our hearts to You, God.
In Your name, Jesus~"

✳ Do not focus on Be Kind earthly thing. Forgive one another.

Please read Luke 1.

Meditate on verses 1-4.

> *Inasmuch as many have undertaken to compile an account*
> *of the things accomplished among us,*
> *just as they were handed down to us*
> *by those who from the beginning*
> *were eyewitnesses and servants of the Word,*
> *it seemed fitting for me as well,*
> *having investigated everything carefully from the beginning,*
> *to write it out for you in consecutive order,*
> *most excellent Theophilus;*
> *so that you may know the exact truth*
> *about the things you have been taught.*

Meticulous Luke wrote a consecutive account of the life of Jesus and the church. It is recorded in the Bible in the books of Luke and Acts. For the next 52 days, you will read and pray exact Truth, the chapters written by God through Luke, His servant of the Word (Luke 1:2). What a gift God gave you in His Word!

Luke 1 is filled with treasures to pray. Take time to find the verses God wants you to pray specifically for those you love. For example, Luke 1:17 is good to pray over someone who needs to be brought to obedience to Christ. "LORD, turn the heart of _____ back to their children and turn _____, who is disobedient, to the attitude of the righteous. Make them people prepared for You."

Pray Luke 1:6 over yourself and those for whom you stand guard as a faithful, prayerful watchman (Isaiah 62:6-7).

*"LORD, please let _____ and me
be like Zacharias and Elizabeth,
righteous in Your sight,
walking blamelessly in all the commandments
and requirements of You.
In Your name, Jesus~"*

Please read Luke 2.

Meditate on verse 26.

*And it had been revealed to him by the Holy Spirit
that he would not see death before he had seen the LORD's Christ.*

Simeon could depart this earthly life in peace once he had seen God's salvation. As he held Jesus in his arms, he blessed God for allowing him to see the LORD's Christ before he saw death (Luke 2:26-30).

There is only one way to depart this earthly life in peace. You must see God's salvation. You must hold Jesus in your arms as the gift of grace that is salvation. You must see the LORD's Christ before you die.

Think of the people you know who would not depart in peace if they were to die today. Pray Luke 2:26 over them as their faithful, prayerful watchman (Isaiah 62:6-7).

*"Holy Spirit, let _____ see Christ
before they see death.
In Your name, Jesus~"*

Please read Luke 3.

Meditate on verse 8a.

Therefore bear fruits in keeping with repentance.

John the Baptist was an "in your face" preacher. He called the people a "brood of vipers" (Luke 3:7) and told them not to rely on their pedigree for salvation (Luke 3:8). The people responded by asking John what they should do to bear fruits in keeping with repentance and to be in a state of expectation for the coming of Christ (Luke 3:10, 15).

Contrast the people's reaction to Herod's response when John reprimanded him for the wicked things he had done. Herod added to his wicked deeds by locking John up in prison (Luke 3:19-20).

How do you respond when God confronts you about sin? Do you ask Him what to do to bear fruits in keeping with repentance? Or in rebellion to the Holy Spirit, do you add to the wicked things you are doing by continuing in disobedience to God?

Pray Luke 3:8,10,15, and 20 over yourself and those for whom you stand guard as a faithful, prayerful watchman (Isaiah 62:6-7).

> *"LORD, as _____ and I live*
> *in a state of expectation of Your return,*
> *tell us what to do to bear*
> *fruits in keeping with repentance.*
> *Do not let us add to the wicked things we have done.*
> *In Your name, Jesus~"*

Please read Luke 4.

Meditate on verse 1.

Jesus, full of the Holy Spirit, returned from the Jordan
and was led around by the Spirit in the wilderness.

Luke recorded interesting contrasts in this chapter. Jesus, full of the Holy Spirit, was being led in the power of the Holy Spirit (Luke 4:14). The people in Nazareth were full of rage and driving Jesus out of their city (Luke 4:28-29). The people in Capernaum were amazed by Christ's teaching and did not want Him to go away from them (Luke 4:32,42).

What are you full of? How are you responding to Jesus Christ?

Pray Luke 4:1, 14, and 42 over yourself and those for whom you stand guard as a faithful, prayerful watchman (Isaiah 61:6-7).

"LORD, please let _____ and me
be full of Your Holy Spirit;
let us be led by Your Spirit
in the power of Your Spirit.
May we be like those from Capernaum,
never wanting You to leave us.
In Your name, Jesus~"

Please read Luke 5.

Meditate on verse 5.

> *Simon answered and said,*
> *"Master, we worked hard all night and caught nothing,*
> *but I will do as You say and let down the nets."*

Have you ever worked hard and accomplished nothing? Peter was frustrated that his hard work had not paid off. But Peter was willing to obey his Master Jesus and do whatever He told him to do. Peter's obedience to Jesus paid off; the nets were so full of fish they began to break. James and John were with Peter, and these three men were so seized with amazement by Jesus Christ they left everything and followed Him.

This is the appropriate response to Jesus when He intersects your life:

- Be seized with amazement
- Do as He says
- Leave everything (from your old life)
- Follow Him

Pray Luke 5:1,5,9, and 11 over yourself and those for whom you stand guard as a faithful, prayerful watchman (Isaiah 61:6-7).

> *"LORD, may _____ and I listen to Your Word.*
> *Let us be seized with amazement*
> *by what You are doing in our lives.*
> *May we do as You say,*
> *leave everything, and follow You.*
> *In Your name, Jesus~"*

Read Luke 6. As you do, notice the timing of events and everything that Jesus does. Remember Luke wrote in consecutive order (Luke 1:3-4).

Meditate on verse 46.

Why do you call Me, "LORD, LORD,"
and do not do what I say?

Do you call Jesus "LORD"? Do you obey Him? A *lord* is a master, a person possessing supreme power and authority. No wonder Jesus questioned His disciples about why they were calling Him "LORD." They called Jesus their LORD, but they did not obey Him as a LORD must be obeyed. After asking the question, Jesus immediately defined what it meant to call Him "LORD." If Jesus is your LORD, you will:

- Come to Him
- Hear His Words
- Do His Words

Pray Luke 6:46-48 over yourself and those for whom you stand guard as a faithful, prayerful watchman (Isaiah 62:6-7).

"May _____ and I call You "LORD"
and do what You say.
Jesus, help us come to You,
hear Your Words, and act on them.
Jesus, build our spiritual houses.
May we dig deep and lay our foundation on You, our Rock.
When a flood occurs and the torrent bursts against our homes,
may they be unshakeable
because we have built in Your name, Jesus~"

JANUARY 9

Please read Luke 7.

Meditate on verse 30a.

But the Pharisees and the lawyers
rejected God's purpose for themselves.

In this chapter, God taught about soldiers and slaves who obeyed their Roman centurion master (Luke7:8). He taught about a sinful woman who loved Jesus so much she wept at His feet, wiped His feet with her hair, and anointed His feet with perfume that traditionally might have been bought by her family for her wedding day (Luke 7:37-38). Contrast the response of the Pharisees when Christ intersected their lives.

God had Luke weave these events together in his carefully written account (Luke 1:3) so you can decide who you are going to be like: those who acknowledged God in faith and received His healing, forgiveness, and peace, or those who chose to take offense at Jesus and rejected God's purpose for their lives.

Pray Luke 7:8, 30, and 50 over yourself and those for whom you stand guard as a faithful, prayerful watchman (Isaiah 62:6-7).

> *"LORD, may _____ and I*
> *be faithful servants of Yours,*
> *obeying Your commands to*
> *"Go!" "Come!" and "Do this!"*
> *Do not let us reject Your purpose for our lives.*
> *May we hear You say,*
> *"Your faith has saved you; go in peace."*
> *In Your name, Jesus~"*

Please read Luke 8.

Pay careful attention to the repeated words *hear* and *listen*.

Meditate on this phrase from verse 18.

So take care how you listen.

Have you ever been told you have ears that look like a member of your family? Our daughter has one ear that looks like her daddy's ear and one ear that looks like mine—it is obvious she is our daughter! Jesus said those who hear the Word of God and do it are His mother and brothers (Luke 8:21). The way you listen makes it obvious whether or not you belong to Christ. So, do you have ears that look like the ears of Jesus?

Did you notice in verse 25 that even the winds and the water hear and obey Jesus Christ? "Oh, LORD, may I listen and obey You like the wind and water do!"

Pray Luke 8:15 over yourself and those for whom you stand guard as a faithful, prayerful watchman (Isaiah 62:6-7).

> *"LORD, please let _____ and me be seed in good soil.*
> *Let us hear Your Word with honest and good hearts;*
> *let us hold it fast and bear fruit with perseverance.*
> *In Your name, Jesus~"*

I encourage you to go back and read this chapter with the purpose of finding verses that specifically speak to the needs of your family. I have made several notes in the margin of my Bible that say, "LORD, please do this in my family!"

Please read Luke 9.

Meditate on verse 23.

> *And He was saying to them all,*
> *"If anyone wishes to come after Me,*
> *he must deny himself,*
> *and take up his cross daily*
> *and follow Me"*

In this chapter, Jesus taught what it means to follow Him:

- 9:1 — Know that Jesus will give you the power and authority you need to follow Him.
- 9:3 — Be willing to leave all your earthly belongings.
- 9:20 — Know who you are following – The Christ of God.
- 9:23 — Deny yourself, die to yourself daily, and follow Jesus.
- 9:57-62 — Follow Jesus with no "buts"—no "buts" about your stuff, your routine, your traditions, or your relationships.

Pray Luke 9:44 and the above verses over yourself and those for whom you stand guard as a faithful, prayerful watchman (Isaiah 62:6-7).

> *"LORD, let these Words sink into _____ and my ears.*
> *Let us be willing to deny ourselves,*
> *take up our cross daily,*
> *(dying to things, routines, traditions, and*
> *what other people might think),*
> *and follow You.*
> *You will give us all the power and authority we need.*
> *Thank You, Jesus~"*

Please read Luke 10 with the purpose of finding verses to pray specifically for those you are guarding. The chapters in Luke are long, but if you take about 15 minutes to prayerfully read a chapter, you and those you love will reap eternal results.

Meditate on verse 39.

> *She had a sister called Mary,*
> *who was seated at the LORD's feet,*
> *listening to His Word.*

Picture Mary gazing into the loving eyes of her LORD, watching His lips form every Word, listening intently, not wanting to miss even an inflection. She was so absorbed by what Jesus said, she did not hear the preparations going on in the kitchen. Martha wanted Jesus to scold her sister for not helping. He instead admonished Martha for being worried and bothered and had Luke describe her as distracted.

Who are you? If the LORD were describing you, what would He say? Would He call you distracted, worried, and bothered? Or would He say you are choosing the one necessary thing, the good part of living life with Jesus—the privilege of listening to His Word?

Pray Luke 10:39-42 over yourself and those for whom you stand guard as a faithful, prayerful watchman (Isaiah 62:6-7).

> *"LORD, let _____ and me not be distracted, worried,*
> *and bothered about so many things.*
> *Let us not take for granted*
> *the privilege of listening to Your Word.*
> *Your Word is the one thing necessary for living.*
> *It is the good part.*
> *Thank You that Your Word*
> *will never be taken away from us.*
> *In Your name, Jesus~"*

Please read Luke 11.

Meditate on verses 21 and 28b.

When a strong man, fully armed, guards his own house,
his possessions are undisturbed.
Blessed are those who hear the Word of God
and observe it.

In this chapter, Jesus addressed people who prided themselves in knowing the Word of God: scribes, Pharisees, lawyers, even Christ's disciples who were hearing the Word of God every day. Jesus wanted people to know they were blessed when they heard the Word of God AND observed it. When you observe the Word of God, you put it into practice; you do what it tells you to do.

Interestingly, the Greek word (the original language of the New Testament) translated as *observe* in Luke 11:28 is the same Greek word that is translated as *guards* in verse 21. Jesus was making the point that to truly guard your home and family, you must observe His Word.

Evaluate your life. Are you merely a deluded hearer of the Word, or are you an effectual doer (James 1:22,25)? Are you guarding yourself and those you love by obeying God and His Word?

Pray Luke 11:21 and 28 over yourself and those for whom you stand guard as a faithful, prayerful watchman (Isaiah 62:6-7).

"LORD, make _____ and me strong in You.
May we be fully armed with Your Word,
so we can guard our homes.
Keep our families undisturbed.
Let us hear AND observe Your Word.
In Your name, Jesus~"

Please read Luke 12.

Meditate on verses 29-32. Jesus is talking.

> *And do not seek what you will eat*
> *and what you will drink, and do not keep worrying*
> *for all these things the nations of the world eagerly seek;*
> *but your Father knows that you need these things.*
> *But seek His Kingdom, and these things will be added to you.*
> *Do not be afraid, little flock,*
> *for your Father has chosen gladly to give you the Kingdom.*

What are you worried about right now? What are you fearful of right now? Read and reread Luke 12:22-35. Keep reading it until you know and believe what Jesus is telling you. The Words of Christ will bring healing to your soul. "Do not be afraid, little flock, for your Father has chosen gladly to give you the Kingdom."

Amazing! God loves you so much!

Pray Luke 12:29-32 over yourself and those for whom you stand guard as a faithful, prayerful watchman (Isaiah 62:6-7).

> *"LORD, You already know what _____ and I need.*
> *Help us stop worrying and being afraid.*
> *Father, You have chosen gladly to give us the Kingdom.*
> *May we constantly seek it.*
> *As we do, thank You for Your promise*
> *to add to us everything we need.*
> *In Your name, Jesus~"*

Please read Luke 13.

Meditate on verse 13.

> *And He laid His hands on her;*
> *and immediately she was made erect again*
> *and began glorifying God.*

Jesus healed a woman bound by Satan for eighteen years. She was bent double and could not straighten up at all.

Sin does the same thing to you. It binds you, bends you double, and makes you unable to straighten up at all. When you allow Christ to take control, He will free you, straighten you up, heal you, and release you from the bondage of sin.

Pray Luke 13:11-16 over yourself and those for whom you stand guard as a faithful, prayerful watchman (Isaiah 62:6-7).

> *"LORD, please free _____ and me*
> *from the sin that has us bent double*
> *and unable to straighten up at all.*
> *Free us from our sin sickness.*
> *Release us from this bond*
> *and make us erect in You.*
> *For Your glory's sake, God~"*

Please read Luke 14.

Meditate on this phrase from verse 35.

He who has ears to hear,
let him hear.

Do you have ears to hear Jesus Christ? Jesus had lots of things for you to hear in this chapter. Please reread it. Before you do, pray for God to give you the ears of Christ that can and will listen to God. Pray to have the heart of Christ that will love God more than self and anyone else. Pray to have the obedience of Christ that will give up any and everything to be His disciple.

Pray Luke 14:10,17,27, and 33 over yourself and those for whom you stand guard as a faithful, prayerful watchman (Isaiah 62:6-7).

"LORD, You have given the invitation:
'Come; for everything is ready now.'
May _____ and I come to You
not seeking a place of honor.
Make us Your disciples
as we come after You,
carrying our cross,
dying to self.
May we come
giving up everything
to be Your disciples.
In Your name, Jesus~"

Please read Luke 15.

Meditate on verse 32.

> *But we had to celebrate and rejoice,*
> *for this brother of yours was dead and has begun to live,*
> *and was lost and has been found.*

Are there people for whom you are praying? Are you praying for them to come to Christ? Perhaps they have wandered away from God like a lost sheep. Perhaps they are lost and need to be found by Jesus like a lost coin. Perhaps they have squandered the riches of the Father and want to return to Him in humility. Perhaps they pride themselves as always being with the Father, yet need a heart of compassion like Christ's.

Pray Luke 15:17 and 20 over yourself and those for whom you stand guard as a faithful, prayerful watchman (Isaiah 62:6-7).

> *"LORD, please let _____ come to their senses!*
> *Thank You for feeling compassion for us*
> *even when we are still a long way off.*
> *Thank You for seeing us,*
> *running to us,*
> *embracing and kissing us.*
> *Father, give me Your compassion for others.*
> *In Your name, Jesus~"*

Please read Luke 16.

Meditate on verse 10.

> *He who is faithful in a very little thing*
> *is faithful also in much;*
> *and he who is unrighteous in a very little thing*
> *is unrighteous in much.*

This chapter contains some teachings that may be difficult to understand. Verse 10, however, is not difficult to understand and tells you what is important to God: faithfulness and righteousness. It is important to God that you are faithful and righteous in the very little things, even the things the world would say are not important. Little things are a big deal to God. Take some time to examine your life. Ask God to show you tiny areas where you need to be more faithful and more righteous.

Pray Luke 16:10 over yourself and those for whom you stand guard as a faithful, prayerful watchman (Isaiah 62:6-7).

> *"LORD, please make _____ and me*
> *faithful in the very little things*
> *so we will be faithful in much.*
> *Make us righteous in little things*
> *so we will be righteous in much.*
> *Because You are faithful and righteous, Jesus~"*

Please read Luke 17.

Meditate on verse 10.

> *So you too, when you do all the things*
> *which are commanded you, say,*
> *"We are unworthy slaves;*
> *we have done only that*
> *which we ought to have done."*

Do you ever get a case of the "oughts"? "I ought to be appreciated." "I ought to get paid." "I ought to be noticed." "I ought to be treated with more respect." "I ought … I ought … I ought …"

The Bible says you ought to do everything God tells you to do. He even gives Himself as the example of how you ought to do it. "Have this attitude in yourselves which was also in Christ Jesus, who … emptied Himself taking the form of a bond-servant" (Philippians 2:5-7).

Serve others for the sake of Christ. Examine your heart. Do you have any ulterior motives?

Pray Luke 17:10 over yourself and those for whom you stand guard as a faithful, prayerful watchman (Isaiah 62:6-7).

> *"Jesus, You ought not to have died for _____ and me.*
> *Help us to follow in Your steps with this attitude:*
> *After we have done everything You commanded us,*
> *may we say, 'We are unworthy slaves;*
> *we have done only that which we ought to have done.'*
> *In Your name, Jesus~"*

Please read Luke 18.

Meditate on verses 1 and 38.

Now He was telling them a parable
to show that at all times
they ought to pray and not to lose heart.
And he called out, saying,
"Jesus, Son of David, have mercy on me!"

Do you ever grow weary in prayer? Satan wants you to give up praying for people and situations. God tells you to wear Him out with your petitions (Luke 18:5). "Give the LORD no rest until He establishes ..." (Isaiah 62:7).

What is weighing heavy on your heart today? God wants you to cry out to Him. The blind man in Luke 18 kept crying out to Jesus to have mercy on him. Jesus responded by asking the blind man what he wanted done for him. The man told Jesus his need to see, and immediately Jesus caused him to regain his sight.

Amazing! It is no coincidence chapter 18 ends with a real life example of someone praying at all times and not losing heart.

Pray Luke 18:38-39 over yourself and those for whom you stand guard as a faithful, prayerful watchman (Isaiah 62:6-7).

"Jesus, Son of David,
have mercy on _____ and me!
Son of David,
have mercy on _____ and me!"

Please read Luke 19.

Meditate on verses 30-31.

> *Go into the village ahead of you;*
> *there, as you enter you will find a colt tied*
> *on which no one yet has ever sat;*
> *untie it and bring it here.*
> *If anyone asks you, "Why are you untying it?"*
> *you shall say, "The LORD has need of it."*

Jesus entered, not only Jerusalem, but the week of His life when He became the sin of all mankind (2 Corinthians 5:21). He walked from Jericho through the desolate Judean wilderness, to a mountain outside of Jerusalem. He then mounted a colt that had never been ridden in its life, rode down the steep mountain on a winding road, through a valley, up another hill into the gates of Jerusalem. He chose to make His triumphal entry into the most important week in the history of the world on an untamed donkey. Twice Luke recorded that the LORD needed that donkey. The moment that donkey's Creator sat on it, the untamed beast maneuvered up and down steep paths, with crowds of people cheering and tossing cloaks and palm branches in front of its face; all the while, performing brilliantly because it was under the control of Christ.

That donkey is the picture of your life. Before Jesus, you were an untamed beast, a wild donkey of a person, but Jesus needed you. He needed to be in a relationship with you, so He chose and tamed you, and He goes with you on the winding up and down paths of life.

You are praying for people who appear to be wild donkeys. Jesus has need of them, too. Pray for them to come under Christ's control.

Pray Luke 19:6, 9, and 48 over those for whom you stand guard as a faithful, prayerful watchman (Isaiah 62:6-7).

"LORD, make _____ like Zaccheus,
who received You gladly.
Let salvation come to their house.
May they hang on to every Word You say.
In Your name, Jesus~"

Please read Luke 20.

Meditate on verse 13.

> *The owner of the vineyard said,*
> *"What shall I do?*
> *I will send my beloved son;*
> *perhaps they will respect him."*

Do you respect Jesus? Do your thoughts, words, and actions show you really respect Jesus Christ, or are you like the spies sent by the scribes and chief priests who pretended to be righteous? God knows your heart. Be honest with yourself and Him.

Pray Luke 20:17-18 over yourself and those for whom you stand guard as a faithful, prayerful watchman (Isaiah 62:6-7).

> *"Jesus, You are the Chief Cornerstone.*
> *Please let _____ and me build our lives on You.*
> *As we fall on You,*
> *break to pieces all the areas of our life*
> *where we are pretending to be righteous.*
> *Rebuild us to live in honor and respect of You.*
> *In Your name, Jesus~"*

Please read Luke 21.

Meditate on verse 28.

> *But when these things begin to take place,*
> *straighten up and lift up your heads*
> *because your redemption is drawing near.*

This chapter is full of end-time prophecies declared by Jesus. Some of them have been fulfilled, like verse 6 in 70 AD, and others are happening even as you read this, like verses 25-26.

This chapter is also filled with commands to you from Jesus, like verse 28. "Straighten up and lift up your heads because your redemption is drawing near."

Ask God to show you areas in your life where you need to straighten up. Your time on earth is short. It is time to lift up your head and fix your eyes on Christ.

Pray Luke 21:8, 28, 31, 34, and 36 over yourself and those for whom you stand guard as a faithful, prayerful watchman (Isaiah 62:6-7).

> *"LORD, do not let _____ and me be misled.*
> *Help us to straighten up, lift up our heads,*
> *and recognize that Your Kingdom is near.*
> *Let us be on our guard,*
> *so our hearts will not be weighed down*
> *with dissipation, drunkenness, and the worries of life.*
> *Let us keep on the alert at all times,*
> *praying at all times*
> *that we may have strength to escape*
> *all these things that are about to take place.*
> *In order to stand before You, Jesus-"*

Please read Luke 22.

Meditate on verse 32.

> *But I have prayed for you,*
> *that your faith may not fail;*
> *and you, when once you have turned again,*
> *strengthen your brothers.*

Imagine Jesus Himself praying for you like He prayed for Peter. Jesus does pray for you that way. Hebrews 7:25 says Jesus is able to save you forever because He always lives to make intercession for you. Jesus is living to always pray for you. Meditate on that truth.

Jesus not only prays for you, He commands you to pray. Twice in Luke 22, Jesus issued a command to pray: "Pray that you may not enter into temptation" (Luke 22:40, 46).

Jesus prayed and prayed and prayed in this chapter. He prayed immediately (v. 41). He prayed fervently (v. 44). He prayed for others (v. 32). He prayed for the will of His Father to be done (v. 42).

Heed the command of Christ to pray and follow His example of how to pray.

Pray Luke 22:40-44 and 46 over yourself and those for whom you stand guard as a faithful, prayerful watchman (Isaiah 62:6-7).

> *"LORD, help _____ and me to pray*
> *so we will not enter into temptation.*
> *Teach us to pray like You,*
> *immediately and fervently.*
> *May Your will be done, not ours.*
> *In Your name, Jesus~"*

Please read Luke 23.

Meditate on verse 21.

> *But they kept on calling out, saying,*
> *"Crucify, crucify Him!"*

How do you respond to Jesus? Are you like the people in Luke 23:21? Does your lifestyle betray Jesus and treat Him as if you wish He were dead?

Or are you like those in Galatians 5:24? "Now those who belong to Christ Jesus have crucified the flesh with its passions and desires."

Have you crucified your sinful passions and desires? Do you live in Christ?

Luke 23 recorded what Christ offered to all mankind and the various ways people responded to Him. The gracious Savior said, "Father, forgive them; for they do not know what they are doing" (v. 34). Some responded by mocking, sneering, and hurling abuse. Others responded by beating their breasts, praising God, and asking Jesus to remember them.

What is your response to the forgiveness of Christ?

Pray Luke 23:34, 42, and 47 over yourself and those for whom you stand guard as a faithful, prayerful watchman (Isaiah 62:6-7).

> *"Father, thank You*
> *for Your undeserved forgiveness.*
> *Remember _____ and me in Your Kingdom*
> *May we live to praise You.*
> *In Your name, Jesus~"*

Please read Luke 24.

Observe references to the Word of God.

Meditate on verse 45.

Then He opened their minds
to understand the Scriptures.

Contrast Luke 24:11 with Luke 24:45. At the beginning of the chapter, the words the disciples heard appeared as nonsense, and they would not believe them. By the end of the chapter, because of being with Jesus, their minds were opened to understand the Scriptures.

The Word of God brings clarity to every aspect of your life. Jesus is asking you the same question He asked His followers, "Why are you troubled, and why do doubts arise in your hearts?" (Luke 24:38).

Read and hear God's Word. Be blessed, worship Him, and praise Him continually (Luke 24:51-53).

Pray Luke 24:45 over yourself and those for whom you stand guard as a faithful, prayerful watchman (Isaiah 62:6-7).

"LORD, open _____ and my mind
to understand the Scriptures.
In Your name, Jesus~"

Please read Acts 1.

Meditate on verse 14a.

> *These all with one mind were continually*
> *devoting themselves to prayer.*

Luke continued his consecutive account to Theophilus of Christ and His church in the book called Acts (Luke 1:1-4; Acts 1:1-2). Acts begins with Christ commissioning His followers to be His witnesses in the power of the promised Holy Spirit. Christ ascended, and as the disciples waited for the Holy Spirit, they continually prayed.

The disciples asked Jesus to teach them to pray in Luke 11:1. Since that day, they had learned through the trials of life the importance of prayer. In obedience, they continued to pray.

God calls you to continually devote yourself to prayer. Ask Him to teach you how to pray. Ask Him to awaken that part of your brain where you can be talking to someone and talking to God at the same time. Ask Him to quicken your ability to memorize a Bible verse and then pray it all day over someone you love. Ask Him to teach you how to pray with the knowledge of His will in all spiritual wisdom and understanding (Colossians 1:9).

 Pray Acts 1:14 over yourself and those for whom you stand guard as a faithful, prayerful watchman (Isaiah 62:6-7).

> *"LORD, may _____ and I be of one mind,*
> *the mind of Christ.*
> *Help us to continually devote ourselves to prayer.*
> *In Your name, Jesus~"*

Please read Acts 2.

Meditate on verse 42.

> *They were continually devoting themselves*
> *to the apostles' teaching and to fellowship,*
> *to the breaking of bread and to prayer.*

Acts 2 is the account of how Christ's church started. Look at the place names in verses 9-11. You will recognize many of them from today's news. The church is people from every nation.

People's reaction to church has not changed in 2000 years. It varies from amazement to perplexity to mocking (Acts 2:12-13).

Peter explained the way a person becomes a part of Christ's church in three steps in verse 38: 1) repent, 2) be baptized in the name of Jesus Christ for the forgiveness of sins, and 3) receive the gift of the Holy Spirit. Then in verse 42, Luke listed four things a disciplined follower of Christ, someone who is part of church, will be devoted to: 1) teaching, 2) fellowship, 3) breaking bread, and 4) prayer.

Verses 46-47 told the results of that kind of devotion.

> *Day by day continuing with one mind in the temple,*
> *and breaking bread from house to house,*
> *they were taking their meals together*
> *with gladness and sincerity of heart,*
> *praising God and having favor with all the people.*
> *And the LORD was adding to their number*
> *day by day those who were being saved.*

To what are you devoted? Pray Acts 2:42 over yourself and those for whom you stand guard as a faithful, prayerful watchman (Isaiah 62:6-7).

"LORD, let _____ and me continually be devoted
to the teaching of Your Word,
to fellowship ,
to the breaking of bread,
and to prayer.
In Your name, Jesus~"

Please read Acts 3.

Meditate on verses 9-10.

> *And all the people saw him walking and praising God; and they*
> *were taking note of him as being the one who used to sit at the*
> *Beautiful Gate of the temple to beg alms, and they were filled*
> *with wonder and amazement at what had happened to him.*

Jesus' church had begun, and a miracle of healing took place. A beggar who had never walked a day in his life was healed in the name of Jesus Christ. His feet and ankles were immediately strengthened, and he entered the temple walking and leaping and praising God.

This physical healing is a picture of the spiritual healing that takes place in every Christian's life. Before Jesus, you were incapable of walking a day of your life with God. Once you were saved in the name of Jesus Christ, the rest of your life is spent walking with Christ praising God. People notice that before Christ you were a spiritual beggar. But, because of what Jesus did and is doing in you, people are amazed and filled with wonder.

Does Acts 3:1-12 describe you? If not, then, "Repent and return, so that your sins may be wiped away, in order that times of refreshing may come from the presence of the LORD; and that He may send Jesus, the Christ appointed for you"(Acts 3:19-20).

Pray Acts 3:19 and 26 over yourself and those for whom you stand guard as a faithful, prayerful watchman (Isaiah 62:6-7).

> *"LORD, please cause* _____ *and me to repent and return,*
> *so our sins may be wiped away,*
> *in order that times of refreshing may come from Your presence.*
> *God, thank You for raising Jesus and sending Him*
> *to bless us by turning every one of us from our wicked ways.*
> *In Your name, Jesus~"*

Please read Acts 4.

Meditate on verse 13.

> *Now as they observed the confidence of Peter and John*
> *and understood that they were uneducated and untrained men,*
> *they were amazed, and began to recognize*
> *them as having been with Jesus.*

Do people recognize you as having been with Jesus? Does the way you act and talk reflect that you know Christ? Peter and John could not stop speaking about what they had seen and heard (Acts 4:20). Continually tell what Jesus has done for you.

Pray Acts 4:29 and 31 over yourself and those for whom you stand guard as a faithful, prayerful watchman (Isaiah 62:6-7).

> *"LORD, may _____ and I be Your bond-servants*
> *and speak Your Word with all confidence.*
> *Fill us with the Holy Spirit*
> *to be able to speak the Word of God with boldness.*
> *In Your name, Jesus~"*

Additional insight:

Acts 4 is a continuation of the event recorded in Acts 3. The man who was walking, leaping, and praising God was standing with Peter and John—he had been lame for more than 40 years (Acts 4:14, 22). By the name of Jesus Christ, the man stood before the people in good health (Acts 4:10). Jesus did the impossible!

What are you believing God for today? The Lord made the heaven and the earth and the sea, and all that is in them (Acts 4:24). Nothing is too difficult for Him!

Please read Acts 5.

Meditate on verse 14.

And all the more believers in the LORD,
multitudes of men and women,
were constantly added to their number.

Christianity is unstoppable. Fighting against the spread of the Gospel of Jesus is fighting against God (Acts 5:39). As a believer in Jesus Christ, Acts 5 is an encouraging chapter. The apostles knew Christ was risen from the dead. They could not stop teaching and preaching Jesus as the Messiah (Acts 5:42). Ask God to give you the same boldness.

Pray Acts 5:20 and 42 over yourself and those for whom you stand guard as a faithful, prayerful watchman (Isaiah 62:6-7).

"LORD, may _____ and I go and speak
the whole message of this Life.
Every day, let us keep right on teaching and preaching
You, Jesus, as the Christ.
In Your name~"

FEBRUARY

On your walls, O Jerusalem,
I have appointed watchmen;
All day and all night they
will never keep silent.
You who remind the LORD,
take no rest for yourselves;
And give Him no rest
until He establishes
And makes Jerusalem a
praise in the earth.
ISAIAH 62:6-7, NASB

Please read Acts 6.

Meditate on verse 10.

> *But they were unable to cope with the wisdom*
> *and the Spirit with which he was speaking.*

If you have been reading the chapters that accompany these devotionals, you are reading Luke's account to Theophilus (Acts 1:1-2) about all Jesus began to do and teach, until the day He was taken up to heaven (the book of Luke) and all Jesus did through the disciples in the power of the Holy Spirit to build His church (the book of Acts). Acts 6:7 described this amazing church growth:

> *The Word of God kept on spreading;*
> *and the number of the disciples*
> *continued to increase greatly in Jerusalem,*
> *and a great many of the priests*
> *were becoming obedient to the faith.*

That is a good verse to pray over the church today.

Acts 6 also contains Godly characteristics of those chosen to serve in the church. Pray those characteristics from Acts 6:3, 5, 8, and 10 over yourself and those for whom you stand guard as a faithful, prayerful watchman (Isaiah 62:6-7).

> *"LORD, let _____ and me be of*
> *good reputation, full of the Spirit,*
> *and full of wisdom.*
> *Put us in charge of Your tasks.*
> *May we be full of faith and the Holy Spirit.*
> *Fill us with Your grace and power.*
> *May we, like Stephen, speak with wisdom and the Spirit.*
> *In Your name, Jesus~"*

Please read Acts 7.

Meditate on verse 55.

But being full of the Holy Spirit,
he gazed intently into heaven
and saw the glory of God
and Jesus standing at the right hand of God.

What a treasure God gave you through this meticulous physician named Luke! Inspired by the Holy Spirit, he wrote a consecutive account of the life of Christ (the book of Luke), a consecutive account of the birth of the church, and a consecutive history of Israel (the book of Acts). The Word of God is fascinating! And if you let it, it will cut you to the quick (Acts 7:54). Acts 7:51 is a convicting verse.

You men, who are stiff-necked
and uncircumcised in heart and ears,
are always resisting the Holy Spirit;
you are doing just as your fathers did.

Pray Acts 7:51 and 54-55 over yourself and those for whom you stand guard as a faithful, prayerful watchman (Isaiah 62:6-7).

"LORD, do not let _____ and me be stiff-necked
and uncircumcised in heart and ears.
Holy Spirit, do not let us resist You.
Let Your Word cut us to the quick.
May we be full of You, Holy Spirit.
Let us gaze intently at You, Jesus.
Show us Your glory, God!
In Your name, Jesus~"

Please read Acts 8.

Meditate on verse 23.

> *For I see that you are in the gall of bitterness*
> *and in the bondage of iniquity.*

In Acts 8, you read that Saul ravaged the church, and the believers scattered. As they were scattered, they preached the Word. God used the scattering caused by persecution to scatter His Word throughout the world. Be aware and thank God for how He is working even in the midst of trials.

Acts 8 also recorded that Peter discerned a man named Simon who had a heart not right before God. Peter described Simon being in the gall (the bile and poison) of bitterness.

The byproduct of bitterness is bilious poison. Allowing bitterness to take root in your life will put you in a toxic prison where God never intended you to dwell. Allow the Holy Spirit to examine your heart and reveal its intentions. Ask Jesus to remove any bitterness and wickedness. God exhorts you in Hebrews 12:15 to make sure no root of bitterness springs up causing trouble and defiling many.

Pray Acts 8:21-23 and 25 over yourself and those for whom you stand guard as a faithful, prayerful watchman (Isaiah 62:6-7).

> *"LORD, my heart and the heart of _____*
> *are not right before you.*
> *Help us repent of wickedness.*
> *Please forgive the intentions of our hearts.*
> *Remove the gall of bitterness*
> *and the bondage of iniquity from us.*
> *LORD, may we solemnly testify and speak Your Word,*
> *preaching the Gospel to many.*
> *In Your name, Jesus~"*

Please read Acts 9.

Meditate on verse 6.

> *Get up and enter the city,*
> *and it will be told you what you must do.*

This verse is Jesus speaking to Saul, giving him his marching orders. Only a moment before, Saul thought he was in charge of his life and in charge of taking the lives of others. Suddenly a light from heaven flashed around him, and Saul quickly learned who was in charge— who was LORD of his life. Jesus is LORD!

In this same chapter, the LORD Jesus told Ananias to "get up and go" (Acts 9:11).

Jesus needed him to minister to Saul. Both Saul and Ananias obeyed because Jesus is LORD.

What about you? Do you call Jesus "LORD"? Do you obey Him when He commands you to "get up and go"? Or do you make up excuses and disobey Him?

Pray Acts 9:5, 6, 11, and 36 over yourself and those for whom you stand guard as a faithful, prayerful watchman (Isaiah 62:6-7).

> *"Jesus, You are LORD.*
> *Help _____ and me listen and obey*
> *Your command to 'get up and go.'*
> *May we hear when we are told*
> *what we must do.*
> *As we go, help us to be like Tabitha,*
> *abounding with deeds of kindness and charity,*
> *doing them continually.*
> *In Your name, Jesus~"*

Please read Acts 10.

Meditate on verse 15.

Again a voice came to him a second time,
"What God has cleansed, no longer consider unholy."

God's salvation is for all people. The LORD made sure Peter understood salvation was not for the Jews alone. God showed Peter that his prejudices were not Godly. "God has shown me that I should not call any man unholy or unclean (Acts 10:28)."

Let the LORD examine your heart. Do you see yourself as better than another person or group of people? Do you secretly say in your heart, "Thank God I am not like one of them?"

Repent of your thoughts that are not from God. Practice seeing and loving others the way God does.

Pray Acts 10:34-36 over yourself and those for whom you stand guard as a faithful, prayerful watchman (Isaiah 62:6-7).

"LORD, help _____ and me to most certainly understand
that You are not one to show partiality,
but in every nation, the one who fears You
and does what is right is welcome to You.
Jesus Christ, You are LORD of all.
May we preach that peace
comes through You.
In Your name, Jesus~"

Please read Acts 11.

Meditate on verse 21.

> *And the hand of the LORD was with them,*
> *and a large number who believed turned to the LORD.*

This chapter starts with a contentious situation. Peter encountered a group of people who took issue with him. He handled the situation by calmly explaining in orderly sequence what happened. The result was the people who had an issue quieted down and glorified God. Following Peter's example may be helpful when others take issue with you.

Pray Acts 11:12, 21, 23, and 24 over yourself and those for whom you stand guard as a faithful, prayerful watchman (Isaiah 62:6-7).

> *"LORD, when your Spirit tells _____ and me to go,*
> *may we obey without misgivings.*
> *Let Your hand be with us.*
> *May large numbers believe and turn to You.*
> *Let us witness Your grace; let us rejoice;*
> *let us encourage others with*
> *resolute heart to remain true to You.*
> *Fill us with Your Holy Spirit and with faith.*
> *In Your name, Jesus~"*

Please read Acts 12.

Meditate on verse 5.

> *So Peter was kept in the prison,*
> *but prayer for him was being made fervently*
> *by the church to God.*

Acts 12 is an action packed chapter. Anyone who claims that the Bible is boring has not read it! With 675 words, Luke described the true events of James dying by the sword, Peter guarded by 16 soldiers in a prison and freed by an angel of the LORD; a king dying because an angel of the LORD struck him, and he was eaten by worms, and Peter miraculously going to a home where many people were praying fervently for him.

Prayer, does it really make a difference? What does fervent prayer mean? How is it different from regular prayer?

Fervently means constantly, without ceasing, earnestly. Webster's 1828 dictionary says that fervent means to boil and to swarm as bees.

I can imagine Peter was thankful God's church was swarming like bees in prayer on his behalf.

Rather than boiling with worry over a situation in your life or the life of someone you love, try praying fervently and watching in faith for God to cause the chains to fall off the person and the situation.

Use Acts 12:5 to keep you constantly praying for someone you stand guard for as a faithful, prayerful watchman (Isaiah 62:6-7).

> *"LORD, thank You that I can come to You in fervent prayer.*
> *Thank You that You desire fervent prayer.*
> *Thank You that You hear and answer fervent prayers.*
> *Knowing these truths, I am bringing _____ to You.*
> *LORD, I will continue to bring*
> *_____ to You until You bring freedom.*
> *In Your name, Jesus~"*

Please read Acts 13.

Meditate on verse 36a.

> *For David, after he had served*
> *the purpose of God in his own generation, fell asleep,*
> *and was laid among his fathers ...*

Acts 13 is another rich chapter in God's Holy Word. It contains interesting details about Israel's history and the spread of the Gospel of Jesus Christ.

King David's epitaph is in Acts 13. While David was alive, he served the purpose of God. Can you imagine that on your tombstone?

What is your purpose in life? Why do you wake up in the morning? Do you live to please God and do whatever He says?

Is it the cry of your heart to serve the purpose of God? Is that your desire for those you love? What will be on your tombstone?

Pray Acts 13:12, 36, and 43 over yourself and those for whom you stand guard as a faithful, prayerful watchman (Isaiah 62:6-7).

> *"LORD, I am amazed at Your teaching.*
> *Please let _____ and me serve*
> *Your purpose in our generation.*
> *May we continue in Your grace.*
> *In Your name, Jesus~"*

Please read Acts 14.

Observe all God did to establish His church.

Meditate on verse 3.

Therefore they spent a long time there
speaking boldly with reliance upon the LORD,
who was testifying to the Word of His grace,
granting that signs and wonders be done by their hands.

The more you grow in Christ the more aware you become that nothing good comes from you except what Christ does in and through you. Acts 14:3 said it was the LORD who was testifying to the Word of His grace. Paul and Barnabas were merely vessels entrusted to the grace of God for the work they were accomplishing (Acts 14:26). The establishment and existence of Christ's church was because God caused it to happen.

Pray Acts 14:3 and 26 over yourself as you serve by the grace of God. Pray Acts 14:15 and 27 over someone who needs to turn from vain things to the living God as their faithful, prayerful watchman (Isaiah 62:6-7).

"LORD, I am relying on You.
Help me speak boldly testifying to the Word of Your grace.
I commend myself to Your grace for the work to be accomplished.
God, You are the Maker of heaven and earth,
the sea and all that is in them.
Please cause _____ to turn
from vain things to You, the living God.
Open the door of faith to them.
In Your name, Jesus."

FEBRUARY 10

Please read Acts 15.

Meditate on verse 40.

> *But Paul chose Silas and left,*
> *being committed by the brethren*
> *to the grace of the LORD.*

As you read through the book of Acts, be aware of and thank God for the miracles He performed to start His church. The resurrection of Jesus proved nothing was too difficult for God. Faithful believers like Paul, Barnabas, and Silas traveled great distances to share the Gospel and to get church questions answered by the leadership at Jerusalem. Peter and James were not swayed by their Judaism but listened to the Holy Spirit to answer questions according to the will of God. God used a divisive situation for good, sending Paul and Silas to Greece to start new churches rather than returning to familiar places.

Christianity exists and thrives because of the grace of God. It is God's grace, His merciful kindness and favor, which saves and keeps you as a child of His. Think about God's grace in your life today, and as you thank Him for it, commit your loved ones to it.

Pray Acts 15:11 and 40 over yourself and those for whom you stand guard as a faithful, prayerful watchman (Isaiah 62:6-7).

> *"Jesus, thank You for saving me through Your grace.*
> *Through Your grace, please save _____.*
> *I commit us to Your grace, LORD.*
> *For the sake of Your name, Jesus~"*

Please read Acts 16.

Meditate on verses 6-7.

They passed through the Phrygian and Galatian region,
having been forbidden by the Holy Spirit
to speak the Word in Asia;
and after they came to Mysia,
they were trying to go into Bithynia,
and the Spirit of Jesus did not permit them.

In Acts 15, you observed how God used a disagreement between Paul and Barnabas to start moving Paul and Silas in the geographical direction He needed them to go. In Acts 16, you observed the Holy Spirit forbade Paul and Silas from speaking the Word in Asia. The Spirit of Jesus would not permit them to go into Bithynia. Then in verse 9, God used a vision to show Paul where to go. Acts 16:10 said when Paul saw the vision, he immediately started making plans to get there. The rest of the chapter records the results of Paul and Silas' immediate obedience to the will of God, the salvation of many.

This passage may be helpful in determining God's will for your life. Do you yield to the Spirit when He forbids you to do something? Do you immediately go when the Spirit of Jesus tells you to move? Eternal results in your life and the life of others will be the result as you obey the LORD.

Pray Acts 16:6-7 and 10 as you seek the Holy Spirit's guidance in your life and the life of those for whom you stand guard as a faithful, prayerful watchman (Isaiah 62:6-7)..

"LORD, please help _____ and me recognize
and obey when Your Spirit forbids us to speak.
Help us submit when You do not permit us to go.
God, when you call us,
may we immediately go and preach according to Your will.
In Your name, Jesus~"

Please read Acts 17.

Meditate on verse 11.

> *Now these were more noble-minded*
> *than those in Thessalonica,*
> *for they received the Word*
> *with great eagerness,*
> *examining the Scriptures daily*
> *to see whether these things were so.*

Acts 17 is an enlightening chapter for living and sharing God's Word. Pay attention to the facts God wants you to know. It was Paul's custom to reason with people using the Word of God (vs. 2,17). Jesus was changing people's lives in such a way that nonbelievers described Paul and Silas as "men who have upset the world" (v. 6). The worship of false gods exasperated Paul (v. 16). The sermon Paul boldly preached in Athens was to the men considered the wisest in the land (vs. 22-31). God overlooks your times of ignorance and allows you to repent (v. 30).

Pray Acts 17:11 over yourself and those for whom you stand guard as a faithful, prayerful watchman (Isaiah 62:6-7).

> *"LORD, please make _____ and me more noble-minded.*
> *May we receive Your Word with great eagerness,*
> *examining the Scriptures daily*
> *to see whether the things we hear are true.*
> *In Your name, Jesus~"*

Please read Acts 18.

Meditate on verse 24.

> *Now a Jew named Apollos,*
> *an Alexandrian by birth,*
> *an eloquent man, came to Ephesus,*
> *and he was mighty in the Scriptures.*

This is a good chapter to practice your observation skills of God's Word. Notice names of places and time phrases. Acts 18 started with Aquila and Priscilla being kicked out of Rome because they were Jews. They moved to Corinth where they were discipled by Paul. Aquila and Priscilla later moved to Ephesus where they taught Apollos. Apollos was mighty in the Scriptures, but he needed to learn God's Word more accurately. Instead of being prideful about his Biblical knowledge, Apollos was willing to learn more about God's ways. He then went to Achaia and discipled believers there. Discipleship family trees are beautiful. Paul—Aquila and Priscilla—Apollos—Believers in Achaia.

Is a mature Christian teaching you? To whom have you explained the way of God? Who are you currently discipling? What does your discipleship family tree look like?

Pray Acts 18:24-28 over yourself and those for whom you stand guard as a faithful, prayerful watchman (Isaiah 62:6-7).

> *"Jesus, please make _____ and me*
> *mighty in the Scriptures.*
> *Instruct us in Your way, LORD.*
> *Make us fervent in spirit, speaking and teaching accurately*
> *the things concerning You.*
> *May we greatly help those who have believed through grace.*
> *Let us demonstrate by the Scriptures*
> *that You, Jesus, are the Christ.*
> *For the sake of Your name~"*

Please read Acts 19.

Meditate on verse 20.

> *So the Word of the LORD*
> *was growing mightily and prevailing.*

In Acts 19, you read that all of Asia and the pagan world worshipped the goddess Diana (Acts 19:27). Paul, Apollos, and other disciples were in Ephesus at this time calmly and daily reasoning with these idolaters. They did not blaspheme the name of Diana (Acts 19:37); they simply reasoned from the Scriptures for two years in Ephesus, "so that all who lived in Asia heard the Word of the LORD, both Jews and Greeks" (Acts 19:10).

How do you share your faith in Christ? God's Word is powerful. In Ephesus, reasoning from the Word of God caused heathens to burn their pagan books with a combined worth of 136 years of wages (Acts 19:19). That is incredible! Let God's Word burn years' worth of junk out of your life and share that Good News with others.

Pray Acts 19:17 and 20 over yourself and those for whom you stand guard as a faithful, prayerful watchman (Isaiah 62:6-7).

> *"LORD Jesus, let Your name*
> *be magnified in _____ and me.*
> *Let Your Word grow mightily*
> *and prevail in our lives.*
> *In Your name, Jesus~"*

Please read Acts 20.

Meditate on verse 28.

> *Be on guard for yourselves and for all the flock,*
> *among which the Holy Spirit has made you overseers,*
> *to shepherd the church of God which He*
> *purchased with His own blood.*

Paul said good-bye to the people (flock) to whom he had faithfully taught the Word of God. He had not shrunk back from declaring to them anything that was profitable for living obediently in the LORD Jesus Christ (Acts 20:20-21). Paul's last exhortation to these believers was to go and shepherd the flock God had given them.

Who has God given you to shepherd? Your wife, your husband, your children, grandchildren, a friend, a Sunday School class, a small group, the people who sit beside you at the office, your next door neighbor, the waiter at the restaurant ... Teach, admonish, and encourage with the Word of God, so your flock can grow up in Christ and shepherd well the flock God will entrust to them. Do not shrink from declaring to them the whole purpose of God (Acts 20:27).

Pray Acts 20:19-21 and 32 over yourself and those for whom you stand guard as a faithful, prayerful watchman (Isaiah 62:6-7).

> *"LORD, help _____ and me serve You*
> *with all humility, tears, and trials.*
> *May we not shrink from declaring anything*
> *profitable concerning repentance and faith in You, Jesus.*
> *LORD, I commend _____ to You and to the Word of Your grace*
> *which is able to build them up and give them*
> *the inheritance among all those who are sanctified.*
> *In Your name, Jesus~"*

FEBRUARY 16

Please read Acts 21.

Meditate on verse 29.

*For they had previously seen Trophimus, the Ephesian, in the city
with him, and they supposed that Paul had
brought him into the temple.*

Paul told James and the other elders of the Jerusalem church about the Gentiles being saved; James told Paul about the thousands of Jews who believed. God was glorified, and His church was growing.

But where good things happened, suppositions abounded. People supposed Paul had taken Greeks into the temple. They supposed he was an Egyptian who stirred up a revolt. These rumors provoked the entire city of Jerusalem.

What about you? Do you ever presume and suppose something to be true? Do you allow suppositions to swirl around in your head all day until they become truth to you then you tell it to another as if it were truth, and your suppositions provoke many?

2 Corinthians 10:5 is the antidote to that kind of poisonous thinking:

*We are destroying speculations
and every lofty thing raised up against the knowledge of God,
and we are taking every thought captive to the obedience of Christ.*

Pray Acts 21:20, 29, and 2 Corinthians 10:5 over yourself and those for whom you stand guard as a faithful, prayerful watchman (Isaiah 62:6-7).

*"LORD, please let _____ and me glorify You by what we say.
Let us handle suppositions carefully.
Let us destroy speculations and every lofty thing
raised up against the knowledge of You, God.
May we take every thought captive to the obedience of You.
In Your name, Jesus~"*

Please read Acts 22.

Meditate on verse 14.

> *And he said, "The God of our fathers has appointed you*
> *to know His will and to see the Righteous One*
> *and to hear an utterance from His mouth."*

God used the false suppositions from Acts 21 to give Paul an opportunity to share his testimony in Acts 22. As Paul made his defense that he was not a riotous Egyptian, he told a multitude of Jews about the Righteous One, Jesus Christ (Acts 21:36-22:2, 14-15). Paul boldly shared his testimony and his assignment from God.

God can turn sinful situations into opportunities to give Him glory. Be mindful of how God wants you to witness for Christ even in the midst of difficult times. Remember God will never leave you or forsake you; He is your Helper; do not be afraid of what man might do to you (Hebrews 13:5-6).

Pray Acts 22:14-15 asking God to share His Testimony through you and those for whom you stand guard as a faithful, prayerful watchman (Isaiah 62:6-7).

> *"LORD, appoint _____ and me to know Your will*
> *and to see You, the Righteous One.*
> *May we hear an utterance from Your mouth.*
> *Let us be a witness for You to all men*
> *of what we have seen and heard.*
> *In Your name, Jesus~"*

FEBRUARY 18

Please read Acts 23.

Meditate on verse 1.

> *Paul, looking intently at the council, said,*
> *"Brethren, I have lived my life with a*
> *perfectly good conscience before God up to this day."*

The man who murdered believers and after becoming a Christian, still struggled with sin (Romans 7:14-25) said, "I have lived my life with a perfectly good conscience before God up to this day."

Was he delusional or in denial? No! Paul knew the forgiveness of God covers not only sin, but also conscience. Paul knew "as far as the east is from the west, so far has God removed our transgressions from us" (Psalm 103:12).

Paul knew this truth about God, "God has kept my soul from the pit of nothingness, for You have cast all my sins behind Your back" (Isaiah 38:17).

Paul knew that God cast all of his sins into the depths of the sea (Micah 7:19). The blood of Jesus Christ cleansed him from ALL sin (1 John 1:7), and that included the sin of his guilty conscience.

Confess your sins and repent in obedience to your LORD Jesus Christ. Know with confidence that God not only casts your sin into the depths of the sea, but also your guilt and shame. Now, armed with the truth of God's Word, you can say, "because of the blood of Jesus Christ, I have lived my life with a perfectly good conscience before God up to this day."

Pray Acts 23:1 over yourself and those for whom you stand guard as a faithful, prayerful watchman (Isaiah 62:6-7).

> *"God, thank You for Your forgiveness that gives _____ and me*
> *a perfectly good conscience before You.*
> *In Your name, Jesus~"*

Please read Acts 24.

Meditate on verse 16 NIV.

So I strive always to keep my conscience
clear before God and man.

How do you get and keep a clear conscience? Meditate on and take
to heart these truths from the Word of God:

How much more, then, will the blood of Christ,
who through the eternal Spirit
offered Himself unblemished to God,
cleanse our consciences from acts that lead to death,
so that we may serve the living God!
—Hebrews 9:14 NIV

Let us draw near to God with a sincere heart
and with the full assurance that faith brings,
having our hearts sprinkled to cleanse us from a guilty conscience
and having our bodies washed with pure water.
—Hebrews 10:22 NIV

Therefore, since through God's mercy we have this ministry,
we do not lose heart.
Rather, we have renounced secret and shameful ways;
we do not use deception, nor do we distort the Word of God.
On the contrary, by setting forth the truth plainly,
we commend ourselves to everyone's conscience in the sight of God.
—2 Corinthians 4:1-2 NIV

Satan wanted Paul stuck in his guilty conscience so kings, governors, high priests, lawyers, Jews, Gentiles, you, and I would not hear the truth about God's great salvation. Paul let the blood of Christ cleanse him from acts that lead to death. He let the blood of Christ cleanse him from his guilty conscience. He knew by God's mercy he was given this ministry, and he renounced (formally gave up) secret and shameful ways and plainly set forth the truth of God's Word.

It is the will of God for you to do the same.

Pray Acts 24:16 over yourself and those for whom you stand guard as a faithful, prayerful watchman (Isaiah 62:6-7).

> *"LORD, let _____ and me maintain always*
> *a blameless conscience before You and man.*
> *In Your name, Jesus."*

Please read Acts 25.

Meditate on verses 8 and 18-19.

Paul said in his own defense,
"I have committed no offense either against the Law of the Jews
or against the temple or against Caesar."
When the accusers stood up,
they began bringing charges against him, not
of such crimes as I was expecting,
but they simply had some points of disagreement with him
about their own religion and about a dead man,
Jesus, whom Paul asserted to be alive.

Power. The Roman sea city of Caesarea was a huge military fortress strategically located to prevent attacks against Rome by sea from hostile countries in the East. When Festus became the Roman governor, he inherited in his prison, Paul, whom the previous governor, Felix, was holding to protect and to appease the Jewish leadership in Jerusalem. As Festus took the mantle of power, the Jewish leaders who wanted to kill Paul approached him. But Paul had "… committed no offense against the Law of the Jews, or against the temple, or against Caesar" (Acts 25:8). He was what he would later command Timothy and all elders to be, "above reproach" (1 Timothy 3:2).

Power. Paul was being held for believing Jesus was alive. He knew Jesus was alive. He talked with Him. He had Jesus in his life. He was filled with the Holy Spirit. He talked to the LORD without ceasing. He was being accused of believing in the resurrection. Power.

Power. Paul stood before the governor, his military leaders, all of the important civic leaders; then King Agrippa and his wife Bernice walked in, all there to witness Paul's testimony, to see if they could even have charges filed against him.

Power. Many of you face trials with both just and unjust court systems, fair and unfair laws, and abuses of power. Many of you are falsely accused or are separated from your loved ones due to national catastrophes. You may be reading this in a refugee camp or in prison awaiting trial. Find power in the Holy Spirit and pray. The LORD is always with you, and He is more powerful than all of the kings of the earth. As a Christian, you are already spiritually resurrected. Power!

Pray Acts 25:8 and 19 over yourself and those you know in distress as a faithful, prayerful watchman (Isaiah 62:6-7)

> *"LORD, help _____and me to live as Paul,*
> *committing no offense against the law*
> *and with the courage to assert before others that You are alive.*
> *In Your name, Jesus~"*

Please read Acts 26.

Meditate on verse 28.

Agrippa replied to Paul,
"In a short time you will persuade
me to become a Christian."

Paul used every opportunity to tell others about Jesus. Rather than being overcome by circumstances, he focused on Christ. Paul loved to share his story of what Jesus did for him. He was not ashamed of the Gospel (Romans 1:16).

Open your eyes to the opportunities God gives you to tell others about Christ. Unexpected inconveniences or a change of plans can actually be God's plans for you to share Jesus. Stay expectant for what God is doing.

As a faithful, prayerful watchman (Isaiah 62:6-7), pray Acts 26:18 over someone who needs Jesus Christ.

"LORD, open the eyes of _____
so they may turn from darkness to light
and from the dominion of Satan to You, God,
that they may receive forgiveness of sins
and an inheritance among those
who have been sanctified by faith in You.
In Your name, Jesus~"

Please read Acts 27.

Meditate on verse 25.

> *Therefore, keep up your courage, men,*
> *for I believe God that it will turn out*
> *exactly as I have been told.*

Everything happening around Paul screamed that he and the other 275 people on board the storm tossed ship were going to die. An angel of God told Paul every person would survive. Paul boldly relayed the message from the LORD to his shipmates.

If you read the entire chapter, you know the rest of the story: "And so it happened that they all were brought safely to land" (Acts 27:44).

What do you believe God will do for you and your family? What has He promised you in His Word that you believe by faith will come to sight? 1 Chronicles 5:20 says: "He answered their prayers because they trusted in Him."

God loves it when you have faith in Him. In fact, it is impossible to please Him without faith (Hebrews 11:6). Cling to Christ and His Word and wait expectantly for Him.

> *But as for me, I will watch expectantly for the LORD;*
> *I will wait for the God of my salvation.*
> *My God will hear me.*
> —Micah 7:7

Pray Acts 27:25 over a situation you believe God for as a faithful, prayerful watchman (Isaiah 62:6-7).

> *"God, help me keep up my courage*
> *as I believe You for _____.*
> *In Your name, Jesus~"*

Please read Acts 28.

Meditate on verse 31.

> *He was preaching the kingdom of God*
> *and teaching concerning the LORD Jesus Christ*
> *with all openness, unhindered.*

The last 52 devotionals took you through the writings of Luke. You read the exact Truth (Luke 1:4) of how Christianity started. This exact Truth was so powerful it even changed the heart of Paul, who had all appearances of being impossible to save.

Truth about Jesus saved Paul so much that Luke ended his story with Paul, from morning until evening, "solemnly testifying about the kingdom of God and trying to persuade others concerning Jesus" (Acts 28:23).

Paul taught about the LORD Jesus Christ even though Christianity was spoken against everywhere (Acts 28:22). Your situation is similar to Paul's. Christianity is still spoken against, but the exact Truth must be told, and now God has given you the privilege to be a Paul. Christ saved you. He wants you to share that Good News with others, even the impossible ones.

Pray Acts 28:31 over all of us who call ourselves Christians as a faithful, prayerful watchman (Isaiah 62:6-7).

> *"Help _____and _____and me*
> *preach Your Kingdom, God,*
> *and teach concerning You, LORD Jesus Christ,*
> *with all openness, unhindered.*
> *In Your name, Jesus~"*

Please read Isaiah 1.

Meditate on these two phrases from verses 2 and 10.

The LORD speaks.
Hear the Word of the LORD.

For the next 66 days, you will read and pray through the book of Isaiah. Isaiah's name means Jehovah Saves. In this book, you will see Jesus as your Messiah, the Suffering Servant, and the Conquering King. Isaiah gives more prophecies than any other book in the Bible about Christ's coming.

God wants you to know there is no God besides Him. He tells you what to do so He will listen to your prayers. The LORD is speaking ... hear what He is saying to you.

Pray Isaiah 1:18-20 over yourself and those for whom you stand guard as a faithful, prayerful watchman (Isaiah 62:6-7).

"LORD, truly Your mouth has spoken,
and You invite _____and me to reason with You.
LORD, our sins are as scarlet and red like crimson.
Make them as white as snow, white like wool.
Help us not to refuse and rebel against You.
We do not want to be devoured by the sword.
Thank You for Your promise that if we consent and obey,
we will eat the best of the land.
In Your name, Jesus~"

Please read Isaiah 2.

Meditate on verse 11.

> *The proud look of man will be abased*
> *and the loftiness of man will be humbled,*
> *and the LORD alone will be exalted in that day.*

Isaiah 2 sets the stage for why you need a Savior. The people in Isaiah's day were consumed with themselves. They were influenced by the world instead of God. They had lots of stuff, and they worshipped their accomplishments instead of worshipping God. It's amazing how nothing has changed in 2,700 years! "LORD, save us from ourselves!"

Verses 19-20 say men will go into caves and holes in the ground. They would rather hang out with moles and bats than humble themselves before the LORD. Pride drives people to pathetic places.

God promises a day of reckoning against everyone who is proud, lofty, and lifted up.

Pray Isaiah 2:5, 11, and 22 over yourself and those for whom you stand guard as a faithful, prayerful watchman (Isaiah 62:6-7).

> *"LORD, help _____and me stop*
> *regarding and esteeming man instead of You.*
> *May we remove our proud looks*
> *and humble our loftiness.*
> *Let us exalt You, LORD.*
> *May we walk in Your Light.*
> *In Your name, Jesus~"*

Please read Isaiah 3.

Look for parallels between Isaiah's world (739 BC – 681 BC) and your world today.

Meditate on verses 8 and 9.

Jerusalem has stumbled and Judah has fallen
because their speech and their actions are against the LORD,
to rebel against His glorious presence.
The expression of their faces bears witness against them,
and they display their sin like Sodom;
they do not even conceal it.
Woe to Them!
For they have brought evil on themselves.

God promised to remove everything the people trusted in instead of trusting Him. Instead of sweet perfume, there would be a putrid stench (Isaiah 3:24). It would go badly for the wicked; what they deserved would be done to them (Isaiah3:11). The LORD said He would arise to contend and to judge the people for their pride and rebellion against Him.

In the midst of the calamity, God made a promise to the righteous: "it will go well with them, for they will eat the fruit of their actions" (Isaiah 3:10).

Pray Isaiah 3:10 over yourself and those for whom you stand guard as a faithful, prayerful watchman (Isaiah 62:6-7).

"LORD, make _____ and me righteous
that it will go well with us.
May we eat the fruit of our actions.
In Your name, Jesus-"

Please read Isaiah 4.

Meditate on verse 3.

> *It will come about that he who is left in Zion*
> *and remains in Jerusalem will be called holy—*
> *everyone who is recorded for life in Jerusalem.*

Isaiah 4 is a short chapter beautifully describing salvation. You desperately need someone to take away your shame. The women in verse 1 pathetically grasped at anyone to take away their disgrace.

Thankfully, Jesus Christ came. He is beautiful and glorious. Because of who He is, you can be called holy if your name is recorded for life by letting Him wash away the filth and purge the bloodshed from your life. The LORD not only cleanses you from sin, but gives you shelter, refuge, and protection (Isaiah 4:6). What an awesome God you serve!

Pray Isaiah 4:3 and 6 over those for whom you stand guard as a faithful, prayerful watchman (Isaiah 62:6-7).

> *"LORD, please let _____*
> *be called holy and recorded for life.*
> *Give them shelter from the heat by day,*
> *and refuge and protection from the storm and the rain.*
> *In Your name, Jesus~"*

Please read Isaiah 5.

Meditate on verses 20-22.

> *Woe to those who call evil good and good evil;*
> *who substitute darkness for light and light for darkness;*
> *who substitute bitter for sweet and sweet for bitter!*
> *Woe to those who are wise in their own*
> *eyes and clever in their own sight!*
> *Woe to those who are heroes in drinking wine*
> *and valiant men in mixing strong drink,*
> *who justify the wicked for a bribe,*
> *and take away the rights of the ones who are in the right!*

God gave the people of Judah everything they needed to be productive. He compared them to a vineyard that had been perfectly cared for; all it needed to do was produce good grapes. God's people chose to produce worthless grapes despite God's provision for their lives. God was mad and pronounced six "woes" on them in Isaiah 5.

Examine your life. Are you producing good or worthless grapes for the sake of Christ? Is God pronouncing "woes" on you like He did the people 2,700 years ago?

God's standards have not changed. The world around you may call evil "good," and good "evil," but take care that you do not. Be obedient to the Knowledge of God.

Pray Isaiah 5:2, 12, 13, and 16 over yourself and those for whom you stand guard as a faithful, prayerful watchman (Isaiah 62:6-7).

"LORD of hosts, You will be exalted in judgment,
and You will show Yourself holy in righteousness.
Let _____ and me pay attention to Your deeds
and consider the work of Your hands.
We want Your knowledge, LORD!
You expect us to produce good grapes;
help us not to produce worthless ones.
For the sake of Your name, Jesus~"

Please read Isaiah 6.

Meditate on verse 3b.

> *Holy, Holy, Holy is the LORD of hosts;*
> *the whole earth is full of His glory.*

When you take your eyes off yourself and focus on the LORD, your life will change. Isaiah saw the King, the LORD of hosts, and he was immediately aware of his sinfulness. His immediate response to his sin was to confess it. God's immediate response to Isaiah's confession was forgiveness. His iniquity was taken away! Isaiah's immediate response to the LORD's amazing forgiveness was surrender to do whatever God wanted Him to do.

Notice the path of a life submitted to God.

- Focus on the LORD.
- Humbly and quickly confess your sin.
- Immediately accept God's forgiveness.
- Respond to God's forgiveness by obeying Him.

Pray Isaiah 6:5-8 over yourself and those for whom you stand guard as a faithful, prayerful watchman (Isaiah 62:6-7).

> *"LORD, _____ and I are ruined*
> *because we are people of unclean lips.*
> *Please burn the sin out of our lives.*
> *Thank You for taking away our iniquity*
> *and forgiving our sin.*
> *LORD, You ask, 'Whom shall I send,*
> *and who will go for Us?'*
> *Our response is 'Here we are. Send us!'*
> *In Your name, Jesus~"*

On your walls, O Jerusalem,
I have appointed watchmen;
All day and all night they
will never keep silent.
You who remind the LORD,
take no rest for yourselves;
And give Him no rest
until He establishes
And makes Jerusalem a
praise in the earth.
ISAIAH 62:6-7, NASB

Please read Isaiah 7.

Meditate on verse 13, inserting your family's name in place of "David."

Then he said, "Listen now, O house of David!
Is it too slight a thing for you to try the patience of men,
that you will try the patience of my God as well?"

Judah was terrorized by Aram (Syria). The king of Aram planned evil against Judah. As you can imagine, Ahaz (the king of Judah) and the people were scared. Isaiah described their fear like this: "His heart and the hearts of the people shook as the trees of the forest shake with the wind" (Isaiah 7:2).

Can you relate? Have you been that fearful? Is your heart shaking like that right now?

God made a promise to Judah that the threats coming from Aram would not stand nor come to pass (Isaiah 7:7). God wanted King Ahaz to trust Him and to ask Him for a sign, but Ahaz refused to obey. God told him, "If you will not believe, you surely shall not last" (Isaiah 7:9).

The LORD is saying the same thing to you. Trust and obey Him.

Pray Isaiah 7:4 and 13 over yourself and those for whom you stand guard as a faithful, prayerful watchman (Isaiah 62:6-7).

"LORD, do not let _____ and me try Your patience.
Help us as we trust You
to take care, be calm, have no fear,
and not be fainthearted because of _____.
In Your name, Jesus~"

Please read Isaiah 8.

Meditate on verses 12-14a.

> *You are not to say, "It is a conspiracy!"*
> *In regard to all that this people call a conspiracy,*
> *and you are not to fear what they fear or be in dread of it.*
> *It is the LORD of hosts whom you should regard as holy.*
> *And He shall be your fear, and He shall be your dread.*
> *Then He shall become a sanctuary.*

What are you afraid of? What conspiracy theory causes your heart to race? What do you believe about Almighty God?

God told His people to stop listening to the latest conspiracy theory and to stop being afraid. The LORD said to fear and dread Him; He is holy! Once you focus on the LORD rather than surrounding circumstances and people, He will become your sanctuary, your place of refuge from all the craziness going on around you.

Pray Isaiah 8:8, 10, 17, and 19-20 over yourself and those for whom you stand guard as a faithful, prayerful watchman (Isaiah 62:6-7).

> *"Immanuel, God with us, help _____ and me wait for You.*
> *May we eagerly look for You.*
> *Let us NEVER consult mediums and spiritists*
> *who whisper and mutter.*
> *Let us consult You, God,*
> *not the dead on behalf of the living.*
> *May we test everything we hear by Your Law and Testimony.*
> *In Your name, Jesus~"*

Please read Isaiah 9.

Meditate on this repeated phrase from verses 12, 17, and 21.

> *In spite of all this, His anger does not turn away,*
> *and His hand is still stretched out.*

God's anger burns and His hand is stretched out against sin. 2,700 years ago, the people were proud and arrogant. They were godless evildoers, and every mouth spoke foolishness (Isaiah 9:17). Wickedness burned like a fire (Isaiah 9:18). Oh, how things have not changed in 2,700 years!

God had Isaiah precede these verses about His wrath and judgment with the promise of His grace given to you with the birth of a Child—the birth of your Wonderful Counselor, Mighty God, Eternal Father, Prince of Peace (Isaiah 9:6). The LORD's zeal for you fulfilled this prophecy with the coming of Messiah!

You desperately need a Savior! Thankfully, in Christ, God's anger is turned away, and His hand is not stretched out against you.

Pray Isaiah 9:2 over someone who still walks in darkness for whom you stand guard as a faithful, prayerful watchman (Isaiah 62:6-7).

> *"LORD, _____ walks in darkness.*
> *Let them see Your great light.*
> *They live in a dark land.*
> *Let Your light shine on them.*
> *In Your name, Jesus-"*

MARCH 4

Please read Isaiah 10.

Meditate on verse 12.

> *So it will be that when the LORD has completed*
> *all His work on Mount Zion and on Jerusalem,*
> *He will say, "I will punish the fruit of the arrogant heart*
> *of the king of Assyria and the pomp of his haughtiness."*

God used the Assyrians to punish Israel for being disobedient to Him. God then punished the Assyrians for being prideful about how God had used them. They took credit for the things God did through them. Reread Isaiah 10:13-14 and notice all the uses of "my" and "I." "By the power of <u>my</u> hand and by <u>my</u> wisdom <u>I</u> did this" (Isaiah 10:13a).

God hates pride. Never forget when God is working through you, He is doing it for His purposes and His glory. Nothing good comes from yourself; the only good in you is Jesus. He alone is worthy of praise.

Pray Isaiah 10:12 over yourself and those for whom you stand guard as a faithful, prayerful watchman (Isaiah 62:6-7).

> *"LORD, You are the One doing and completing all Your work.*
> *Let _____ and me produce fruit for Your Kingdom,*
> *not fruit of an arrogant heart.*
> *LORD, keep us from the pomp of haughtiness.*
> *In Your name, Jesus~"*

Please read Isaiah 11.

Meditate on verse 10.

> *Then in that day the nations will resort to the root of Jesse,*
> *who will stand as a signal for the peoples;*
> *and His resting place will be glorious.*

Isaiah 11 describes Jesus (vs. 1-5) and what the world will be like under His rule (vs. 6-16). Christ will reign in righteousness. His unshakeable Kingdom will be characterized by peace. By the LORD's hand, Israel will be recovered. The earth will be full of the knowledge of the LORD. It will be glorious!

As you wait for Christ's return, you are to become more like Him. Pray for the characteristics in Isaiah 11:2 to be true in your life and in those for whom you stand guard as a faithful, prayerful watchman (Isaiah 62:6-7).

> *"LORD, let Your Spirit rest upon _____ and me,*
> *the spirit of wisdom and understanding,*
> *the spirit of counsel and strength,*
> *the spirit of knowledge and the fear of You, LORD.*
> *In Your name, Jesus~"*

Please read Isaiah 12.

Meditate on verse 2.

> *Behold, God is my salvation,*
> *I will trust and not be afraid;*
> *for the LORD God is my strength and song,*
> *and He has become my salvation.*

The time phrase "that day" found in Isaiah 12:1 refers to the future salvation of Israel. If you are a Christian, it refers to the day you already have the privilege of living because of what Jesus did in your life. Reread Isaiah 12; it is only six verses long, and see if it is a description of your life.

Pray Isaiah 12:1-2 in thanksgiving to your LORD.

> *"I will give thanks to You, O LORD;*
> *for although You were angry with me,*
> *Your anger is turned away,*
> *and You comfort me.*
> *Behold, God, You are my salvation.*
> *I will trust and not be afraid;*
> *for You, LORD God, are my strength and song,*
> *and You have become my salvation.*
> *Thank You, Jesus~"*

Please read Isaiah 13.

Meditate on verse 11.

> *Thus I will punish the world for its evil*
> *and the wicked for their iniquity;*
> *I will also put an end to the arrogance of the proud*
> *and abase the haughtiness of the ruthless.*

The next several chapters of Isaiah contain oracles. An oracle was a message God gave Isaiah. It was a burden within Isaiah until he expressed what the LORD told him. An oracle was a message of doom. This first oracle is to Babylon, present day Iraq. God said it was also a message to the entire world.

God promised to exterminate the sinners from the land. Destruction was coming from the Almighty. The day of the LORD, the day of God's judgment, was described as cruel, with fury and burning anger.

Oh, how you need a Savior! Thanks be to God you have a Savior through Jesus Christ your LORD! Are you willing to share that Good News before Isaiah 13 is fulfilled?

Pray Isaiah 13:2-3 over yourself and those for whom you stand guard as a faithful, prayerful watchman (Isaiah 62:6-7).

> *"LORD, make _____ and me Your consecrated ones,*
> *Your mighty warriors.*
> *Let us lift up Your standard on the bare hill*
> *and raise our voice to tell others about You.*
> *Let us wave our hand that others*
> *may see to enter the door of Your Kingdom.*
> *In Your name, Jesus~"*

Please read Isaiah 14.

Meditate on verse 24.

> *The LORD of hosts has sworn saying,*
> *"Surely, just as I have intended so it has happened,*
> *and just as I have planned so it will stand."*

Isaiah 14 is a great chapter for building your trust in God. It contains prophecy fulfilled: the destruction of Babylon, its king and inhabitants, and the destruction of Assyria; all things that history records as true. The chapter also contains prophecy yet to be fulfilled concerning the oppressor. I believe God gave the prophecy concerning the oppressor, the king of Babylon, to also be prophecy about the coming destruction of the oppressor, Satan. Read the chapter again carefully and decide what you believe.

However you interpret the prophecies, the theme of the chapter is clear:

> *The LORD of hosts has planned, and who can frustrate it?*
> —Isaiah 14:27

Let that be a theme in your life.

Pray Isaiah 14:7, 24, and 27 over yourself and those for whom you stand guard as a faithful, prayerful watchman (Isaiah 62:6-7).

> *"LORD, I trust You for my life and the life of _____ ,*
> *that no one can frustrate the plans You have planned for us.*
> *We look forward to the day the whole earth is at rest and is quiet,*
> *when we break forth into shouts of joy. As we wait, we rest*
> *in the confidence that just as You have planned, so it will stand.*
> *In Your name, Jesus~"*

MARCH 9

Please read Isaiah 15.

Meditate on verse 5a.

My heart cries out for Moab.

Moab is present-day Jordan. Isaiah spoke about the burden (oracle) God had for the people of this country.

All of the inhabitants of Moab, even their armed men, wailed in distress over their ruin rather than mourning over their sin, which caused their ruin. Sadly, they went up to their idolatrous temples in their devastation and shame instead of turning to Almighty God. Amazingly, the heart of God cried out for these people who were so blinded by their sin.

Do you have the heart of the Father? What is your attitude toward others who are suffering the consequences of sin? Does your heart break for them?

Pray for God to show you the sin in your own life. After you confess and repent, ask God to give those for whom you stand guard as a faithful, prayerful watchman (Isaiah 62:6-7) a heart to return to Him. Pray for them with the heart of God (Isaiah 15:5a).

"LORD, my heart cries out for _____ .
In Your name, Jesus~"

Please read Isaiah 16.

Meditate on verse 5.

> *A throne will even be established in lovingkindness,*
> *and a judge will sit on it in faithfulness in the tent of David;*
> *moreover, he will seek justice and be prompt in righteousness.*

The burden God had for Moab continues in Isaiah 16. God was burdened for Moab because of the people's pride, arrogance, and fury. God described Moab's pride as excessive and his idle boasts as false (v. 6). Yet again, you see God weeping bitterly for Moab (v. 9). God hates sin, and it breaks His heart when He sees people wearying themselves in it (vs. 11-12).

In the middle of God's oracle concerning Moab, He prophesied the coming of Messiah. The throne of Christ is established in lovingkindness, faithfulness, justice, and righteousness; exactly what you need to counter pride, arrogance, fury, and idle boasts.

Pray Isaiah 16:4 over yourself and those for whom you stand guard as a faithful, prayerful watchman (Isaiah 62:6-7).

> *"LORD, make extortioners, oppressors, and destruction*
> *cease from the lives of _____ and me.*
> *Be a hiding place to us from the destroyer.*
> *In Your name, Jesus~"*

Please read Isaiah 17.

Meditate on verses 10-11.

For you have forgotten the God of your salvation
and have not remembered the rock of your refuge.
Therefore, you plant delightful plants
and set them with vine slips of a strange god.
In that day that you plant it, you carefully fence it in,
and in the morning, you bring your seed to blossom;
but the harvest will be a heap
in a day of sickliness and incurable pain.

God told of the burden (oracle) He had for Damascus, Syria in Isaiah 17. He also reiterated a theme of Isaiah that idol worship is futile.

God will not put up with idols in your life. What are you planting in your life that is more important to you than your relationship with God? What are you carefully tending and caring for that is not pleasing to your LORD? Be honest with God. Listen to the Holy Spirit and ask Him to show you things in your life that are going to end up in a heap unless you uproot them now.

Pray Isaiah 17:7-8 over yourself and those for whom you stand guard as a faithful, prayerful watchman (Isaiah 62:6-7).

"LORD, let _____ and me have regard for You as our Maker.
May our eyes look to You, the Holy One of Israel.
May we stop having regard for the altars, the work of our hands.
Let us not look to that which our fingers have made.
May we only have eyes for You, LORD.
In Your name, Jesus~"

MARCH 12

Please read Isaiah 18.

Meditate on verse 7a.

> *At that time a gift of homage*
> *will be brought to the LORD of hosts*
> *from a people tall and smooth,*
> *even from a people feared far and wide.*

Isaiah 18 tells about a future time when God will cut away and remove those who refuse to honor Him. Compare Isaiah 18:5-6 with Revelation 19:17-21.

Notice what God says about Himself in Isaiah 18:4. "I will look from My dwelling place quietly like dazzling heat in the sunshine, like a cloud of dew in the heat of harvest."

The LORD is patiently waiting for people to come to Him in repentance before He uses His pruning knives to cut off those who oppose Him. Let Him prune the junk in your life that keeps you from wholeheartedly honoring Him.

Pray Isaiah 18:5 and 7 over yourself and those for whom you stand guard as a faithful, prayerful watchman (Isaiah 62:6-7).

> *LORD, use Your pruning knives*
> *to cut off everything keeping*
> *_____ and me from following You.*
> *May our lives be the gift of homage*
> *we bring to You.*
> *In Your name, LORD of hosts~"*

MARCH 13

Please read Isaiah 19.

Meditate on verse 22.

The LORD will strike Egypt, striking but healing;
so they will return to the LORD,
and He will respond to them and will heal them.

The LORD was burdened for Egypt. He was so burdened for them He was going to cause their water to dry up, their crops to be gone, their fish to be gone, their manufacturing to be gone, their leaders and wisest men to be stupid fools ...

God has ways of getting your attention, doesn't He? Isaiah 19:20 said Egypt would "cry to the LORD because of oppressors, and He will send them a Savior and a Champion, and He will deliver them."

Is the LORD trying to get your attention? Is He trying to get the attention of someone you love?

Pray Isaiah 19:20-22 and 24 over yourself and those for whom you stand guard as a faithful, prayerful watchman (Isaiah 62:6-7).

"LORD, _____ and I need a Savior and a Champion.
We need You to deliver us.
LORD, make Yourself known to us.
May we worship You with sacrifice and offering;
may we make a vow to You and perform it.
I know You are striking but healing us,
so we will return to You.
You will respond to us
and heal us when we return to You.
LORD, make us a blessing in the midst of the earth.
In Your name, Jesus~"

Please read Isaiah 20.

Meditate on verse 5.

> *Then they will be dismayed and ashamed*
> *because of Cush their hope and Egypt their boast.*

The northern kingdom of Israel was destroyed by Assyria. The southern kingdom of Judah was fearful of the same fate. They were trusting in Egypt and Cush (present-day Ethiopia and Sudan) to save them from Assyria instead of trusting in the LORD. The LORD had Isaiah dramatize the foolishness of Judah's decision. Isaiah walked naked and barefoot for three years to show the people they were trusting in nations that were going to be taken captive themselves and led away with their buttocks uncovered.

The image is vivid and so is the point God is making. The LORD says, "Trust Me! Anyone or anything else you trust more than you trust Me is going to leave you in captivity with your hind end exposed. You will end up humiliated and looking foolish."

Use Isaiah 20:5-6 as a prayer of confession for yourself and those for whom you stand guard as a faithful, prayerful watchman (Isaiah 62:6-7).

> *"LORD, I confess that _____ and I have*
> *fled to _____ for help to be delivered from _____ .*
> *Now, how are we going to escape?*
> *LORD, forgive us for making them our hope and our boast.*
> *Almighty God, You are our hope and our boast.*
> *You are our Deliverer.*
> *In Your name, Jesus~"*

Please read Isaiah 21.

Meditate on verse 10.

O my threshed people and my afflicted of the threshing floor!
What I have heard from the LORD of hosts,
the God of Israel, I make known to you.

God gave Isaiah a harsh vision, which caused his loins to be full of anguish, for him to have pains like a woman in labor, and for him to be so bewildered and terrified he could not hear or see. Isaiah was overwhelmed with horror at the vision of God's impending judgment.

The watchman in Isaiah 21 announces that morning is coming but also night. God's final judgment is coming. It will bring morning for believers, but it will bring the darkest night to nonbelievers. The LORD's judgment will be horrific for those who do not know Jesus.

Who has God placed in your life that is threshed and afflicted? Will they be in trembling, eternal darkness when Christ returns? Pray for God to give you the opportunity to make known to them what you have heard from the LORD of hosts.

Pray Isaiah 21:10 and 14 over yourself as a faithful, prayerful watchman (Isaiah 62:6-7).

"LORD, I want to bring water to
the thirsty and bread to the fugitive.
Jesus, You are the Living Water, the Bread of Life.
Give me the courage and the opportunity
to say to the threshed and afflicted,
'What I have heard from the LORD of hosts,
the God of Israel, I make known to you.'
In the name of Jesus~"

Please read Isaiah 22.

Meditate on verses 5a and 11b.

> *For the LORD God of hosts has a day of panic,*
> *subjugation, and confusion in the valley of vision.*
> *But you did not depend on Him who made it,*
> *nor did you take into consideration*
> *Him who planned it long ago.*

Isaiah 22 is a prophecy concerning Jerusalem that was fulfilled over 2,500 years ago. The LORD made sure it was written down for you to take to heart today. The people of Jerusalem depended on weapons, resources, and other people to meet their needs instead of depending on God. They refused to repent and return to the LORD. It resulted in panic, confusion, and destruction.

History does not have to repeat itself in your life. Are you in the process of creating a vision for your future? Have you taken into consideration Him who already has the plan for your life and will reveal it to you if you depend on Him? If you are experiencing a day of panic and confusion, repent and turn to the LORD for His vision.

Pray for yourself and those for whom you stand guard as a faithful, prayerful watchman (Isaiah 62:6-7) to have the opposite of an Isaiah 22:11-13 attitude.

> *"LORD, remove the attitude from _____ and me of*
> *'Let us eat and drink, for tomorrow we die.'*
> *May we come to You in repentance*
> *as You call us to weeping and wailing over sin in our lives.*
> *LORD, we depend on You.*
> *We want to live Your plan for our lives.*
> *In Your name, Jesus~"*

MARCH 17

Please read Isaiah 23.

Meditate on verse 9.

The LORD of hosts has planned it,
to defile the pride of all beauty,
to despise all the honored of the earth.

Isaiah 23 was addressed to Tyre, present-day Lebanon. Read Ezekial 28 for a description of the king of Tyre, the ultimate example of pride.

This chapter concludes the oracles, the burden God has for people who refuse to acknowledge Him. Isaiah 13-23 teaches you these things:

- God reigns supreme.
- God has and will judge the nations that have oppressed Israel.
- The nations will bow and bend the knee to the LORD.
- Do not look to world powers or fear them.
- Fear God.

Use Isaiah 23:9, 12, and 18 to pray for the humility God desires in your life as a faithful, prayerful watchman (Isaiah 62:6-7).

"LORD, I do not want to exult in myself.
You defile the pride of beauty
and despise the honored of the earth.
I want to dwell in Your presence, LORD.
In Your name, Jesus~"

Please read Isaiah 24.

Meditate on verses 4 and 5.

> *The earth mourns and withers, the world fades and withers,*
> *the exalted of the people of the earth fade away.*
> *The earth is also polluted by its inhabitants,*
> *for they transgressed laws, violated statutes,*
> *broke the everlasting covenant.*

Isaiah 24 gives a vivid description of God's coming judgment on all the inhabitants of the earth who do not know Him as LORD and Savior. "Therefore, a curse devours the earth, and those who live in it are held guilty. Therefore, the inhabitants of the earth are burned, and few men are left" (Isaiah 24:6).

The party is over in verses 7-13; the worldly party will end and glorifying the Righteous One will fill the earth (Isaiah 24:14-16). Isaiah 24 is a great chapter to share with people about the coming wrath of God; the only way of escape is through a relationship with Jesus Christ.

Pray Isaiah 24:16 over yourself and those for whom you stand guard as a faithful, prayerful watchman (Isaiah 62:6-7).

> *"LORD, let _____ and me be singing this song,*
> *'Glory to the Righteous One.'*
> *In Your name, Jesus~"*

90 | *The* WATCHMAN *on the* WALL

Please read Isaiah 25.

Say verse 1 to your LORD.

O LORD, You are my God;
I will exalt You,
I will give thanks to Your name;
For You have worked wonders,
plans formed long ago,
with perfect faithfulness.

Isaiah 25 is a sigh of relief. God is in control! His plans were formed long ago in perfect faithfulness. His plans will prevail!

This chapter of Isaiah gives you a glimpse into some of God's future plans: the silencing of the ruthless, a lavish banquet being prepared for you and all believers, the swallowing up of death for all time, the LORD Himself wiping away your tears … Reread these precious 12 verses of Isaiah 25 and rest in God's promises.

Pray Isaiah 25:9 as a faithful, prayerful watchman (Isaiah 62:6-7). You will be saying the very words you are going to say that day you see the LORD face to face.

LORD, please bring _____
into a saving relationship with You,
so together we will say,
'Behold, this is our God for whom
we have waited that He might save us.
This is the LORD for whom we have waited;
let us rejoice and be glad in His salvation.'
In Your name, Jesus~"

Please read Isaiah 26.

Meditate on verses 3-4.

> *The steadfast of mind You will keep in perfect peace*
> *because he trusts in You.*
> *Trust in the LORD forever, for in God the LORD,*
> *we have an everlasting Rock.*

In Isaiah 26:3, *steadfast* means to lean upon, brace yourself, rest yourself. God promises perfect peace to those who rest upon Him. Would you describe yourself as a person who leans and rests on God? Do you trust in yourself to accomplish tasks or do you trust in the LORD? Isaiah confesses in verse 12, "LORD, You will establish peace for us, since You have also performed for us all our works."

Keep your mind steadfast on the LORD today. Recognize it is Christ in you who performs all your works.

Pray Isaiah 26:7-9 over yourself and those for whom you stand guard as a faithful, prayerful watchman (Isaiah 62:7-9).

> *"LORD, make _____ and me righteous and may we say:*
> *'The way of the righteous is smooth;'*
> *O Upright One, make the path of the righteous level.*
> *Indeed, while following the way of Your judgments, O LORD,*
> *we have waited for You eagerly;*
> *Your name, even Your memory, is the desire of our souls.*
> *At night my soul longs for You,*
> *indeed my spirit within me seeks You diligently;*
> *for when the earth experiences Your judgments,*
> *the inhabitants of the world learn righteousness.*
> *In Your name, Jesus~"*

Please read Isaiah 27.

Meditate on verse 5.

> *Or let him rely on My protection.*
> *Let him make peace with Me.*
> *Let him make peace with Me.*

Isaiah 27 tells you about the future destruction of the serpent/dragon (Satan, see Revelation 12:9; 20:2, 10), God's forgiveness and restoration of Israel, and the gathering of people from the nations to worship Him. It is exciting to read and think about end time prophecies. It is also sobering because like the dragon, the end of time will be a day of destruction for those who do not know the LORD.

Pray Isaiah 27:5 and 9 over those for whom you stand guard as a faithful, prayerful watchman (Isaiah 62:6-7).

> *"LORD, I pray for _____ to come to You*
> *to forgive their iniquity.*
> *Jesus, thank You for paying*
> *the full price for pardoning their sin.*
> *May they rely on Your protection.*
> *Let them make peace with You.*
> *Let them make peace with You.*
> *In Your name, Jesus~"*

Please read Isaiah 28.

Meditate on verse 15.

> *Because you have said, "We have made a covenant with death,*
> *and with Sheol we have made a pact.*
> *The overwhelming scourge will not reach us when it passes by,*
> *for we have made falsehood our refuge*
> *and we have concealed ourselves with deception."*

This is a powerful chapter from God's Word. God addressed people who, in their pride, made covenants with death instead of the God of Life. They were deceived and full of lies; they thought they could escape God's judgment. They were so overcome with wine and strong drink they were reeling, and their tables were full of filthy vomit without a single clean place (Isaiah 28:7-8).

Without being in a saving covenant relationship with Jesus Christ, your life is nothing more than confusing, staggering, and vomit filled. Why would anyone choose to make a covenant with death when God offers everyone the covenant with LIFE through Christ Jesus the LORD?

Pray Isaiah 28:21, 26, and 29 over yourself and those for whom you stand guard as a faithful, prayerful watchman (Isaiah 62:6-7) to put an end to the covenant of death in your lives.

> *"LORD, rise up and be stirred up to do Your task,*
> *Your unusual task, and to work Your work,*
> *Your extraordinary work in _____ and me.*
> *Instruct and teach us properly.*
> *Your counsel is wonderful and Your wisdom is great.*
> *In Your name, Jesus~"*

Please read Isaiah 29.

Meditate on 13.

Then the LORD said,
"Because this people draw near with their words
and honor Me with their lip service,
but they remove their hearts far from Me,
and their reverence for Me consists of
tradition learned by rote ..."

It is time to ask yourself some questions. How would you describe your Christianity? Is it going to church, saying the Apostle's Creed, and the LORD's Prayer then returning home to do your own thing the rest of the week? Or is it walking every moment of every day in love and in conversation with the Savior of your soul?

Is your Christianity a relationship with Jesus Christ, or is it merely the traditions of your church?

God does not like tradition without relationship. In Isaiah 29, God pronounced a woe to Ariel (Jerusalem). The people performed their religious rituals, but they were not reading and understanding the Word of God. They removed their hearts far from the LORD.

Are you like the people of Jerusalem? Do you know someone who is like the people God is addressing in Isaiah 29?

Pray Isaiah 29:18 and 24 over yourself and those for whom you stand guard as a faithful, prayerful watchman (Isaiah 62:6-7).

"LORD, remove spiritual deafness from _____ and me.
Let us hear the Words of Your Book.
Out of our gloom and darkness, let our blind eyes see.
Let us not err in mind but know the truth.
Help us not criticize but accept instruction.
In Your name, Jesus~"

Please read Isaiah 30.

Meditate on verses 1, 9, and 10.

> *"Woe to the rebellious children," declares the LORD,*
> *"who execute a plan, but not Mine, and make an*
> *alliance, but not of My Spirit, in order to add sin to*
> *sin." For this is a rebellious people, false sons, sons who*
> *refuse to listen to the instruction of the LORD;*
> *who say to the seers, "You must not see visions"; and to the prophets,*
> *"You must not prophesy to us what is right,*
> *speak to us pleasant words, prophesy illusions."*

God's Word is timeless. Isaiah was prophesying 2,700 years ago, yet these words describe people living today. How often do you execute a plan without making sure it is God's plan for your life? Do you listen to the LORD's instructions? Do you want to hear what is right in the sight of Almighty God, or would you rather hear teaching that is pleasant to your ears, so you can continue in the illusion you are doing okay with God? Would God describe you as a true child of His or as a rebellious, false child?

Pray Isaiah 30:15 and 21 over yourself and those for whom you stand guard as a faithful, prayerful watchman (Isaiah 62:6-7).

> *"LORD God, the Holy One of Israel,*
> *in repentance and rest _____ and I will be saved,*
> *in quietness and trust is our strength.*
> *Make us willing to live that truth.*
> *Tune our ears to hear and obey Your Word when it says,*
> *'This is the way, walk in it,'*
> *whenever we turn to the right or to the left.*
> *In Your name, Jesus~"*

Please read Isaiah 31.

Meditate on verse 1.

> *Woe to those who go down to Egypt*
> *for help and rely on horses,*
> *and trust in chariots*
> *because they are many*
> *and in horsemen*
> *because they are very strong,*
> *but they do not look to the Holy One of Israel,*
> *nor seek the LORD!*

In the first part of Isaiah, God declared oracles (His burdens) for the people. In this section of Isaiah, the LORD pronounced woes on them. A "woe" from the LORD implies great disapproval. You do not want to get "woe-d" by God.

Take heed to the Word of the LORD. Placing your trust, reliance, and confidence in anyone or anything more than Almighty God will always be met with a "woe" from Him. Trusting in anything besides God to save you is idolatry, and the LORD will not put up with it.

Examine your life. In whom or what do you put your trust? From the salvation of your soul to the decision of what to do in the next five minutes, on what or whom are you relying?

Pray Isaiah 31:6 over yourself and those for whom you stand guard as a faithful, prayerful watchman (Isaiah 62:6-7).

> *"LORD, may _____ and I return to You*
> *from whom we have deeply defected.*
> *In Your name, Jesus~"*

Please read Isaiah 32.

Meditate on verse 17.

> *And the work of righteousness will be peace,*
> *and the service of righteousness,*
> *quietness and confidence forever.*

Isaiah 32 described the desolate wilderness that was Jerusalem. Her only hope was for the Spirit to be poured out on the people. This is the description of your life without the Holy Spirit, an abandoned, forsaken wilderness.

When the Spirit is poured out upon you, your wilderness of a life becomes a fertile field, a forest. Justice and righteousness dwell in you bringing peace, quietness, and confidence forever.

Being in a saving relationship with Jesus Christ is amazing! You do not have to remain in your wilderness.

Pray Isaiah 32:3-4 over yourself and those for whom you stand guard as a faithful, prayerful watchman (Isaiah 62:6-7).

> *"LORD, pour Your Spirit upon _____ and me.*
> *Let our eyes not be blinded, and let our ears listen.*
> *Let our hasty mind discern the truth*
> *and our stammering tongue hasten to speak clearly.*
> *In Your name, Jesus~"*

Please read Isaiah 33.

Meditate on verse 6a.

And He will be the stability of your times.

You live in a world that appears unstable. Just reading a news article can cause your heart to race with anxiety.

Reread Isaiah 33. Isaiah's words penned 2,700 years ago are intended to comfort and encourage you, today. The world 2,700 years ago appeared as unstable as it does today, perhaps even more so.

Here is the truth:

> The LORD is still our judge.
>
> The LORD is still our lawgiver.
>
> The LORD is still our king.
>
> He will save us (Isaiah 33:22).

Stop being afraid when you read the news; instead pray Isaiah 33:2 and 6 over yourself and those for whom you stand guard as a faithful, prayerful watchman (Isaiah 62:6-7).

"O LORD, be gracious to _____ and me
as we wait for You.
Be our strength every morning,
our salvation also in the time of distress.
You will be the stability of our times,
a wealth of salvation, wisdom, and knowledge;
the fear of You is our treasure.
In Your name, Jesus~"

Please read Isaiah 34.

Meditate on verse 5.

For My sword is satiated in heaven;
behold it shall descend for judgment upon Edom
and upon the people whom I have devoted to destruction.

Isaiah 34 describes the LORD's coming day of vengeance. It is a time when the LORD's indignation and wrath will be poured out on all of mankind. God hates it when people, like Edom (Esau), despise the birthright He has given them to become a child of His and sell it for a bowl of the world's "red stuff" (Genesis 25:30-34; Malachi 1:3). People who choose the way of the world rather than the way of Jesus Christ are forewarned in Isaiah 34:2 that they will be utterly destroyed and given over to slaughter.

Yet God desires for all men to be saved and come to knowledge of the truth (1 Timothy 2:3-4). Salvation is why the LORD invites all people to hear and listen in Isaiah 34:1.

Pray Isaiah 34:1 and 16 over those in your life who are Edoms and need to be saved from the coming wrath of the LORD. Pray for them as their faithful, prayerful watchman (Isaiah 62:6-7).

"LORD, please let _____ hear and listen to You.
Holy Spirit, gather them.
May they seek and read from Your Book.
In Your name, Jesus~"

Please read Isaiah 35.

Meditate on verse 4.

> *Say to those with anxious heart,*
> *"Take courage, fear not.*
> *Behold, your God will come with vengeance;*
> *the recompense of God will come,*
> *but He will save you."*

Isaiah 35 tells about a time when the wilderness and the desert will have pools and springs of water and will blossom profusely. There will be a roadway called the Highway of Holiness, and the redeemed will walk on it. Everlasting joy will radiate from the faces of the redeemed.

This chapter is like a breath of fresh air in the midst of God's burdens and woes for people. You may have someone in your life who is a burden and a woe to you because you do not know for sure they are counted with the redeemed who will be walking the Highway of Holiness. Pray for them to ask Christ, the Living Water (John 7:38), to come and forever change their desert of a life.

Pray Isaiah 35:5-6 and 10 over those for whom you stand guard as a faithful, prayerful watchman (Isaiah 62:6-7).

> *"LORD,_____ is spiritually*
> *blind, deaf, lame, and mute.*
> *Let Your waters break forth in the wilderness of their life.*
> *Open their eyes, unstop their ears,*
> *let them leap like a deer and shout for joy.*
> *LORD, ransom them.*
> *May everlasting joy be upon their head.*
> *Let them find gladness and joy,*
> *and let sorrow and sighing flee away from them.*
> *In Your name, Jesus~"*

Please read Isaiah 36.

Meditate on verse 21.

> *But they were silent and answered him not a word;*
> *for the king's commandment was, "Do not answer him."*

Enter Rabshakeh, the Assyrian bully. Sennacherib, king of Assyria, sent him to Judah. Rabshakeh seized the fortified cities of Judah and taunted the people about trusting in God. He bragged about coming up against Judah without the LORD's approval. He threatened the people not to believe King Hezekiah.

Do you have a Rabshakeh in your life? Someone who tries to "shake" your confidence in Christ? Someone who wants you to question the LORD's miraculous provision and care for you and your family? Someone who tells you that God is not trustworthy, and you need to be doing something different rather than waiting and depending on the LORD?

Sometimes Rabshakeh is a person who is trying to talk you into doing something that is not God's will for your life. Sometimes Rabshakeh is the voice in your head that doubts God and His promises.

Rabshakehs need to be ignored. You do not owe them an answer, and if Rabshakeh is in your head, stop conversing with him. Pray without ceasing to the One who is your only source of strength and provision.

Pray Isaiah 36:7 and 21 over yourself and those for whom you stand guard as a faithful, prayerful watchman (Isaiah 62:6-7).

> *"Father, may _____ and I say, 'We trust in the LORD, our God.'*
> *Give us the wisdom not to answer the Rabshakehs in our lives.*
> *We only have to answer to You, Jesus,*
> *In whose name I pray~"*

Please read Isaiah 37.

Meditate on verse 21.

> *Then Isaiah the son of Amoz sent word to Hezekiah, saying,*
> *"Thus says the LORD, the God of Israel,*
> *'Because you have prayed to Me about*
> *Sennacherib king of Assyria...'"*

"Because you have prayed to Me ..." Does prayer make a difference? God tells you in Isaiah 37 that it does. The LORD handled Hezekiah's difficult situation because he prayed. God told Hezekiah the reason He spoke against King Sennacherib was because Hezekiah spread out the threatening letter before the LORD and prayed, asking God for deliverance.

What situation is threatening you or someone you love? In your human eyes, what looks impossible? God takes great delight in doing the impossible for His own sake, so everyone will know the LORD alone is God.

As a faithful, prayerful watchman (Isaiah 62:6-7), spread out the impossible before the LORD praying Isaiah 37:16–20.

> *"O LORD of hosts, the God of Israel,*
> *who is enthroned above the cherubim, You are the God,*
> *You alone, of all the kingdoms of the earth.*
> *You have made heaven and earth.*
> *Incline Your ear, O LORD, and hear;*
> *open Your eyes, O LORD, and see;*
> *and listen to all the words of my impossible situation.*
> *Truly, O LORD, I feel devastated, and it*
> *looks like we will be destroyed.*
> *Now, O LORD our God, deliver us from _____ that*
> *everyone may know that You alone, LORD, are God.*
> *In Your name, Jesus~"*

APRIL

On your walls, O Jerusalem,
I have appointed watchmen;
All day and all night they
will never keep silent.
You who remind the LORD,
take no rest for yourselves;
And give Him no rest
until He establishes
And makes Jerusalem a
praise in the earth.
Isaiah 62:6-7, NASB

Please read Isaiah 38.

Meditate on verse 14b.

> *O LORD, I am oppressed;*
> *be my security.*

King Hezekiah was sick and about to die. Just as he spread out the threatening letter from the Assyrians before the LORD (Isaiah 37), he spread his life out before the Almighty and begged God to heal him. Hezekiah knew to whom he must go if he was really going to get the help he needed.

Just as God was his security against the Assyrian threats, God was his security for all of life. The LORD heard King Hezekiah's prayer and added 15 years to his life.

What oppression are you or someone you love facing today? Go to your only real security and pray Isaiah 38:3, 17, and 20 as a faithful, prayerful watchman (Isaiah 62:6-7).

> *"LORD, it is You who has kept _____ and my soul*
> *from the pit of nothingness,*
> *for You have cast all our sins behind Your back.*
> *Remember now, O LORD, I beseech You,*
> *how we have walked before You in truth*
> *and with a whole heart,*
> *and have done what is good in Your sight.*
> *LORD, I know You will surely save us.*
> *For Your name's sake, Jesus~"*

APRIL 2

Please read Isaiah 39.

Meditate on verse 5.

Then Isaiah said to Hezekiah,
"Hear the Word of the LORD of hosts."

God gave Hezekiah an additional fifteen years to live. Then Hezekiah got full of himself. Hezekiah's story was recorded for all eternity, so you can learn from his prideful mistakes. Hezekiah showed the king of Babylon ALL his treasure house. When the Babylonians attacked Jerusalem less than 100 years after King Hezekiah's show and tell, they knew exactly what the treasures of Jerusalem were and where they were located.

Do you ever get carried away? Do you ever talk too much, brag too much, show off too much? Be mindful of who you are lifting up. Do your words and actions exalt your glorious LORD Jesus Christ, or do they exalt self?

The inhabitants of Jerusalem paid dearly for a king who got full of himself. Notice Hezekiah's selfishness in Isaiah 39:8. Isaiah told Hezekiah of the coming punishment of God even on his own children, and Hezekiah's response was, "Well, at least there will be peace and truth in my days."

Pray Isaiah 39:5 and 8 over yourself and those for whom you stand guard as a faithful, prayerful watchman (Isaiah 62:6-7).

"LORD, the Word you have spoken is indeed good.
May _____ and I hear it and obey.
Keep our foolish pride in check.
In Your name, Jesus~"

Please read Isaiah 40.

Meditate on verse 31.

Yet those who wait for the LORD will gain new strength;
They will mount up with wings like eagles;
they will run and not get tired;
they will walk and not become weary.

Have you ever watched an eagle soar? These powerful birds do not soar on their own strength; they spread their wings and ride thermals upward. They don't have to beat their wings; they effortlessly lift heavenward as they trust in another source of power instead of their own. What a perfect comparison God gives you! Honestly, you are not going to accomplish anything on your own strength, but when you soar on the strength of the Creator of the universe and the Resurrector of the dead, you can do all things through Christ who gives you strength (Philippians 4:13).

Pray Isaiah 40:31 over yourself and those for whom you stand guard as a faithful, prayerful watchman (Isaiah 62:6-7).

"LORD, let _____ and me wait for You.
Thank You that as we do, we will gain new strength;
we will mount up with wings like eagles;
we will run and not get tired;
we will walk and not become weary.
In Your strong name, Jesus~"

APRIL 4

Please read Isaiah 41.

Meditate on verse 10.

> *Do not fear, for I am with you;*
> *Do not anxiously look about you, for I am your God.*

Isaiah has 66 chapters like there are 66 books in the Bible. The fortieth chapter of Isaiah begins with these words, "'Comfort, O comfort My people,' says your God."

The fortieth book of the Bible is Matthew. Matthew begins with these words, "The record of the genealogy of Jesus, the Messiah."

The remainder of Isaiah talks about the coming salvation of the LORD. The LORD promised the Messiah would come in Isaiah. God keeps His Word.

Isaiah 41:10-13 contains more promises from God. Pray these verses over a situation where you or someone you stand guard for as a faithful, prayerful watchman (Isaiah 62:6-7) needs the LORD's help.

> *"LORD, I believe You when You tell me these words:*
> *'Do not fear, for I am with you;*
> *Do not anxiously look about you, for I am your God.*
> *I will strengthen you, surely I will help you,*
> *surely I will uphold you with My righteous right hand.*
> *Behold all those who are angered at you*
> *will be shamed and dishonored;*
> *those who contend with you will be as nothing and will perish.*
> *You will seek those who quarrel with you, but will not find them.*
> *Those who war with you will be as nothing and non-existent.*

For I am the LORD your God who upholds your right hand,
who says to you, "Do not fear; I will help you."'
Thank You, Father, in the name of Jesus–"

Author's Note (from Marsha): I prayed these verses everyday when my husband was in Iraq. They brought me much comfort, and God was faithful to bring them to pass.

APRIL 5

Please read Isaiah 42.

Meditate on verses 8-9.

> *I am the LORD; that is My name;*
> *I will not give My glory to another;*
> *nor My praise to graven images.*
> *Behold, the former things have come to pass.*
> *Now I declare new things;*
> *Before they spring forth, I proclaim them to you.*

This chapter begins with prophecies of the LORD's servant coming and establishing justice on the earth. This servant would be a covenant to the people and a light to the nations. Jesus fulfilled these prophecies. In Him, everything you need is accomplished and provided.

The LORD addressed Israel and others who were spiritually blind and deaf. He was searching for people who would observe, hear, and heed His Words. Are you paying attention to God? Ask Him to give you ears to hear and eyes to see.

Pray Isaiah 42:16 over yourself and those for whom you stand guard as a faithful, prayerful watchman (Isaiah 62:6-7).

> *"LORD, lead blind _____ and me*
> *by a way we do not know;*
> *in paths we do not know, guide us.*
> *Make darkness into light before us*
> *and rugged places into plains.*
> *Thank You that You do not leave us undone.*
> *For the sake of Your glory and praise, Jesus~"*

Read Isaiah 43.

Meditate on verse 25.

> *I, even I, am the One who*
> *wipes out your transgressions*
> *for My own sake,*
> *and I will not remember your sins.*

There are amazing verses in this chapter about who God is. He is the LORD. There is no Savior besides Him. Even from eternity, He is God. None can deliver out of His hand. He acts and who can reverse it? He is your Redeemer, your Holy One, your Creator, your King (Isaiah 43:11-15).

Meditate on these truths. Enjoy worshipping and praising your LORD.

Pray Isaiah 43:11-15, 21, and 25 as a faithful, prayerful watchman (Isaiah 62:6-7).

> *"LORD, You formed _____ and me for Yourself.*
> *We will declare Your praise.*
> *Thank You for wiping out our transgressions for Your own sake*
> *and for not remembering our sins.*
> *You are:*
> *God*
> *LORD*
> *Savior*
> *Redeemer*
> *Holy One*
> *Creator*
> *King*
> *You are Jesus in whose name I pray-"*

APRIL 7

Please read Isaiah 44.

Meditate on verses 6 and 8.

> *Thus says the LORD, the King of Israel and his Redeemer,*
> *the LORD of hosts:"I am the first and I am the last,*
> *and there is no God besides Me. Do not tremble and*
> *do not be afraid. Have I not long since announced it to*
> *you and declared it? And you are My witnesses.*
> *Is there any God besides Me, or is there any other Rock?*
> *I know of none."*

Isaiah 44:9-20 talks about the foolishness and irrationality of trusting in idols, of putting your hope in anyone or anything besides Almighty God. A deceived heart turns you aside from trusting in the LORD. You think you can deliver yourself. You do not recognize what you are holding onto is a lie in your right hand (Isaiah 44:20). The only thing that should be in your right hand is the LORD's hand: "For I am the LORD your God, who upholds your right hand, Who says to you, 'Do not fear; I will help you'" (Isaiah 41:13).

Pray the promises of Isaiah 44:3-5 over yourself and those for whom you stand guard as a faithful, prayerful watchman (Isaiah 62:6-7).

> *"LORD, please pour out these promises on _____ and me today.*
> *'I will pour out water on the thirsty land and streams on*
> *the dry ground. I will pour out My Spirit on your offspring*
> *and My blessing on your descendants, and they will*
> *spring up among the grass like poplars by streams of water.*
> *This one will say, "I am the LORD's;" And that one will*
> *call on the name of Jacob; And another will*
> *write on his hand, "'Belonging to the LORD,'"*
> *And will name Israel's name with honor.'*
> *In Your name, Jesus~"*

Please read Isaiah 45.

Meditate on verse 5.

I am the LORD, and there is no other;
besides Me there is no God.

God talked to Cyrus in this chapter. The LORD told Cyrus He called him by name. Anything Cyrus had, God gave to him. The things Cyrus did were because the LORD took Cyrus by the right hand to do what God desired.

The LORD had Isaiah pen these words concerning King Cyrus the Great of Persia 175 years before Cyrus was born. Cyrus conquered Babylon where the Israelites were in exile for 70 years. He issued the decree for the Israelites to return to Israel and rebuild the temple (2 Chronicles 36:22-23). Cyrus, the great pagan king of Persia, who did not know God (Isaiah 45:4), was an instrument in the hand of The Almighty.

As a faithful, prayerful watchman (Isaiah 62:6-7), pray Isaiah 45:21-24 over those who need to bow the knee to Almighty God.

"You are the LORD.
There is no God besides You.
You are a righteous God and a Savior;
there is none except You.
Please let_____ turn to You,
for You are God, and there is no other.
Your Word has gone forth from Your mouth
in righteousness and will not turn back.
Let_____ bow their knee and swear allegiance to you.
Let them say, 'Only in the LORD are righteousness and strength.'
In Your name, Jesus-"

Please read Isaiah 46.

Meditate on verses 9-10.

> *Remember the former things long past,*
> *for I am God, and there is no other;*
> *I am God, and there is no one like Me,*
> *declaring the end from the beginning,*
> *and from ancient times things which have not been done,*
> *saying, "My purpose will be established,*
> *and I will accomplish all My good pleasure."*

In Isaiah 46, God challenges you to examine your life and determine what you are trusting to save and deliver you. Isaiah 46:1 names two idols, Bel and Nebo. Bel was the main deity of the Babylonians, and Nebo was the god of learning, writing, and astronomy. People hoped these idols would rescue them from their burdens.

What are you investing time, money, and energy into hoping it will rescue you and bring you relief? God says to you, "Listen to Me! You have been borne by Me from birth and have been carried from the womb; even to your old age; I will be the same, and even to your graying years, I will bear you. I have done it, and I will carry you; and I will bear you, and I will deliver you" (Isaiah 46:3-4).

Deliverance comes when you acknowledge your total dependence on Almighty God. Relief comes when you humbly return to the only One who can save and rescue you.

Pray Isaiah 46:12-13 over yourself and those for whom you stand guard as a faithful, prayerful watchman (Isaiah 62:6-7).

> *"LORD, please help _____and me*
> *stop being stubborn-minded*
> *and far from righteousness and listen to You.*
> *Bring us near to Your righteousness, salvation, and glory.*
> *In Your name, Jesus~"*

APRIL 10

Please read Isaiah 47.

Meditate on verse 4.

Our Redeemer, the LORD of hosts is His name,
The Holy One of Israel.

God used the Babylonians to punish Israel for their idolatrous disobedience to Him. Babylon was merciless in their dealings, so God was mad. "Judgment will be merciless to one who has shown no mercy; mercy triumphs over judgment" (James 2:13).

The Babylonians did not show mercy. They felt secure in their wickedness and knowledge. They were arrogant. "I am, and there is no one besides me," they said (Isaiah 47:8, 10).

God said, "I am the LORD, and there is no other. I am God, and there is no other" (Isaiah 45:5, 6, 18, 21, 22).

The LORD destroyed Babylon. That world power ceased to exist overnight (Daniel 5:30-31).

There are lessons to be learned from Babylon. God will punish a Babylonian attitude: merciless, arrogant, god of your own life, shamelessly living in wickedness, and wandering in your own way.

As a faithful, prayerful watchman (Isaiah 62:6-7), cry out Isaiah 47:4 for yourself and others who need to be saved from their Babylonian existence.

"Our Redeemer, the LORD of hosts,
The Holy One of Israel, save _____ and me!
For the sake of Your name, Jesus~"

Please read Isaiah 48.

Meditate on verses 3-5.

> *I declared the former things long ago, and they went forth from*
> *My mouth, and I proclaimed them. Suddenly I acted,*
> *and they came to pass. Because I know that you are obstinate,*
> *and your neck is an iron sinew and your forehead bronze;*
> *therefore, I declared them to you long ago. Before they took place,*
> *I proclaimed them to you, so that you would not say,*
> *"My idol has done them, and my graven image*
> *and my molten image have commanded them."*

To whom do you give credit for what is happening in your life? God told Israel if they had paid attention to His commandments, their well-being would have been like a river, and their righteousness like the waves of the sea (Isaiah 48:18).

God wants you to pay attention to Him. Blessings come when you do.

Pray Isaiah 48:17-19 over yourself and those for whom you stand guard as a faithful, prayerful watchman (Isaiah 62:6-7).

> *"LORD, You are _____ and my Redeemer,*
> *the Holy One of Israel. You are God who teaches us what*
> *is best for us. You lead us in the way we should go.*
> *LORD, help us to pay attention to Your commandments,*
> *so our well-being will be like a river and our righteousness*
> *like the waves of the sea. Let our descendants be like the sand;*
> *our offspring like its grains. May their name never be cut off*
> *or destroyed from Your presence.*
> *In Your name, Jesus~"*

Please read Isaiah 49.

Meditate on verses 23b and 26b.

> *And you will know that I am the LORD;*
> *those who hopefully wait for Me will not be put to shame.*
> *And all flesh will know that I, the LORD, am your Savior*
> *and your Redeemer, the Mighty One of Jacob.*

Through the prophet Isaiah, God told the future of Israel. Isaiah 49 is a good news chapter for this beloved nation of His. At different times in history, Israel thought God forgot her, but God promised never to forget Israel (Isaiah 49:15).

If you are a child of God, the LORD never forgets you either. You have the promises of Israel because in Christ, you have been grafted into this relationship with Him (Romans 11). God saved you and redeemed you for His renown and glory, so all flesh will know He is the LORD. In all your ways acknowledge Him (Proverbs 3:6). He loves it when you choose to recognize Him.

Pray Isaiah 49:1-2 and 5 over those for whom you stand guard as a faithful, prayerful watchman (Isaiah 62:6-7).

> *"LORD, You called _____ from the womb.*
> *From the body of their mother, You named them.*
> *Make their mouth like a sharp sword.*
> *In the shadow of Your hand conceal them.*
> *Make them a select arrow; hide them in Your quiver.*
> *LORD, You have formed them from the womb to be Your servant.*
> *God, be their strength.*
> *In Your name, Jesus~"*

Please read Isaiah 50.

Meditate on verse 10.

> *Who is among you that fears the LORD,*
> *That obeys the voice of His servant,*
> *That walks in darkness and has no light?*
> *Let him trust in the name of the LORD and rely on his God.*

Isaiah 50:4-9 contains prophecy about the coming of Messiah. Without Christ, you are sold into slavery to sin. No man can do anything about it, but God's hand is not too short that He cannot ransom, and He has the power to deliver (Isaiah 50:1-2). Christ set His face like flint to do whatever it took to save you (Isaiah 50:6-7). What it took was His life given for yours in horrific abuse and death on the cross. The only appropriate response to that sacrifice is to fear the LORD, trust in His name, obey the voice of Jesus, and rely on God (Isaiah 50:10).

Isaiah 50:4-5 is a description of Christ. Pray these verses over yourself and those for whom you stand guard as a faithful, prayerful watchman (Isaiah 62:6-7), asking God to make you more like Jesus.

> *"LORD God, give _____ and me the tongue of disciples*
> *that we may know how to sustain the weary one with a word.*
> *Awaken us morning by morning.*
> *Awaken our ear to listen as a disciple.*
> *Open our ear and*
> *do not let us be disobedient or turn back.*
> *In Your name, Jesus-"*

APRIL 14

Please read Isaiah 51.

Meditate on verses 1 and 4.

Listen to me, you who pursue righteousness, who seek the LORD;
Look to the rock from which you were hewn
and to the quarry from which you were dug.

Pay attention to Me, O My people, and give ear to Me,
O My nation; for a law will go forth from Me,
And I will set My justice for a light of the peoples.

The prophet Isaiah spoke in the first verse giving you Godly advice. God spoke in the fourth verse commanding you to pay attention to Him.

To whom do you pay attention? Where do you turn for advice? What is your first reaction to a troubling or a joyous situation? Do you thank the LORD and ask for His wisdom and help? Are your thoughts filled with the Word of God?

Pray Isaiah 51:7, 12-13, and 15-16 over yourself and those for whom you stand guard as a faithful, prayerful watchman (Isaiah 62:6-7).

"LORD, You are God our Maker.
The LORD of hosts is Your name.
You stretched out the heavens
and laid the foundation of the earth.
You are the One who comforts _____ and me.
Do not let us be afraid of man who dies
or of the fury of the oppressor.
Put Your Words in our mouth.
Cover us with the shadow of Your hand.
Make us know righteousness
and put Your Law in our heart.
In Your name, Jesus~"

APRIL 15

Please read Isaiah 52.

Meditate on verse 8.

> *Listen! Your watchmen lift up their voices;*
> *they shout joyfully together,*
> *for they will see with their own eyes*
> *when the LORD restores Zion.*

Answered prayer is cause for rejoicing. God told about a future time when watchmen for Israel will rejoice because of Israel's restoration. God promised comfort, redemption, and salvation for His people. Because of Jesus Christ, these promises are for you and those for whom you are a watchman. Your comfort is abundant through Christ (2 Corinthians 1:3). You have redemption through the blood of Jesus (Ephesians 1:7). And there is salvation in no other name except Jesus Christ (Acts 4:12).

Keep praying for those God needs to restore. The rejoicing will be worth the time you spend faithfully watching over them in prayer.

Pray Isaiah 52:7 over yourself and those for whom you stand guard as a faithful, prayerful watchman (Isaiah 62:6-7).

> *"LORD, make the feet of _____ and me*
> *lovely on the mountains.*
> *Let us bring good news.*
> *May we announce peace and salvation*
> *and bring good news of happiness.*
> *Let us say to Zion and the rest of the world,*
> *'Our God reigns!'*
> *Because of Your name, Jesus~"*

Please read Isaiah 52:13-53:12.

Meditate on Isaiah 53:6.

> *All of us like sheep have gone astray, each of us has turned*
> *to his own way; but the LORD has caused the iniquity*
> *of us all to fall on Him.*

This is the "Suffering Servant" passage of Scripture. It actually begins in Isaiah 52:13. When Isaiah asks, "Who has believed our message?" (Isaiah 53:1), the message is in Isaiah 52:13-15.

Acts 8:26-40 tells about an Ethiopian who believed the message. He was reading this passage from Isaiah when he met Philip. Philip preached Jesus to him by explaining this Suffering Servant Scripture. These are good verses to use when witnessing to Jews about Jesus. Many have come to faith in Christ when this part of their Bible is explained to them.

Reread these verses from Isaiah praying Isaiah 53:5 and 12 to thank your Suffering Servant for pouring Himself out to death for you and those for whom you stand guard as a faithful, prayerful watchman (Isaiah 62:6-7). Tell those you are guarding what Jesus did for them.

> *"LORD, You were pierced through*
> *for _____ and my transgressions.*
> *You were crushed for our iniquities.*
> *The chastening for our well-being fell on You.*
> *By Your scourging we are healed.*
> *Jesus, You poured Yourself out to death.*
> *You were numbered with transgressors.*
> *You bore the sins of many,*
> *and You interceded for us, the transgressors.*
> *Thank You, Jesus, for loving us that much."*

Please read Isaiah 54.

Meditate on verse 8.

> *"In an outburst of anger*
> *I hid My face from you for a moment,*
> *but with everlasting lovingkindness,*
> *I will have compassion on you,"*
> *says the LORD your Redeemer.*

God tells you about two of His attributes in Isaiah 54:8, His lovingkindness and His compassion. The LORD's lovingkindness is His attitude toward you which contains mercy. Lovingkindness leads you to repentance. God's compassion soothes, cherishes, and loves you deeply like a parent loves a child.

You may feel afflicted, storm-tossed, and not comforted today (Isaiah 54:11). Let the LORD's promises encourage you. The LORD who has compassion on you says, "My lovingkindness will not be removed from you, and my covenant of peace will not be shaken" (Isaiah 54:10).

Pray Isaiah 54:13-14 over yourself and those for whom you stand guard as a faithful, prayerful watchman (Isaiah 62:6-7).

> *"LORD, thank You that*
> *You will teach _____ and me,*
> *and our well-being will be great.*
> *Establish us in righteousness*
> *and keep us far from oppression.*
> *Do not let us fear*
> *and do not let terror come near us.*
> *In Your name, Jesus."*

Please read Isaiah 55.

Meditate on verses 1-2.

> *Ho! Every one who thirsts, come to the waters;*
> *and you who have no money come, buy and eat.*
> *Come, buy wine and milk without money and without cost.*
> *Why do you spend money for what is not bread,*
> *and your wages for what does not satisfy?*
> *Listen carefully to Me and eat what is good,*
> *and delight yourself in abundance.*

Do you ever think about the invitation God gives to you?

You are Invited

What: A Banquet

Host: The LORD

Cost: No cost to you

Come and drink from the waters and eat what is good.
Delight yourself in abundance.
If you accept this invitation,
The LORD will make an everlasting covenant with you!

Isaiah 55 is a beautiful invitation to enter into a covenant relationship with Jesus Christ. Once you have that relationship with Christ, you commemorate it with a covenant meal, the LORD's Supper/Communion. What is your reply to this invitation? Do you choose to delight in the LORD's abundance?

Pray Isaiah 55:6-7 over yourself and those for whom you stand guard as a faithful, prayerful watchman (Isaiah 62:6-7).

"LORD, please let _____ and me seek You
while You may be found.
Let us call upon You while You are near.
Let the wicked forsake their way
and the unrighteous their thoughts.
Let us return to You, LORD.
God, thank You that You have compassion on us,
and You abundantly pardon.
In Your name, Jesus."

Please read Isaiah 56.

Meditate on verses 6 and 7.

> *Also the foreigners who join themselves to the LORD,*
> *to minister to Him, and to love the name of the LORD,*
> *to be His servants, every one who keeps from profaning*
> *the Sabbath and holds fast My covenant; even those I will*
> *bring to My holy mountain and make them joyful in*
> *My house of prayer. Their burnt offerings and their sacrifices*
> *will be acceptable on My altar; for My house will be called a*
> *house of prayer for all peoples.*

God caused the iniquity of all people to fall on Jesus (Isaiah 53:6). Jesus was pierced through and crushed for the transgressions and iniquities of everyone (Isaiah 53:5). Because of Jesus, even foreigners (those who are not Jewish) can join themselves to the LORD. When you join yourself to Christ, you become the house/temple of God (Hebrews 3:6; 1 Corinthians 6:19).

As a house of prayer, spend this day talking to God. Ask Him to examine your life in light of the Truth, which is His Word.

Pray Isaiah 56:1-2 over yourself and those for whom you stand guard as a faithful, prayerful watchman (Isaiah 62:6-7).

> *"LORD, let _____and me preserve justice and do righteousness.*
> *Let us accept Your salvation and righteousness.*
> *Bless us as we do this,*
> *as we take hold of Your salvation and righteousness.*
> *Keep us from profaning Your Sabbath,*
> *and keep our hands from doing any evil.*
> *In Your name, Jesus~"*

Please read Isaiah 57.

Meditate on verse 21.

"There is no peace," says my God, "for the wicked."

There are precious promises and dire warnings in Isaiah 57. God said in the first two verses that the righteous man is taken away from evil and enters into peace. The high and exalted One who lives forever, whose name is Holy, also said, "I dwell on a high and holy place, and also with the contrite and lowly of spirit in order to revive the spirit of the lowly and to revive the heart of the contrite" (v. 15).

It is amazing to think the God of the universe resides with you when you are humble and sorrowful about your sin. He stays with you to revive you, so you can live for and with Him forever.

But with those who continue in the pride of their sin, God is angry and hides His face from them. The LORD says they will have no peace (Isaiah 57:21).

Pray Isaiah 57:14-15 over yourself and those for whom you stand guard as a faithful, prayerful watchman (Isaiah 62:6-7).

"High and exalted One, who lives forever, whose name is Holy,
please build up and prepare the way for _____ and me.
As Your people, remove every obstacle out of our way.
Give us a contrite and lowly spirit,
so we will dwell with You on a high and holy place.
Revive our hearts.
In Your name, Jesus~"

Please read Isaiah 58.

Meditate on verse 6.

Is this not the fast which I choose,
to loosen the bonds of wickedness, to undo the bands of the yoke,
and to let the oppressed go free and break every yoke?

Isaiah 58 is a soul-searching chapter. God spoke to people who used religious ritual in hopes of manipulating Him to give them what they wanted. They gave up eating food so God would notice them. However, God knew what was in their hearts; the people fasted to find their own desires, not God's. Fasting made them "hangry," so they were mean to their workers, striking them with a wicked fist, and creating contention and strife (Isaiah 58:3-4).

God gave His definition of fasting in Isaiah 58. Fasting is giving up wickedness. Fasting is freeing and loosening. Fasting is not depriving yourself of something to make God feel sorry for you in order to get you what you want. God's fast is:

- Loosen the bonds of wickedness
- Break every yoke
- Let the oppressed go free
- Share your bread with the hungry
- Bring the homeless poor into your house
- Cover the naked
- Do not hide from yourself—get honest about yourself before God

Who or what in your life does God want you to give freedom? What could you fast; what could you give up that would bring life to those around you? Do you need to fast anger, abusive speech, and selfishness?

Get honest before the LORD and pray Isaiah 58:9-11 over yourself and those for whom you stand guard as a faithful, prayerful watchman (Isaiah 62:6-7).

"LORD, help _____ and me remove the yoke from our midst.
Let us stop pointing the finger and speaking wickedness.
When we do, then You will answer when we call.
We will cry, and You will say, 'Here I am.'
Help us give ourselves to the hungry and
satisfy the desire of the afflicted.
Then let our light rise in the darkness and
our gloom become like midday.
LORD, continually guide us and satisfy
our desire in scorched places.
Give strength to our bones.
Let us be like a watered garden and like a spring
of water whose waters do not fail.
In Your name, Jesus~"

Please read Isaiah 59.

Meditate on verses 1-2.

> *Behold, the LORD's hand is not so short that it cannot save;*
> *nor is His ear so dull that it cannot hear.*
> *But your iniquities have made a separation*
> *between you and your God,*
> *and your sins have hidden His face from*
> *you so that He does not hear.*

Isaiah 59 is your story. It is the story of every person who has and who will ever live on earth. Sin separates you from God. Sin in your life means no righteousness, no hope, no salvation, only darkness and gloom.

God saw your hopeless situation, and it was displeasing in His sight. He saw there was no man to intercede on your behalf. So the LORD Himself brought salvation. He put on righteousness, salvation, zeal, and vengeance. The LORD came as your Redeemer. All you have to do is turn from your transgression to your Redeemer LORD and fear His Name (Isaiah 59:15-20).

Reread this chapter. It is your salvation story.

Pray Isaiah 59:21 over yourself and those for whom you stand guard as a faithful, prayerful watchman (Isaiah 62:6-7).

> *"LORD, Your covenant is with _____ and me.*
> *Let Your Spirit be upon us.*
> *Put Your Words in our mouth.*
> *Do not let Your Words depart from our mouth,*
> *nor from the mouth of our offspring,*
> *nor from the mouth of our offspring's offspring, now and forever.*
> *In Your name, Jesus~"*

Please read Isaiah 60.

Meditate on verse 1.

Arise, shine; for your light has come,
and the glory of the LORD has risen upon you.

Isaiah 60 contains prophecy about the coming of Christ; both His first coming and His future return to earth. A key day in Christ's first coming, was the Sunday before Christ's crucifixion. It is often called Palm Sunday, but it was actually Lamb Selection Day. 2,000 years ago Jesus came into Jerusalem on the day thousands of people were there to select their Passover lambs. They would choose a lamb and watch it for four days to make sure it was acceptable for sacrifice (Exodus 12:1-6). It was no accident Jesus arrived on Lamb Selection Day. The Lamb of God who takes away the sin of the world came into Jerusalem on the day people chose their lambs to die for their sins. God asked, "Will you choose My Lamb; the only Lamb that can take away your sins?"

Isaiah announced that the glory of the LORD had come. God announced that He is the LORD, the Savior, the Redeemer (Isaiah 60:1,16).

Which lamb do you choose? Choose the Lamb of God who takes away the sin of the world (John 1:29).

Pray Isaiah 60:16, 19, and 21 over those for whom you stand guard as a faithful, prayerful watchman (Isaiah 62:6-7).

"LORD, please let _____ know
You are their Savior, Redeemer, and Mighty One.
Let them choose You to be their everlasting light and glory.
Make them righteous.
In Your name, Jesus~"

Please read Isaiah 61.

Meditate on verse 10.

> *I will rejoice greatly in the LORD. My soul will exult in my God; for He has clothed me with garments of salvation; He has wrapped me with a robe of righteousness, as a bridegroom decks himself with a garland, and as a bride adorns herself with her jewels.*

This is a chapter filled with good news. The LORD is able to take all of your hopeless situations and turn them into victories: freedom for prisoners; comfort for those who mourn; rising up from former devastations; a double portion replacing shame and humiliation.

God even calls you an oak of righteousness, the planting of the LORD, that He may be glorified. What an amazing God you serve!

Pray Isaiah 61:3 over those for whom you stand guard as a faithful, prayerful watchman (Isaiah 62:6-7). Then pray Isaiah 61:10 in thanksgiving for what God has done.

> *"LORD, grant comfort to _____who is mourning.*
> *Give them a garland instead of ashes,*
> *the oil of gladness instead of mourning,*
> *the mantle of praise instead of a spirit of fainting.*
> *Let them be called oaks of righteousness,*
> *the planting of the LORD, that You may be glorified.*
> *I rejoice greatly in You, LORD.*
> *My soul exults in You, my God;*
> *for You have clothed us with garments of salvation.*
> *You have wrapped us with a robe of righteousness,*
> *as a bridegroom decks himself with a garland,*
> *and as a bride adorns herself with her jewels.*
> *Thank You, Jesus, for all You have done for us."*

APRIL 25

Please read Isaiah 62.

Meditate on verses 6-7.

On your walls, O Jerusalem, I have appointed watchmen;
all day and all night they will never keep silent.
You who remind the LORD, take no rest for yourselves,
and give Him no rest until He establishes
and makes Jerusalem a praise in the earth.

Today marks the 116th devotional in *The Watchman on the Wall*, 116 days of tirelessly praying for God to establish you and yours. How are you doing? Are you remaining steadfast in prayer? Are you talking to God day and night? Is your faith in your faithful God increasing?

On day 116, please read Psalm 116. It starts like this:

I love the LORD, because He hears
my voice and my supplications.
Because He has inclined His ear to me;
therefore, I shall call upon Him as long as I live.

Do not grow weary and lose heart! As you continually remind the LORD of those He needs to establish, He continually hears your voice; He hears your cry. Spend this day loving Jesus because He hears you. Because He hears you, recommit to call upon Him as long as you live.

Pray Psalm 116:1-2, 5-9, and 12-13 as a faithful, prayerful watchman (Isaiah 62:6-7).

"I love You, LORD, because you hear
my voice and my supplications.
You have inclined Your ear to me;
therefore, I shall call upon You as long as I live.
Gracious are You, LORD, and righteous.
Yes, God, You are compassionate.
You preserve the simple.
I was brought low, and You saved me.
Return to your rest, O my soul,
for the LORD has dealt bountifully with you.
For You have rescued my soul from death,
my eyes from tears, my feet from stumbling.
I shall walk before You, LORD, in the land of the living.
What shall I render to You, LORD,
for all Your benefits toward me?
I shall lift up the cup of salvation
and continue to call on Your name, LORD."

APRIL 26

Please read Isaiah 63.

Meditate on verse 8.

> *For He said, "Surely, they are My people,*
> *sons who will not deal falsely."*
> *So He became their Savior.*

There are two interesting time phrases in Isaiah 63:4: "the day of vengeance" and "God's year of redemption." Thankfully the LORD's anger is but for a moment; His favor is for a lifetime (Psalm 30:5). Two thousand years ago, your Savior was preparing for the greatest act of lovingkindness and compassion in history; dying for your sins so you could enter into His year of redemption and not have to face His day of vengeance.

As you meditate on your Savior, thank Him that His own arm brought salvation (Isaiah 63:5). Thank Him for being your Savior (Isaiah 63:8). Thank Him for putting His Holy Spirit in the midst of you (Isaiah 63:11).

Pray Isaiah 63:7-8 over yourself and those for whom you stand guard as a faithful, prayerful watchman (Isaiah 62:6-7).

> *"I will make mention of Your*
> *lovingkindness and praises, LORD,*
> *according to all that You have granted us,*
> *and Your great goodness which You have granted*
> *according to Your compassion*
> *and the abundance of Your lovingkindness.*
> *Thank You that _____ and I are Your people,*
> *sons who will not deal falsely.*
> *Thank You for becoming our Savior.*
> *In Your name, Jesus~"*

Please read Isaiah 64.

Meditate on verse 6.

For all of us have become like one who is unclean,
and all our righteous deeds are like a filthy garment,
and all of us wither like a leaf,
and our iniquities, like the wind, take us away.

Two thousand years ago, your Savior literally sweat blood for you. Why did He sweat blood as He prayed in agony for God's will to be done? Was it because He dreaded the beatings? Was it because He dreaded death by crucifixion? Or did another reality torment Him?

Memorize and meditate on this verse for the rest of eternity:

He made Him who knew no sin to be sin on our behalf
so that we might become the righteousness of God in Him.
—2 Corinthians 5:21

Jesus, the perfect, sinless Son of God did not just wear your sin 2,000 years ago; He literally **BECAME** your sin. No wonder God the Father had to forsake Him. He actually **WAS** your sin, shame, and guilt. Why? Why would the God of the universe **BECOME** everything that is detestable about you? So that you could literally, actually, in reality, **BECOME** righteousness! If you are in Christ, you **ARE** the righteousness of God. Just like Christ did not simply wear your sins on the cross, you do not simply wear God's righteousness; you **ARE** His righteousness!

Live this truth for the rest of your days. You **ARE** the righteousness of God in Christ Jesus. There should be no doubt by the way you think, talk, and act who you **ARE**.

Pray Isaiah 64:5 and 9 over yourself and those for whom you stand guard as a faithful, prayerful watchman (Isaiah 62:6-7).

"LORD, You meet _____ and me
who rejoice in doing righteousness,
who remember You in Your ways.
You were angry when we sinned
and continued in them a long time.
Thank You for saving us.
Thank You for not being angry beyond measure.
Thank You for not remembering our iniquity forever.
Thank You for making us Your people.
In Your name, Jesus~"

APRIL 28

Please read Isaiah 65.

Meditate on verses 1-2.

I permitted Myself to be sought by those who did not ask for Me;
I permitted Myself to be found by those who did not seek Me.
I said, "Here am I, here am I,"
to a nation which did not call on My name.
I have spread out My hands all day long to a rebellious people
who walk in the way which is not good,
following their own thoughts.

Jesus Christ became your sin, so you could become His righteousness (2 Corinthians 5:21). He did that for you because it was a life or death situation. If Jesus had not willingly become your sin, you would be eternally dead. But because of His great love for you, He died for you, so you could be eternally living.

God said in Isaiah 65, He came to you even though you were not seeking Him, asking for Him, or calling on His name. That is how much the LORD loves you. In the midst of your rebellion, God spread out His hands on the cross so you do not have to walk in a way, which is not good, following your own thoughts.

"How deep the Father's love for us, how vast beyond all measure,
that He should give His only Son to make a wretch His treasure."
—Stuart Townend

Thank the LORD for what He did for you 2,000 years ago. Pray for someone who needs to know Christ became their sin, so they can become His righteousness. Pray Isaiah 65:1, 13, and 14 over yourself and them as a faithful, prayerful watchman (Isaiah 62:6-7).

"LORD, thank You for seeking me
before I even knew I needed You.
Please let _____ find You.
Make us Your servants,
so we can eat and not be hungry.
Make us Your servants,
so we can drink and not be thirsty.
Make us Your servants,
so we can rejoice and not be put to shame.
As Your servant, I shout joyfully with a glad heart.
I no longer cry with a heavy heart,
nor wail with a broken spirit.
Only because of You, Jesus~"

Please read Isaiah 66.

Meditate on verses 1 and 2.

> *Thus says the LORD,*
> *"Heaven is My throne and the earth is My footstool.*
> *Where then is a house you could build for Me?*
> *And where is a place that I may rest?*
> *For My hand made all these things,*
> *thus all these things came into being,"*
> *declares the LORD.*
> *"But to this one I will look,*
> *to him who is humble and contrite in spirit,*
> *and who trembles at My Word."*

God concluded Isaiah by offering you a choice. Humbly choose God and see His glory, or choose your own way and experience His fiery judgment. God will not force Himself on you. Christ died and rose again, so you can live eternally with Him. But He will not force you to live with Him forever. You must humbly come to the LORD broken because of your sin and revering His Word, then He will show you His favor and glory.

Examine your life. God already knows your works and thoughts (Isaiah 66:18), so you can be honest with yourself and Him. Will you endure before the LORD, or will He say, "You have transgressed against Me, so your worm will not die, and your fire will not be quenched, and you will be an abhorrence to all mankind" (Isaiah 66:22, 24)?

Pray Isaiah 66:2 over yourself and those for whom you stand guard as a faithful, prayerful watchman (Isaiah 62:6-7).

"LORD, Your hand has made all things,
thus all these things came into being.
God, You will look to _____ and me
when we are humble, contrite of spirit,
and tremble at Your Word.
Make us that way.
Because of Your name, Jesus~"

This concluded praying through Isaiah, the book about God saving sinners. You read it during this holy season called Easter. It is the time of remembering Christ's life, death, resurrection, and ascension. It is remembering everything Jesus did so you can be raised up with Him.

APRIL 30

Please read Colossians 3.

Meditate on verse 1.

> *Therefore if you have been raised up with Christ,*
> *keep seeking the things above,*
> *where Christ is,*
> *seated at the right hand of God.*

You have concluded praying through the book of Isaiah, and on this last day of April, I have asked you to read Colossians 3. It begins by making you ask yourself a question: Have you been raised up with Christ?

Jesus Christ your LORD was raised up 2,000 years ago. With His miraculous resurrection came the miraculous opportunity for you to be a child of God, a child of the resurrection (Luke 20:36).

Jesus presented Himself alive by many convincing proofs (Acts 1:3). If you have been raised up with Christ, there will be evidence to prove the fact. Reread Colossians 3 and find the convincing proofs that "you have died, and your life is hidden with Christ in God" (Colossians 3:3).

Pray for the evidence of resurrection to be apparent in your life and the lives of those you for whom you are praying as a faithful watchman (Isaiah 62:6-7).

Pray Colossians 3:1-17.

> *"Christ, as people raised up with You,*
> *let _____ and me keep seeking the things above,*
> *where You are seated at the right hand of God.*
> *Help us to set our mind on the things above,*
> *not on the things that are on earth.*
> *Our life is hidden with You in God.*

Christ, You are our life.
Help us consider the members of our earthly body as dead to:
immorality, impurity, passion, evil desire, and greed.
Do not let us be sons of disobedience!
Let us put aside:
anger, wrath, malice, slander, and
abusive speech from our mouths.
Do not let us lie to one another,
since we have laid aside the old self with its evil practices,
and have put on the new self,
who is being renewed to the true knowledge
according to Your image, God.
As those who have been chosen of You, holy and beloved, let us
put on a heart of compassion, kindness, humility, gentleness, and
patience; bearing with one another, and forgiving each other,
whoever has a complaint against anyone;
just as You, LORD, forgave us.
Beyond all these things, let us put on love,
which is the perfect bond of unity.
Let Your peace, Christ, rule in our hearts,
to which indeed we were called in one body, and let us be thankful.
Let Your Word, Christ, richly dwell within us,
with all wisdom, teaching and admonishing one another
with psalms and hymns and spiritual songs,
singing with thankfulness in our hearts to You, God.
Whatever we do in word or deed,
let us do all in Your name, LORD Jesus,
giving thanks through You to God the Father."

On your walls, O Jerusalem,
I have appointed watchmen;
All day and all night they
will never keep silent.
You who remind the LORD,
take no rest for yourselves;
And give Him no rest
until He establishes
And makes Jerusalem a
praise in the earth.
ISAIAH 62:6-7, NASB

MAY 1

Please read Proverbs 1.

Meditate on verse 7.

> *The fear of the LORD is the beginning of knowledge;*
> *fools despise wisdom and instruction.*

Over the month of May, you will read through the book of Proverbs. Proverbs is packed with verses you can pray to the LORD concerning issues in your life and in the lives of those you love. A *proverb* is a short sentence that expresses a truth. Each chapter of Proverbs is a treasure chest of truths for following God and growing in character.

True wisdom is best defined as: having God's perspective about something. If you have God's perspective, then your mind is being transformed to think like God thinks (Romans 12:2).

Pray Proverbs 1:2-7 over yourself and those for whom you stand guard as a faithful, prayerful watchman (Isaiah 62:6-7).

> *"LORD, help _____ and me*
> *to know wisdom and instruction,*
> *to discern the sayings of understanding,*
> *to receive Your instruction in*
> *wise behavior, righteousness, justice, and equity;*
> *to give prudence to the naive,*
> *to give the youth knowledge and discretion.*
> *Make us wise so we will hear and increase in learning.*
> *Make us understanding so we will receive wise counsel.*
> *Help us understand these proverbs.*
> *Help us understand the wise and their riddles.*
> *Help us to fear You, LORD, as the first step in knowledge.*
> *Let us not be fools who despise wisdom and instruction.*
> *In Your name, Jesus~"*

MAY 2

Please read Proverbs 2.

Meditate on verses 4-7a.

If you seek her as silver
and search for her as for hidden treasures,
then you will discern the fear of the LORD
and discover the knowledge of God.
For the LORD gives wisdom;
from His mouth come knowledge and understanding.
He stores up sound wisdom for the upright.

The treasure hunt continues! Every verse in this chapter could be a prayer for yourself or someone you love.

Many people are seeking truth but have not found the open treasure chest of God as their source. Believers in God are often searching for His will for their lives. Proverbs 2 is full of answers and hope for anyone who is seeking truth.

The Bible is very clear that God is the source, owner, and distributor of wisdom. James 1:5-6a and 17a say, "But if any of you lacks wisdom, let him ask of God, who gives to all generously and without reproach, and it will be given to him. But he must ask in faith without any doubting. Every good thing given and every perfect gift is from above, coming down from the Father of lights."

When you pray a promise of God, such as the promise to give wisdom, pray with faith. One of the key ways God reveals His wisdom to you is in His Word. Read Proverbs 2 again and focus on the value of wisdom in the life of the upright.

Pray Proverbs 2:1-7 over yourself and those for whom you stand guard as a faithful, prayerful watchman (Isaiah 62:6-7).

"LORD, help _____ and me
to receive Your Words and
treasure Your commandments within us.
Make our ears attentive to Your wisdom;
incline our hearts to understanding.
We cry for discernment and ask for understanding.
Help us seek wisdom as silver and as hidden treasures.
Help us discern the fear of You, LORD,
and discover Your knowledge.
Please give us Your wisdom, knowledge, and understanding.
Store up sound wisdom for us; make us upright.
Be our shield as we walk in integrity.
In Your name, Jesus~"

Please read Proverbs 3.

Meditate on verses 5-6.

> *Trust in the LORD with all your heart*
> *and do not lean on your own understanding.*
> *In all of your ways acknowledge Him,*
> *and He will make your paths straight.*

The words of Proverbs 3:5-6 are foundational truths for walking with God. The word *acknowledge* comes from the Hebrew word *yada* which means to know in a personal, relational way. Here, as opposed to just a mental understanding, is the additional characteristic of relationship in knowing. When Jesus saves you, He does so to bring you into a vibrant relationship with God. The sin in your life is taken away, and you are purified, so you get to have a non-stop relationship with your Creator. You get what Adam and Eve lost—you get to walk with God.

So a good way to state this verse is, "In all your ways know God." In everything you do, in all your ways, you should do it WITH God, knowing Him and yourself better through the journey.

In Proverbs 3 the treasure hunt continues! Note the focus on wisdom being better than silver, gold, and precious jewels. Every verse in this chapter could be a prayer for yourself or someone you love. Topics include: love, faithfulness, discipline, and living with others in a holy way.

Pray Proverbs 3:5-6 over yourself and those for whom you stand guard as a faithful, prayerful watchman (Isaiah 62:6-7).

> *"LORD, help _____ and me*
> *trust in You with all our hearts*
> *and not lean on our own understanding.*
> *In all of our ways, we want to know You.*
> *Thank You for making our paths straight.*
> *In Your name, Jesus~"*

Please read Proverbs 4.

Meditate on verses 3-4.

When I was a son to my father,
tender and the only son in the sight of my mother,
then he taught me and said to me,
"Let your heart hold fast my words; keep
my commandments and live."

This chapter begins with insight into the words of Solomon to his son. These were words his father David gave him. They were words David believed would help Solomon walk in the paths of righteousness.

In Proverbs 4:11-13, Solomon said he led his son in upright paths. Because the son was directed and led by his father, his walking and running would not be impeded. He was not going to stumble.

The words of Proverbs 4:14-17 are about avoiding the path of evil. Do not follow the way of wicked and evil men. Turn away from this path. This path is inhabited with people who cannot be satisfied until you stumble.

In Proverbs 4:18-19, the contrast between the paths of righteousness and evil is illustrated. The righteous path gets brighter and brighter like the rising sun. The path of evil only leads to blind darkness.

The chapter closes with the father continuing to admonish his son to stay on the righteous path.

Let your eyes look directly ahead, and let your
gaze be fixed straight in front of you.
Watch the path of your feet, and all your ways will be established.
Do not turn to the right nor the left; turn your foot from evil.
—Proverbs 4:25-27

There are four important Biblical truths found in Proverbs 4.

- ⁶ Men should train their children in the ways of God.
- ⁶ Good and evil are real and very different.
- ⁶ You are responsible for the steps in life you choose to take.
- ⁶ Choose the way of righteousness, and you will be established in your ways.

Pray Proverbs 4:5 and 26-27 over yourself and those for whom you stand guard as a faithful, prayerful watchman (Isaiah 62:6-7).

*"LORD, may _____ not forget nor turn
away from the words of my mouth.
Establish _____ and me in Your ways and paths.
Keep us from turning to the left or the
right; keep our feet from evil.
In Your name, Jesus~"*

MAY 5

Please read Proverbs 5.

Meditate on verses 18-21.

Let your fountain be blessed, and rejoice in the wife of your youth.
As a loving hind and as a graceful doe,
let her breasts satisfy you at all times;
be exhilarated always with her love.
For why should you, my son be exhilarated with an adulteress,
and embrace the bosom of a foreigner?
For the ways of a man are before the eyes of the LORD,
and He watches all his paths.

This passage of Scripture gives insight into the value of loving one's spouse with Godly joy. God shows the clear consequences of the foolish journey to the bed of someone to whom you are not married. Adultery and fornication bring death. Adultery brings separation. It ruins lives, all for a momentary thrill of someone who has no right to meet that need in your life.

Men, do not invest one moment of your life in the world of pornography. It is a sin against the LORD, your spouse, and yourself. Single men, likewise, do not invest a moment of your mind or time to this sinful, shameful display of base behavior. In addition to sinning against God, it is sinning against the enslaved or misguided people who are showing their bodies and acting in ways that are only appropriate for married people. The actor, dancer, or prostitute is loved by God. Jesus died for them. If they are rescued and their lives turned around, they are somebody else's future spouse and a sister or brother of yours in the LORD.

If you are married, you should be exhilarated by your husband or wife. Seek God in asking for His blessings on your private life with your spouse. Be content with God's gift to you of this person. Open up your heart and mind to love them joyfully. It is God's will for married couples.

Pray Proverbs 5:18-19 over yourself, if married, and those you know who need to have God centered marriages, free from lusts outside of marriage, as a faithful, prayerful watchman (Isaiah 62:6-7).

"LORD, help the marriage of _____and my marriage.
May our fountains be blessed,
and may we rejoice in our spouse.
Let our bodies satisfy our spouse at all times;
let us be exhilarated always with that love.
In Your name, Jesus~"

Please read Proverbs 6.

Meditate on verses 20 and 23.

> *My son, observe the commandment of your father,*
> *and do not forsake the teaching of your mother.*
> *For the commandment is a lamp, and the teaching is light;*
> *and reproofs for discipline are the way of life.*

Proverbs 6 has sets of truth on different subjects that make excellent prayers for you and those you love.

Proverbs 6:1-5 is about not making yourself responsible for paying another's debt. Maybe you know someone who needs prayer to make wise business deals with others or who needs wisdom about co-signing for someone.

The words of Proverbs 6:6-11 address laziness and hard work. Pray for those in your life who are lazy and do not want to work. Ask God to give strength for those around them to not support this sinful behavior.

In Proverbs 6:12-19, characteristics and behaviors of wicked people are revealed. The section ends with a list of these wicked behaviors which God hates. "There are six things the LORD hates; yes, seven which are an abomination to Him:

1. Haughty eyes

2. A lying tongue

3. Hands that shed innocent blood

4. A heart that devises wicked plans

5. Feet that run rapidly to evil

6. A false witness who utters lies

7. One who spreads strife among brothers."

The chapter concludes with the consequences of adultery.

Verses 20-23 are placed between the passages about wicked people and adultery. The words are filled with the benefits of keeping the LORD's commands in your heart continually.

Pray Proverbs 6:20-23 over yourself and those for whom you stand guard as a faithful, prayerful watchman (Isaiah 62:6-7).

"LORD, help _____ and me
to observe Your commandments and not forsake Your teachings.
Bind them continually on our heart and tie them around our neck.
Thank You, LORD, that they will guide us when we walk,
watch over us when we sleep, and talk to us when we awake.
May we make Your commandments and
teachings our lamp and light.
Let us receive Godly reproofs to discipline us on Your way of life.
In Your name, Jesus~"

Please read Proverbs 7.

Meditate on verses 1-5a.

> *My son, keep my words and treasure my*
> *commandments within you.*
> *Keep my commandments and live, and my*
> *teaching as the apple of your eye.*
> *Bind them on your fingers; write them on the tablet of your heart.*
> *Say to wisdom, "You are my sister," and call*
> *understanding your intimate friend;*
> *that they may keep you from an adulteress.*

The first nine chapters of Proverbs start by praising wisdom. You learn God's wisdom when you know His words and commandments. You know God's Word when you keep it, treasure it, bind it around your neck, and write it on the tablet of your heart.

Proverbs 7 gives a vivid description of a foolish boy falling into the trap of the adulteress who heartily encourages him to join her in her sinful ways. It is the same method of the wicked described in Romans 1:18-32. The boy will ruin his life because his carnal passions are not overcome by the wisdom of God. God's Word is not the foundation of his decision making process.

> *How can a young man keep his way pure?*
> *By keeping it according to Your Word.*
> *Your Word I have treasured in my heart,*
> *that I may not sin against You.*
> —Psalms 119:9, 11

God says over and over in Proverbs that wisdom is greater than wickedness; it overcomes evil and makes righteous choices. The treasured wisdom is like family. Proverbs 7:4 describes wisdom as a sibling. In Christ, Jesus is your older brother, and He is wisdom from God (1 Corinthians 1:24). Understanding is your intimate friend. As a Christian, you have a relationship with God's Word that protects you. You do not have to become the prey of an adulteress. God has so much more stored up in life for you!

Pray Proverbs 7:1-4 over yourself and those for whom you stand guard as a faithful, prayerful watchman (Isaiah 62:6-7).

"LORD, help _____ and me
to keep Your Words and treasure Your commandments.
May we experience life as a result of keeping Your commandments
and making your teaching the apple of our eyes.
Bind your commandments on us and write
them on the tablets of our hearts.
May we know Your wisdom and understanding intimately.
In Your name, Jesus~"

Please read Proverbs 8.

Meditate on verse 5.

> *O naive ones, understand prudence.*
> *And, O fools, understand wisdom.*

The LORD possessed wisdom from the beginning, before He created the earth. As revealed in the New Testament, Jesus is the wisdom of God (1 Corinthians 1:24) and the Creator (John 1, Colossians 1, Hebrews 1). Proverbs 8:22-31 is a picture of Christ as wisdom with God at creation. Take note of these characteristics of Christ and thank Him for loving you and revealing Himself to you.

Notice that Jesus delights in the sons of men (Proverbs 8:31). Jesus delights in you! Meditate on that amazing truth today.

Pray Proverbs 8:32-36 over yourself and those for whom you stand guard as a faithful, prayerful watchman (Isaiah 62:6-7). These verses contain prayers for both the saved and the unsaved.

> *"LORD, let _____ and me listen to You.*
> *Bless us as we keep Your ways.*
> *May we heed instruction and be wise.*
> *Do not let us neglect instruction.*
> *Bless us as we listen to You.*
> *Let us watch daily at Your gates,*
> *waiting at Your doorposts for Your wisdom.*
> *And, LORD, please let_____ find You,*
> *so they can find life and obtain Your favor.*
> *Keep them from sinning against You,*
> *so they will not injure themselves.*
> *May they stop hating You and loving death.*
> *For the sake of Your name, Jesus~"*

Please read Proverbs 9.

Meditate on verses 6 and 8b-10.

> *Forsake your folly and live, and proceed*
> *in the way of understanding.*
> *Reprove a wise man, and he will love you.*
> *Give instruction to a wise man, and he will be still wiser.*
> *Teach a righteous man, and he will increase his learning.*
> *The fear of the LORD is the beginning of wisdom,*
> *and the knowledge of the Holy One is understanding.*

Wisdom is seen as having an established mansion with seven sculptured pillars. She has prepared food, wine, and set her table. She has sent out her servants to call all to come. She calls for the naive and for those who lack understanding to come to her home and sit at her table.

She offers a new life that requires forsaking folly. She promises a new way of understanding. That way of wisdom begins with the fear of the LORD, and understanding is described as having knowledge of the Holy One. Those who acquire this understanding have days and years added to their lives. It is a beautiful picture of the LORD's purposeful and sacrificial search and desire for you!

There is a powerful contrast in Proverbs 9:12-18. The man who thinks he is wise, the scoffer, and the woman of folly are on the path of death. Like wisdom, the woman of folly calls out for all to enter her home on the high places of the city. She wants the naive and ones who lack understanding to come to her home. Death and the depths of hell await her guests.

Pray Proverbs 9:5-6 and 8-10 over yourself and those for whom you stand guard as a faithful, prayerful watchman (Isaiah 62:6-7).

"LORD, thank You for Your invitation
to eat Your food and drink Your wine.
Help _____ and me forsake folly and live.
Let us proceed in the way of understanding.
Help us to receive reproof as a wise person and love the reprovers.
May we give instruction and grow wiser in it.
Let us be righteous people who are taught and increase in learning.
Help us to fear You, LORD, so we can understand Your wisdom.
Let us understand You, Holy One, by knowing You.
In Your name, Jesus~"

MAY 10

Please read Proverbs 10.

Meditate on verses 11-13.

The mouth of the righteous is a fountain of life,
but the mouth of the wicked conceals violence.
Hatred stirs up strife,
but love covers all transgressions.
On the lips of the discerning, wisdom is found,
but a rod is for the back of him who lacks understanding.

Chapter 10 begins a series of proverbs that are usually singular verses. These are stand-alone truths that make each chapter a jewelry store (or perhaps a hardware store for the men) of prayers you can say for your loved ones. Imagine as a watchman on the wall, you get to go into the weapon room and select whatever you need for protecting and changing the lives of others as you purposely pray for them.

By now you should be able to pray on your own, but if you are picking up this prayer guide later in the year, this is how it works.

For example, verse 1 says:

A wise son makes a father glad, but a foolish son is a grief to his mother.

As a watchman you may know both of these sons in someone's household. You pray,

Part 1

"LORD, thank you for making _____ a wise son.
Please help him continue to make his father glad.
May he never bring grief to his mother."

Part 2
"Please make _____ a wise son who makes his father glad.
Let him stop being foolish and a grief to his mother."

Pray Proverbs 10:11-13 over yourself and those for whom you stand guard as a faithful, prayerful watchman (Isaiah 62:6-7).

"LORD, give _____ and me the mouth of the righteous
in order to be a fountain of life.
Do not let us conceal violence.
Let us not be hateful, stirring up strife.
In love, let us cover transgressions.
Make us discerning, so wisdom will be found on our lips.
Give us understanding, so we will not need the rod of correction.
In Your name, Jesus~"

MAY 11

Please read Proverbs 11.

Meditate on verses 16a, 22, 25-26, and 30.

> *A gracious woman attains honor.*
> *As a ring of gold in a swine's snout, so is a*
> *beautiful woman who lacks discretion.*
> *The generous man will be prosperous, and he*
> *who waters will himself be watered.*
> *He who withholds grain, the people will curse him,*
> *but blessing will be on the head of him who sells it.*
> *The fruit of the righteous is a tree of life,*
> *and he who is wise wins souls.*

These meditation verses may appear disconnected. Prayerfully study them again and see what the LORD lays on your heart.

In 1930, my great-grandfather was a poor farmer in West Texas. He loved the LORD and was known for his generosity. He had 13 children of his own and also reared a large group of children from his deceased brother's family. A drought came to the land, and soon people no longer had water on their farms. Grandfather had a deep pond and invited all who needed water to get their water from him. As his water supply grew lower, one by one, families left him his remaining water and made the 10-mile wagon ride to get water from the nearest city. Soon there was only one other family getting water from Grandfather's pond. As the pond dried up, the young father of that family said he would get water in the city. Grandfather invited him to share the last of his water with him—and so the pond was dry ... until that afternoon, when an isolated thunderstorm completely refilled the pond, only this generous man's pond. The young father, who was not a believer at the time of the drought, told this story of generosity and the miracle that followed for the rest of his life.

The person who trusts in the LORD for everything, a gracious woman compared to a woman whose beauty demands discretion, a person who is generous and shares water and grain rather than hoarding for themselves, a person who seeks and lives for eternal virtues rather than wicked, selfish, or foolish values is to be honored because in the end he or she is wise—winning souls and the LORD's favor.

Pray Proverbs 11:16-17, 25, and 30 over yourself and those for whom you stand guard as a faithful, prayerful watchman (Isaiah 62:6-7).

> *"LORD, make _____ and me gracious, attaining honor.*
> *Make us merciful, doing good.*
> *As we are generous, may we prosper.*
> *As we water, keep us watered.*
> *May our fruit of righteousness be a tree of life.*
> *Make us wise, winning souls.*
> *In Your name, Jesus~"*

Please read Proverbs 12.

Meditate on verses 3, 7, and 12.

> *A man will not be established by wickedness,*
> *but the root of the righteous will not be moved.*
> *The wicked are overthrown and are no more,*
> *but the house of the righteous will stand.*
> *The wicked man desires the booty of evil men,*
> *but the root of the righteous yields fruit.*

In Proverbs 10:11, you meditated on the mouth of the righteous being a fountain of life. This theme of the righteous continues in Proverbs 12 where, in addition to your meditation verses, the righteous:

- obtain favor from the LORD (v. 2)
- have just thoughts (v. 5)
- have regard for the life of their animal (v. 10)
- will escape from trouble (v. 13)
- are a guide to their neighbor (v. 26)
- walk on the pathway of life where there is no death (v. 28).

Pray Proverbs 12:2-3, 5, 7, 10, 12-13, 26, and 28 over yourself and those for whom you stand guard as a faithful, prayerful watchman (Isaiah 62:6-7).

"LORD, You are our righteousness!
Please make _____ and me righteous so we will:
be good and obtain Your favor;
be established and not moved;
have righteous and just thoughts;
have a house that will stand;
have regard for the life of animals;
yield fruit;
escape from trouble;
be a guide to our neighbor;
walk in the way of life on the path where there is no death.
In Your name, Jesus~"

MAY 13

Please read Proverbs 13.

Meditate on verses 2a-3 and 5.

> *From the fruit of a man's mouth he enjoys good.*
> *The one who guards his mouth preserves his life;*
> *the one who opens wide his lips comes to ruin.*
> *A righteous man hates falsehood,*
> *but a wicked man acts disgustingly and shamefully.*

There are trends that reoccur in Proverbs. Throughout the book, God contrasts the wise, righteous, and disciplined with the foolish, wicked, and sluggards.

The proper use of the mouth or tongue is part of the wise, righteous, and disciplined person's life. Truthfulness governs the mouth of the righteous; they hate falsehood and speak the truth.

James addressed the tongue in his New Testament book, *James*. He came to the conclusion that no one can tame the human tongue; it must be put under the control of the Holy Spirit, so Christ can pilot a person's entire life (James 3:1-12). As a believer, you are to be disciplined, holy, and wise in the things you say.

Continue looking for the theme of speech in each chapter of Proverbs. Ask God to make you holy in what you say.

Pray Proverbs 13:2-3 and 5 over yourself and those for whom you stand guard as a faithful, prayerful watchman (Isaiah 62:6-7).

> *"LORD, may _____ and I enjoy good as*
> *a result of the fruit of our mouths.*
> *Guard our mouths in order to preserve life.*
> *May we be careful to not open wide our lips and come to ruin.*
> *Make us righteous people who hate falsehood.*
> *In Your name, Jesus~"*

Please read Proverbs 14.

Meditate on verses 1, 4, and 34.

> *The wise woman builds her house,*
> *but the foolish tears it down with her own hands.*
> *Where no oxen are, the manger is clean,*
> *but much revenue comes by the strength of the ox.*
> *Righteousness exalts a nation,*
> *but sin is a disgrace to any people.*

In this passage of Scripture the three heroes of Proverbs arise again: Wisdom, Discipline, and Righteousness. The meditation verses illustrate them.

Wisdom

A wise woman is someone who is looking out for her home to build it up. Are you a woman or a man who is doing whatever you can so the ones you love can be more in God's favor? Are you changing the landscape of the Kingdom of God with your prayers? Ask God to show you how to better build up your home.

Discipline

Here is sound wisdom for your business. If you do not have oxen, you will have a clean barn; however, to have a profitable farm, you must invest in and maintain the equipment, tools, training, etc. that go into having a profitable enterprise. Simply put, no oxen mean a clean barn and no food in the kitchen. Shovel the manure, feed the oxen, and your fields are profitable. Expand the illustration to other areas of your life: entertaining in your home—no guests—no mess, but no encouragement of one another. How about ministry at your church—no investment of time—no worry about those people, but no growth in your Christian walk and the lives of others who need to be enriched by your life. How about children—purposely choosing not to have children—no mess, but no Godly offspring to carry on the cause of Christ.

Righteousness

The righteousness of a nation makes it great. Become a prayerful watchman for your country and countries where God may have you currently living. Pray for God's justice to reign and for sin not to rule.

Pray Proverbs 14:1, 4, and 34 over yourself and those for whom you stand guard as a faithful, prayerful watchman (Isaiah 62:6-7).

"LORD, help _____ and me to build our house wisely.
Let us not be foolish and tear it down with our own hands.
Help us not be lazy in the care of the oxen
You have given us to provide our revenue.
And LORD, please make our nation righteous,
so it will be exalted.
Take away the sin, so our disgrace will be removed.
In Your name, Jesus~"

MAY 15

Please read Proverbs 15.

Meditate on verses 1, 18, and 33.

> *A gentle answer turns away wrath,*
> *but a harsh word stirs up anger.*
> *A hot-tempered man stirs up strife,*
> *but the slow to anger calms a dispute.*
> *The fear of the LORD is the instruction for wisdom,*
> *and before honor comes humility.*

A friend of ours, whom I will call Mark, was a pastor. One day, he was having an argument with his wife, whom I will call Ann. Mark had finished his last round of statements, and Ann was returning her salvos of reasons why she was right and he was wrong. Mark was not listening but thinking of what to say next when Ann took a breath to reload.

Mark had been reading Proverbs daily for a long time, and God decided it was time to remind him of that fact. Proverbs 15:1 came to his mind. "A gentle answer turns away wrath, but a harsh word stirs up anger."

He responded, "Not now God, I am arguing!"

The LORD asked him, "Mark, am I dead to you that My promises are not true?"

Mark looked up at Ann who was still arguing and said, "Ann, I love you."

She replied, "What?!"

"Ann, I love you."

They do not remember what the argument was about, but they remember that true wisdom comes from God. When you humble yourself and trust in the LORD's promises and His wisdom, the results are miraculous.

Pray Proverbs 15:1, 18, and 33 over yourself and those for whom you
stand guard as a faithful, prayerful watchman (Isaiah 62:6-7).

"LORD, help _____ and me give a
gentle answer, turning away wrath.
May we stop stirring up anger with harsh words.
Do not let us be hot-tempered, stirring up strife.
Make us slow to anger, so the dispute will be calmed.
Let us fear You, so we can have the instruction of wisdom.
Make us humble; honor will not come until we are.
In Your name, Jesus~"

Please read Proverbs 16.

Meditate on verses 2-3.

> *All the ways of a man are clean in his own sight,*
> *but the LORD weighs the motives.*
> *Commit your works to the LORD,*
> *and your plans will be established.*

Another word for clean in Proverbs 16:2 is innocent. The idea is you make your plans and they appear to you to be right, with no ulterior motives. God however knows you better than you know yourself and is concerned about your deep motives.

To ensure your motives are right and your plans are really God's, you must surrender them to the LORD and prayerfully seek His path. Jesus prayed on the Mount of Olives, "Father, if You are willing, remove this cup from me; yet not My will, but Yours be done" (Luke 22:42).

Jesus said in Luke 9:23-24 that walking with Him required losing one's self, taking up the cross, every day, and following Him. This is Lordship. Are your plans yours or God's? Are they a product of your desires and dreams independent of the LORD, or are they His?

Pray Proverbs 16:2-3 over yourself and those for whom you stand guard as a faithful, prayerful watchman (Isaiah 62:6-7).

> *"LORD, since _____ and my ways are clean in our own sight,*
> *and since You weigh our motives,*
> *help us commit our works to You,*
> *so You will establish Your plans for our lives.*
> *In Your name, Jesus~"*

MAY 17

Please read Proverbs 17.

Meditate on verses 1 and 22.

Better is a dry morsel and quietness with it than a house full of feasting with strife. A joyful heart is good medicine, but a broken spirit dries up the bones.

Chapter 17 is full of individual proverbs to pray over your loved ones. In this chapter many negative characteristics and consequences of those characteristics are revealed. You may know people who are shameful, wicked, contentious, mockers, gossips, fools, and abominations to the LORD. This is a great chapter to slowly journey through and seek God to change them while there is still time.

The meditation verses reflect the value of Godly fruit in your life and in relationships with others. In verse 1, starving in a quiet home is contrasted to a full house of feasting with strife. A feast blessing many in a home of love and peace is the ideal, but strife robs the scene of the joy that ought to be there.

In verse 22, a joyful heart is good medicine to a person, but a broken spirit destroys the fabric of the body. As a believer, you are commanded to be joyful always (1 Thessalonians 5:14). Through the power of the Holy Spirit in you, this is possible despite crushing circumstances that may cause you to feel that your spirit is breaking. Ask God to restore the joy of your salvation and renew your spirit (Psalm 51:10, 12).

Pray Proverbs 17:1 and 22 over yourself and those for whom you stand guard as a faithful, prayerful watchman (Isaiah 62:6-7).

"LORD, let _____ and my house be filled with Your joyful feasting and Your peace. Remove the strife! Give us a joyful heart that is good medicine for others and ourselves. LORD, heal our broken spirits. In Your name, Jesus~"

Please read Proverbs 18.

Meditate on verses 1 and 19.

He who separates himself seeks his own desire;
he quarrels against all sound wisdom.
A brother offended is harder to be won than a strong city,
and contentions are like the bars of a citadel.

The world of church work is often difficult because the flock is often difficult to work with. There are many reasons for this, but it basically boils down to the fact that people are imperfect and want to do what they want to do rather than what God wants them to do. Add to this the spiritual battlefield for the souls of people, and it does not take much for many to take much offense. As humans, who are right in their own eyes, many refuse to forgive until others come to their senses. And until others change, people often separate themselves rather than humbly asking God for the wisdom to know what they need to do to make the situation better.

Being separate from other believers is wrong. If you or someone you love is physically separated from fellowshipping with believers because of sickness, imprisonment, persecution, etc., do not grow weary and lose heart. Stay strong in the LORD, and pray for opportunities to be with other Christians even in adverse circumstances. If you are not in one of those situations, God commands you in Hebrews 10:24-25 to be a part of the church, so you can encourage others, and others can encourage you. As a Christian and part of the bride of Christ, you are gifted by the Holy Spirit to minister to other believers in love and unity.

In Proverbs 18:19, the offended one has fortified their life around the bitterness and hatred that comes from being wronged or perceiving they have been wronged. God can take down walled cities; He enjoys doing the impossible. God wants you to forgive others just as He has forgiven you (Matthew 6:12-15).

You know people who are not living their Christian lives to the fullest because they are not faithfully part of the body of Christ. You may be that person.

You may know someone who is living so offended they refuse to forgive. Ask God to search your heart to see if you are that person.

As a faithful, prayerful watchman (Isaiah 62:6-7), pray Proverbs 18:1 and 19 over yourself and those who need to forgive and be part of church.

> *"LORD, help _____ and me stop separating*
> *ourselves and seeking our own desires.*
> *Help us not quarrel against all sound wisdom.*
> *LORD, win my offended brother who is like a strong city.*
> *Break the contentious bars of this citadel.*
> *By Your strong name, Jesus~"*

Please read Proverbs 19.

Meditate on verses 1, 17, and 22.

Better is a poor man who walks in his integrity
than he who is perverse in speech and is a fool.
One who is gracious to a poor man lends to the LORD,
and He will repay him for his good deed.
What is desirable in a man is his kindness,
and it is better to be a poor man than a liar.

Poor people, management of wealth, and holiness are issues you deal with. You may know people who are destitute and also people who are relatively wealthy in the eyes of the world. Some are thankful for a job that pays the equivalent of a U.S. dollar a day. Some leave their homes and move to other countries where they can make a little more. Millions are displaced by war and natural disasters every year. Many of you are serving them—thank you! You may be in a refugee camp with this book and nothing else but the clothes on your back and God on Your side. He is your hope.

God looks at your heart and establishes a higher standard of life than wealth. It is Godliness. Being poor or rich is not the measure of favor; it is integrity, kindness, truth, compassion, and generosity. There is no difference in the eyes of God between a poor person and a wealthy person. Each will be held accountable for how they live and use their sphere of influence to do good and follow His will for their life. When God calls you to change your community for righteousness, no matter where it is, do it.

If you have relative abundance, there are growth areas for you. If you have extra shoes, what does God want you to do with them? If you have money, use it for missions. Sell things you do not use and support a homeless shelter. If you have breath left in you, serve others!

Pray Proverbs 19:1, 17, and 22 over yourself and those for whom you stand guard as a faithful, prayerful watchman (Isaiah 62:6-7).

"LORD, help _____ and me be people of integrity.
Do not let us be fools with perverse speech.
Let us be gracious to the poor remembering
we are really giving to You, LORD.
Thank You, for telling us You will repay us for our good deeds.
You desire kindness; help us, LORD.
In Your name, Jesus~

Please read Proverbs 20.

Meditate on verses 5, 7, 24, and 27.

> *A plan in the heart of a man is like deep water,*
> *but a man of understanding draws it out.*
> *A righteous man who walks in his integrity—*
> *how blessed are his sons after him.*
> *Man's steps are ordained by the LORD.*
> *How then can man understand his way?*
> *The spirit of man is the lamp of the LORD,*
> *searching all the innermost parts of his being.*

How do you orient your life as a person of God and understand His plans for your life? If you are a Christian, your spirit is resurrected, and the LORD lives in you as His new temple (1 Corinthians 3:16). You live by the Spirit and keep in step with the Spirit (Galatians 5:25). You can set your mind on the Spirit and have the desires of the Spirit. The Spirit Himself testifies with your spirit that you are God's children, and you can cry out, "Abba! Father!" (Romans 8:14-17, 26-27). God reveals Himself and His ways through the Holy Spirit and the Word.

The verses in Proverbs 20 are great foundation stones for you to build upon.

- Your spirit is in communion with the LORD searching out the depths of your life (v. 27).

- God is the one who orchestrates the steps of your life and wants you to understand the way He has planned for you (v. 24).

❧ The plans deep within you, if Godly, can be realized with God's understanding and drawn out like a person at a well bringing up water (v. 5).

❧ Walking with God in integrity has generational blessings (v. 7).

Pray Proverbs 20:5, 7, and 24 over yourself and those for whom you stand guard as a faithful, prayerful watchman (Isaiah 62:6-7).

> *"LORD, give _____ and me the understanding*
> *to draw out the deep plans You have placed in our hearts.*
> *Let us walk in integrity, so our children will be blessed.*
> *Ordain our steps, LORD. Let us understand Your way.*
> *In Your name, Jesus~"*

Please read Proverbs 21.

Meditate on verses 1 and 31.

The king's heart is like channels of water in the hand of the LORD;
He turns it wherever He wishes.
The horse is prepared for the day of battle,
but victory belongs to the LORD.

Good governance is an important goal for countries. It benefits the population if the laws are fair and justly applied, if trade is allowed to flourish, and if there are human freedoms for people to direct their own lives.

In 1 Timothy 2:2, Paul called believers to pray for their leaders. Pray "for kings and all who are in authority, so that we may lead a tranquil and quiet life in all Godliness and dignity."

Christians need to be praying for the LORD's intervention in so many places around the world. He is more powerful than any country or any ruler. Ask Him to make the hearts of the rulers of your nation like His heart. Ask His blessings on rulers who are just and trying to serve the people under their care or authority.

One may have the most powerful military in the region, but victory is for the LORD to decide.

As a faithful, prayerful watchman (Isaiah 62:6-7), pray Proverbs 21:1, 31, and 1 Timothy 2:2 over your leaders.

"LORD, the heart of _____ is like a
channel of water in Your hand.
Turn their heart the way You wish.
Their horse is prepared for the day of battle,
but the victory belongs to You.
Let us lead a tranquil and quiet life in all Godliness and dignity.
In Your name, Jesus~"

Please read Proverbs 22.

Meditate on verses 1 and 6.

> *A good name is to be more desired than great wealth;*
> *favor is better than silver and gold.*
> *Train up a child in the way he should go,*
> *even when he is old, he will not depart from it.*

In today's society, being honorable is often not as important as getting ahead at any cost. In Proverbs 22, God emphasizes the importance of creating and defending a good name for yourself and your family.

Ron's father was an Infantry and Aviation Officer in the U.S. Army. He would say, "Son, it takes a lifetime to make a good name. It only takes a moment to lose it."

Do you desire being honorable more than you desire great riches? Is God's favor on your life more important than silver or gold? Or is your character for sale? How are your choices affecting your children?

"Train up a child in the way he should go" (Proverbs 22:6a). Train your children! This requires work. Parenting is constant. Children will follow in the footsteps of their mother and father. You may be a grandparent; your adult children and grandchildren are learning from you how to behave when they are your age. If you are struggling with a sin, stop it! You can break that sin cycle. For the sake of your children and their children, live righteous, honorable lives. Be a model of Godliness for them. Then the blessings of the fathers will be upon your children to the thousandth generation (Exodus 20:6).

Pray Proverbs 22:1 and 6 over yourself and those for whom you stand guard as a faithful, prayerful watchman (Isaiah 62:6-7).

"LORD, may _____ and I desire a good
name more than great wealth.
Let us want Your favor more than silver and gold.
Help me train up _____ in the way they should go.
When they are old, do not let them depart from it.
In Your name, Jesus~"

MAY 23

Please read Proverbs 23.

Meditate on verses 10-11.

> *Do not move the ancient boundary*
> *or go into the fields of the fatherless,*
> *for their Redeemer is strong;*
> *He will plead their case against you.*

In this passage of Scripture, there are real estate laws that go back to Leviticus 25. In the land of Israel, the ancient boundary markers were similar to survey markers, today. Where you build your fence should be on your own property.

Add to the complexity that in Israel, tribes and clans within the tribes determined these properties. Israeli family land had been marked for 400 years at the time these proverbs were written. It was the inheritance.

In Proverbs 23:10-11, God is the one looking out for the orphan and those being cheated. He opposes cheaters and people so selfish they would take advantage of an orphan.

Do you know people who are being cheated by others seeking their own interests? The LORD knows this is happening. Do you know someone who takes advantage of others? Pray for them to repent and return what they have stolen.

Pray Proverbs 23:10-11 as a faithful, prayerful watchman (Isaiah 62:6-7) for those who are victims and for those who are selfish.

> *"LORD, please stop _____ from moving the*
> *ancient boundary. Stop them from going into the*
> *fields of _____. You are their strong Redeemer.*
> *Plead their case, LORD!*
> *In Your name, Jesus~"*

Please read Proverbs 24.

Meditate on verses 3-4.

By wisdom a house is built, and by understanding it is established;
and by knowledge the rooms are filled with all precious and
pleasant riches.

There are instructions in Proverbs 24 about applying wisdom. Applied wisdom is behavior that comes as a result of seeing things the way God does. For example, God cares about those in need; rescue the helpless and don't make excuses not to help (vs. 11-12). It is displeasing to God when you rejoice in your heart over others stumbling; do not rejoice when your enemy falls (vs. 17-18). God loves justice; judge righteously, so the world can rejoice in proper decisions (vs. 23-24). Reflect on things you observe; you will acquire even more of God's wisdom and be able to apply it (vs. 30-32).

A house is built and established when it is constructed using God's plans. Do you apply the wisdom of God in such a way that His Son, Spirit, and Word are the foundation of your life and the governing current of your life's flow. When people look at your life, do they see a wavering person or do they see granite? It does not matter where you live physically, if your spiritual house is established in God, you are occupying incredibly valuable spiritual real estate, purchased with the blood of Christ and built up in Him.

Pray Proverbs 24:3-4 over yourself and those for whom you stand guard as a faithful, prayerful watchman (Isaiah 62:6-7).

"LORD, let _____ and me build our house by Your wisdom.
Establish it by Your understanding.
By Your knowledge, fill the rooms with
all precious and pleasant riches.
In Your name, Jesus~"

MAY 25

Please read Proverbs 25.

Meditate on verses 26-28.

> *Like a trampled spring and a polluted well*
> *is a righteous man who gives way before the wicked.*
> *It is not good to eat much honey, nor is it*
> *good to search out one's own glory.*
> *Like a city that is broken into and without walls*
> *is a man who has no control over his spirit.*

In the three meditation verses, the heroes of Proverbs (Righteousness, Discipline, and Wisdom) are missing.

The righteous man who falls away is like a polluted well or a trampled spring. The one who was a source of life for others has lost his integrity.

Without discipline, situations in one's life quickly deteriorate to being sickening. Lack of control will rob a person of their virtue and good reputation as if they were an unprotected city.

A person seeking their own glory is recognized as small and selfish. There is no wisdom in such behavior. As a child of the King, seek for Christ to be glorified in your life. As Christ increases and you decrease, your need for compliments and recognition will decrease. There is freedom in performing only for the sake of God and His Kingdom.

A wise person will learn from these scenarios. Your righteous behavior is a well of encouragement to others. Do not pollute it for momentary sinful pleasure. You control what goes into your mouth. You should be hungrier for God's Word than for physically driven desires. As a Christian, you have the fruit of the Spirit which includes self-control. Ask God to help you keep your defenses up, so you will be a well-fortified city.

Ask God to make Righteousness, Discipline, and Wisdom governors in your life and the lives of others.

Pray Proverbs 25:26-28 over yourself and those for whom you stand guard as a faithful, prayerful watchman (Isaiah 62:6-7).

"LORD, let _____ and me not be like a
trampled spring and a polluted well;
do not let us give way before the wicked.
Let us enjoy the gifts You give and eat the right amount of honey.
Do not let us search out our own glory,
nor be like a city that is broken into and without walls.
Let us be people who have control over our spirits.
For the sake of Your name, Jesus~"

MAY 26

Please read Proverbs 26.
Meditate on verses 1, 14, and 26.

Like snow in summer and like rain in harvest,
so honor is not fitting for a fool.
As the door turns on its hinges,
so does the sluggard on his bed.
Though his hatred covers itself with guile,
his wickedness will be revealed before the assembly.

As there are three heroes in Proverbs, there are also three villains: the Fool, the Sluggard, and the Wicked. These three are all present in the parade of sayings found in chapter 26.

The Fool

It is wrong, even hurtful, to honor a foolish person. From the perspective of the whole of Proverbs, the fool cannot change.

The Sluggard

The sluggard is so selfish and lazy that he does not contribute to society. He is only concerned about himself. He does not care about his name or working to take care of others. He is a user of others for the sake of his own laziness. The book of Proverbs does not hold hope for the sluggard to change.

The Wicked

The wicked man is not so lazy. He is actively selfish in furthering his evil agenda. He has a plan to counter all that is good. He hates God and goodness. In the book of Proverbs redemption for the wicked is not discussed.

Thankfully, we have the New Testament perspective where God changes all who believe in Jesus as their LORD and Savior. In 1 Corinthians 1:26-31, God revealed His plan to elevate the lesser things. In verse 27 and following it says, "… but God has chosen the foolish things of the world to shame the wise, and God has chosen the weak things of the world to shame the things which are strong … that no man should boast before God. But by His doing you are in Christ Jesus who became to us wisdom from God, and righteousness and sanctification, and redemption."

Jesus is the hero! He makes the foolish wise. He makes the wicked righteous. He makes the sluggard into a hardworking servant.

As a faithful watchman (Isaiah 62:6-7), pray Proverbs 26:1, 14, and 26 with confidence for those you know God can change.

"LORD, make _____ fitting of honor.
LORD, make _____ get out of bed.
LORD, make _____ cease from wickedness.
In Your name, Jesus~"

Please read Proverbs 27.

Meditate on verses 1, 2, 6, and 17.

> *Do not boast about tomorrow,*
> *for you do not know what a day may bring forth.*
> *Let another praise you, and not your own mouth;*
> *a stranger, and not your own lips.*
> *Faithful are the wounds of a friend,*
> *but deceitful are the kisses of an enemy.*
> *Iron sharpens iron,*
> *so one man sharpens another.*

The Bible has many verses about not being invested in the cares of tomorrow since you are not in control of that day nor much of the one you are in currently. This understanding leads to a humble, constant trust in the LORD throughout each day. Applying that wisdom in unceasing prayer brings blessings to your day with the LORD (I Thessalonians 5:16-18).

Note Proverbs 27:2: "Let another praise you, and not your own mouth." This is a hard one for most people. Often people are insecure and brag so much they appear arrogant. A man from the college we attended asked his date one night, after many dates together, why she never bragged about him. She stated she would start when he stopped bragging about himself.

True friends, described in Proverbs 27:6 as faithful friends, are going to say things to you that are hurtful, but in your best interest. Verse 17 illustrates verse 6: "Iron sharpens iron like one man can sharpens another."

This process of disciplining one another is sometimes hard, but when done among Godly believers, it develops character and increases wisdom and righteousness. Do you have friends in your life who tell you the truth about yourself and love you all the more for letting them help you be the man or woman of God He desires you to be?

Pray Proverbs 27:1-2 and 17 over yourself and those for whom you stand guard as a faithful, prayerful watchman (Isaiah 62:6-7).

> *"LORD, let _____ and me not boast in tomorrow.*
> *Thank You that You know what the day will bring forth.*
> *We trust You! Keep us from praising ourselves, LORD.*
> *Give us friends that will sharpen us and*
> *who will let us sharpen them.*
> *For the sake of Your name, Jesus~"*

MAY 28

Please read Proverbs 28.

Meditate on verses 7a and 9.

> *He who keeps the law is a discerning son.*
> *He who turns away his ear from listening to the law,*
> *even his prayer is an abomination.*

Prayer warriors, this is an important passage of Scripture for you. Your effectiveness in praying and discernment in praying are directly connected to your walk with the LORD.

In 1 Peter 3:7, husbands are told to treat their wives correctly so their prayers are not hindered. In Isaiah, it is not the LORD's capabilities that affect prayers but human sins (Isaiah 59:1-2).

In Proverbs 28, the discerning son is one who keeps the law. But the one who turns his ears from hearing the law will have the consequence of prayers that are an abomination to God.

Pray for divine sensitivity to discern areas of your life where the LORD needs to forgive you for sin, so your prayers will not be hampered.

Pray Proverbs 28:7 and 9 over yourself and those for whom you stand guard as a faithful, prayerful watchman (Isaiah 62:6-7).

> *"LORD, make _____ and me discerning.*
> *Help us keep Your law.*
> *Let us not humiliate You or our earthly fathers.*
> *Do not let us turn our ears from listening to Your law,*
> *so our prayers will not be an abomination.*
> *In Your name, Jesus~"*

MAY 29

Please read Proverbs 29.

Meditate on verse 18.

> *Where there is no vision, the people go unrestrained,*
> *but happy is he who keeps the law.*

"Where there is no vision, the people perish" (Proverbs 29:18 KJV). *Perish* and *unrestrained* are the words used to describe what happens to people without a vision. Without purpose, direction, and focus, people are undisciplined and unruly.

But, when people know God's truth and His vision, they stop wandering aimlessly; they stop trying to figure out life on their own.

Herb Hodges describes the importance of churches having vision for the direction they are to go in his book, *Tally Ho, the Fox!* He used the foxhunt illustration for understanding. At the start of the hunt, the dogs are meeting each other; some of the riders are talking; some are dismounted and working with their gear. Then the horn blows, and the fox is released. "Tally ho! The fox!" Everyone, every horse, and every dog is now focused on the common goal of chasing the fox.

In the same way, congregations need to have a common focus in following the LORD's will for their church. Individual families should have vision from the LORD on why they exist and what their purpose is.

Pray Proverbs 29:18a over your family, your church, and others for whom you stand guard as a faithful, prayerful watchman (Isaiah 62:6-7).

> *"LORD, give _____ and me Your vision.*
> *Help us stay focused on it,*
> *so we are not unrestrained*
> *and so we will not perish.*
> *In Your name, Jesus—"*

Please read Proverbs 30.

Meditate on verses 3-4.

> *Neither have I learned wisdom, nor do I have*
> *the knowledge of the Holy One.*
> *Who has ascended into heaven and descended?*
> *Who has gathered the wind in His fists?*
> *Who has wrapped the waters in His garment?*
> *Who has established all the ends of the earth?*
> *What is His name or His Son's name?*
> *Surely you know!*

Here is Agur, who described himself as the stupidest man on earth. Despite being inspired by God to write down his brilliant observations, he sees himself as not very smart; so stupid in fact, he is less than a man in his understanding (Proverbs 30:2).

However, he asks some important questions.

- ✑ Who has ascended into heaven and descended?
- ✑ Who can gather the wind in His fists or wrap the waters in His garment?
- ✑ Who has established all the ends of the earth?
- ✑ What is His name?
- ✑ What is His Son's name? Surely you know!

Maybe Agur was not so stupid after all.

Well, as a result of your privileged place in history, you know the answer to Agur's questions. His name is Jesus!

Paul asked similar questions in 1 Corinthians 2:11 and 16:

Who among men knows the thoughts of a man except the spirit of the man which is in him? And who has known the mind of the LORD, that he will instruct Him?

Paul concluded that the Holy Spirit knows. And, as a Christian, you have the Holy Spirit; therefore, you know because you have the mind of Christ!

With your New Testament understanding of the LORD, who has revealed Himself to you through Jesus Christ by the power of the Holy Spirit, pray with confidence Proverbs 30:3-4 over yourself and those for whom you stand guard as a faithful, prayerful watchman (Isaiah 62:6-7).

"LORD, thank You for giving _____ and me
wisdom and knowledge of You, the Holy One.
You have ascended into heaven and descended.
You have gathered the wind in Your fists.
You have wrapped the waters into Your garment.
You have established all the ends of the earth.
It is You, YAHWEH, and Your Son's name is Jesus!
Surely we know!"

MAY 31

Please read Proverbs 31.

Meditate on verses 10-11 and 30.

> *An excellent wife, who can find? For her worth is far above jewels.*
> *The heart of her husband trusts in her,*
> *and he will have no lack of gain.*
> *Charm is deceitful, and beauty is vain,*
> *but a woman who fears the LORD, she shall be praised.*

Just as the virtues in Titus 1:6-9 make a good list for a man to be or for a woman to look for in a husband, Proverbs 31:10-31 is a list of virtues to aspire to as a woman and characteristics to look for in a wife. This woman can inspire us all!

It can be a difficult passage of Scripture for many women because it lays out a woman of such high standards they feel defeated by it. The characteristics of a Godly, hard working wife and mother are displayed with a climactic ending that summarizes the book of Proverbs and explains why this woman was a success.

> *But a woman who fears the LORD, she shall be praised.*
> —Proverbs 31:30b

Proverbs ends with the truth God used to start the book, the truth He wanted you to learn as you prayed this book:

> *The fear of the LORD is the beginning of knowledge.*
> —Proverbs 1:7a

Fear of Almighty God is the only way to gain true wisdom and success in this life.

This woman's fear of God even brought her praise in the gates of the city (Proverbs 31:31).

The city gate was where the elders, nobles, judges, and leaders would sit and do the business of the city or region. It was the official gathering place. It was here that her Godly behaviors were being upheld and praised. Throughout Proverbs men have been valued for wisdom, discretion, and righteousness. It is fitting that Proverbs ends with the woman of virtue being praised.

Two final thoughts:

- Husband, let your wife be all God wants her to be, and do not envy her praise, for it is yours as well.

- See the value of Godly behavior as a public witness to God's work in your life. May God be praised in the city gates!

Pray Proverbs 31:10-11 and 30-31 over yourself and those for whom you stand guard as a faithful, prayerful watchman (Isaiah 62:6-7).

"LORD, make _____ an excellent wife,
whose worth is far above jewels.
Let her husband trust her.
May this couple have no lack of gain.
LORD, charm is deceitful and beauty is vain;
may we be people who fear You.
May what we do bring You praise in the gates.
For the sake of Your Kingdom, Jesus~"

On your walls, O Jerusalem,
I have appointed watchmen;
All day and all night they
will never keep silent.
You who remind the LORD,
take no rest for yourselves;
And give Him no rest
until He establishes
And makes Jerusalem a
praise in the earth.
ISAIAH 62:6-7, NASB

JUNE 1

Please read Romans 1.
Meditate on verse 16.

For I am not ashamed of the Gospel,
for it is the power of God for salvation to everyone who believes,
to the Jew first and also to the Greek.

Gospel means good message, specifically the good news of salvation through Jesus Christ. In his letter to the church in Rome, Paul examined the Gospel of Jesus Christ from every angle in order to prove salvation is by the grace of God through faith in Christ alone. Paul was not ashamed of the Gospel because he knew it was the power of God for salvation to everybody who believes it.

In the Gospel, God's righteousness is revealed. God also reveals His wrath against everyone who suppresses the truth of the Gospel by living in unrighteousness.

A person who refuses to honor God and exchanges the truth of God for a lie is in a horrific place. God tells you in Romans 1 that every human knows God, yet some will become fools and deny God. The punishment for such a deadly decision is that God gives fools over to their lusts, degrading passions, and depraved minds (Romans 1:24, 26, 28).

Pray Romans 1:16 and 21 over those for whom you stand guard as a faithful, prayerful watchman (Isaiah 62:6-7).

"LORD, let _____ not be ashamed of the Gospel.
Let them believe, so they can have Your power for salvation.
Let them know You, honor You, and give thanks to You.
Do not let them become futile in their thinking
or let their hearts be darkened and foolish.
In Your name, Jesus~"

For the next four months, you will read and pray the 21 letters of the New Testament. The LORD wrote these letters to teach you the truth about who He is and how you as a Christian are to live in relationship with Him and others.

Please read Romans 2.

Meditate on verse 4.

> *Do you think lightly of the riches of His*
> *kindness and tolerance and patience,*
> *not knowing that the kindness of God leads you to repentance?*

Do you presume upon the LORD's kindness, forbearance, and longsuffering patience? The LORD is kind to you because He wants you to repent of your stubborn selfishness.

Examine yourself in the light of Romans 2. Do you obey the truth or do you obey unrighteousness? Are you a hearer of the Word and not a doer of it? Are you a corrector of the foolish, yet you refuse to correct yourself? Do you take the LORD's kindness and patience for granted?

The day of God's wrath is coming for those with a stubborn and unrepentant heart.

Do not take His longsuffering over you lightly. The LORD's patience will one day cease for those who refuse His glory, honor, immortality—His offer of eternal life.

Pray Romans 2:4-7 over yourself and those for whom you stand guard as a faithful, prayerful watchman (Isaiah 62:6-7).

> *"LORD, may _____ and I stop taking lightly*
> *the riches of Your kindness, tolerance, and patience.*
> *Please forgive our stubborn and unrepentant hearts.*
> *We do not want to store up wrath for ourselves in*
> *the day of Your wrath and revelation of*
> *Your righteous judgment, God.*
> *Help us to persevere in doing good.*
> *May we seek Your glory, honor, and immortality, Your eternal life.*
> *In Your name, Jesus~"*

Please read Romans 3.

Meditate on verses 23-24.

For all have sinned and fall short of the glory of God,
being justified as a gift by His grace
through the redemption which is in Christ Jesus.

Try to wrap your mind around salvation. God's Word says:

There is none righteous, not even one;
there is none who understands, there is none who seeks for God.
All have turned aside, together they have become useless;
there is none who does good, there is not even one.
Their throat is an open grave;
with their tongues they keep deceiving.
The poison of asps is under their lips;
whose mouth is full of cursing and bitterness.
Their feet are swift to shed blood;
destruction and misery are in their paths,
and the path of peace they have not known.
There is no fear of God before their eyes.
—Romans 3:10-18

That is the description of the people Jesus came to save. That is the description of you apart from Jesus. That is the description of every single life separate from the gift of God's grace through the redemption in Christ Jesus. Amazing, absolutely amazing! If God Himself had not said it, it would be unbelievable. Why? Why would the God of the universe love you so much to offer you the gift of Himself? Why would any human refuse the gift of God's grace, and why would anyone boast in themselves once they received it?

Pray Romans 3:24-26 over those for whom you stand guard as a faithful, prayerful watchman (Isaiah 62:6-7).

"Christ Jesus, please let _____ be justified
by accepting the gift of Your grace through Your redemption.
Bring them to faith in You.
Demonstrate Your righteousness and forbearance
by passing over their previously committed sins.
In Your name, Jesus~"

Please read Romans 4.

Meditate on verses 18 and 21.

In hope against hope he believed,
so that he might become a father of many nations
according to that which had been spoken,
"So shall your descendants be."
And being fully assured that what God had promised,
He was able also to perform.

What do you believe God says? Are you waiting for something or someone God has promised? Your human reason for hoping is gone, yet you are hoping in faith.

Abraham did not waver in unbelief when it came to the promises of God. While he waited for God to fulfill His promises, Abraham grew stronger in faith. Abraham's growth gave glory to God.

Without faith it is impossible to please God (Hebrews 11:6). Do not grow weary and lose heart (Hebrews 12:3). The LORD has called you to be a watchman for someone. There is at least one person in your life who appears hopeless. God calls you to grow strong in faith for them, to be fully assured that what God has promised He is able to perform. God calls you to pray without ceasing for Him to establish their hearts without blame in holiness (1 Thessalonians 3:13).

Pray Romans 4:17 over the person for whom God has called you to be a faithful, prayerful watchman (Isaiah 62:6-7).

"LORD, You give life to the dead and call
into being that which does not exist.
Please give spiritual life to _____.
Let them exist and have their being in You.
In Your name, Jesus~"

Please read Romans 5.

Meditate on verse 6.

For while we were still helpless,
at the right time, Christ died for the ungodly.

Without Christ you are helplessly hopeless. At the right time, while you were still a sinner, Christ died for you so you could be saved from the wrath of God by the life of Christ. What an amazing gift He has given you! In Jesus Christ you receive the abundance of God's grace, the gift of His righteousness, and the privilege of reigning in life through Him (Romans 5:17).

Pray for those in your life who have not yet received this gift from God.

Pray Romans 5:3-5 over yourself and those for whom you stand guard as a faithful, prayerful watchman (Isaiah 62:6-7).

"LORD, help _____ and me to exult in our tribulations,
knowing that tribulation brings about perseverance.
Let perseverance prove our character.
May our proven character bring hope.
Hope does not disappoint
because Your love has been poured out within our hearts
through the Holy Spirit who was given to us.
In Your name, Jesus~"

Please read Romans 6.

Meditate on verse 11.

Consider yourselves to be dead to sin
but alive to God in Christ Jesus.

Romans 6 is a freeing chapter. If you are in Christ, this is the truth about you:

- You have died to sin.
- You cannot still live in sin.
- You can walk in newness of life.
- Your old self was crucified with Christ.
- Your body of sin can be done away with.
- You are no longer a slave of sin.
- You are freed from sin.
- You live with Christ.
- You live to God.
- Sin will not be master over you.
- You are a slave of righteousness.

Satan did not want you to know those facts about yourself, but now you do. Satan wants you to believe the lie that you will spend the rest of your time on earth struggling with your old nature instead of victoriously living your new identity in Christ to the glory of the Father. Now that you know the truth about yourself, you can obey the first exhortation in Romans: "Consider yourself to be dead to sin, but alive to God in Christ Jesus" (Romans 6:11).

Pray Romans 6:12-13 over yourself and those for whom you stand guard as a faithful, prayerful watchman.

"LORD, help _____ and me not let sin reign in our mortal body
so that we obey its lusts.
Do not let us go on presenting the members of our body
as instruments of unrighteousness,
but help us present ourselves to You, God,
as people alive from the dead,
and our members as instruments of righteousness to You.
In Your name, Jesus~"

JUNE 7

Please read Romans 7.

Meditate on verses 24-25a.

Wretched man that I am!
Who will set me free from the body of this death?
Thanks be to God through Jesus Christ our LORD!

In Romans 6, Paul commanded you to consider yourself dead to sin and alive to God in Christ Jesus. He exhorted you not to let sin reign in your mortal body and not go on presenting the members of your body to sin but to present yourself as an instrument of righteousness to God. In chapter 7, Paul illustrated the only way you can keep those commands. Paul used the pronouns "I," "me," and "my" nearly 50 times in Romans 7. They are used in the context of frustration and apparent defeat in Paul's battle with sin. "My flesh;" "I practice the very evil;" "sin dwells in me;" "wretched man that I am!"

If you are united with Christ, then "I," "me," and "my" should no longer be your focus. If you are the focus of your life, then Romans 7 probably describes you. Like Paul, you must come to the end of yourself and realize it is ALL about Jesus Christ your LORD. The struggle with sin is born out of selfishness. Paul realized he could not conquer sin in his life. Jesus Christ was the only one who ever conquered sin. Let Him conquer yours today.

Pray Romans 7:24-25 over yourself and those for whom you stand guard as a faithful, prayerful watchman (Isaiah 62:6-7).

"LORD, _____ and I are wretched people apart from You.
Only You can set us free from this body of death.
Thank You, God, through Jesus Christ our LORD,
we can be free from sin!"

JUNE 8

Please read Romans 8.

Meditate on verse 1.

> *Therefore there is now no condemnation*
> *for those who are in Christ Jesus.*

If you are in a covenant relationship with Jesus Christ, say this aloud inserting your name in the blank. "There is now no condemnation for _____."

That is the truth. God does not condemn you, and He tells you in Romans 8 how to stop the condemnation you heap on yourself. Set your mind on the things of the Holy Spirit.

Use the Bible to change your mindset. Every time your mind starts to wander to your past, say "there is now no condemnation for me because I am in Christ Jesus." Say it hundreds of times until your mindset changes. God wants you to live in His life and peace.

Pray Romans 8:5-11 over yourself and those for whom you stand guard as a faithful, prayerful watchman (Isaiah 62:6-7).

> *"LORD, please help _____ and me no longer*
> *set our minds on the things of the flesh.*
> *Let us set our minds on the things of the Spirit.*
> *For the mind set on the flesh is death,*
> *but the mind set on the Spirit is life and peace.*
> *Those who are in the flesh cannot please You, God.*
> *LORD, let Your Spirit dwell in _____ and me.*
> *We want to belong to You.*
> *Make our spirits alive because of righteousness.*
> *Spirit of God, You raised Jesus from the dead.*
> *Dwell in us. Give life to our mortal bodies.*
> *In Your name, Jesus~"*

Please read Romans 9.

Meditate on verse 15.

> *For He says to Moses, "I will have mercy on whom I have mercy,*
> *and I will have compassion on whom I have compassion."*

God is sovereign. God's purpose according to His choice will stand (Romans 9:11).

God calls (Romans 9:11). God has mercy on whom He desires, and He hardens whom He desires (Romans 9:18).

These are truths about God that can be difficult to comprehend, but they are still the truth. He is the Molder; you are the molded (Romans 9:20). And amazingly, He invites you to be a prayerful watchman as He molds those you love (Isaiah 62:6-7).

Pray Romans 9:15, 17, and 23 over those you are faithfully guarding.

> *"LORD, please choose to have*
> *mercy and compassion on _____.*
> *Raise them up to demonstrate Your power in them,*
> *that Your name might be proclaimed throughout the whole earth.*
> *Please make known the riches of Your glory*
> *upon them as vessels of mercy,*
> *which You prepared beforehand for glory.*
> *In Your name, Jesus~"*

Please read Romans 10.

Meditate on verse 1.

> *Brethren, my heart's desire and my prayer*
> *to God for them is for their salvation.*

Paul loved the Jewish people and desired for them to be saved. They were disobedient and obstinate, but Paul knew from personal experience that God could even save them (Romans 10:13, 21).

Who has God placed in your life that is disobedient, obstinate, and in desperate need of the righteousness of Jesus Christ? As their faithful, prayerful watchman (Isaiah 62:6-7), pray Romans 10:9, 13, 15, and 17 over yourself and them.

> *"LORD, faith comes from hearing Your Word.*
> *May my feet take the Good News of good things to _____.*
> *Please let them confess with their mouth You, Jesus, as LORD,*
> *and believe in their heart that God raised You from the dead.*
> *Save them, Jesus! Let them call on Your name!"*

JUNE 11

Please read Romans 11.

Meditate on verses 33-34.

Oh, the depth of the riches both of the
wisdom and knowledge of God!
How unsearchable are His judgments and unfathomable His ways!
For who has known the mind of the LORD,
or who became His counselor?

Romans 11 is full of truth about God that can be difficult for humans to comprehend. "God gave them a spirit of stupor ..." (v. 8). "By their transgression salvation has come to the Gentiles to make them jealous" (v. 11). "All Israel will be saved ..." (v. 26).

Rest in the fact that the LORD's sovereignty rules over all (Psalm 103:19). His gifts and calling are irrevocable (Romans 11:29). Examine your life today. What has the sovereign LORD gifted and called you to do? Choose to be obedient to God and the calling He has on your life.

Pray Romans 11:29 and 36 over yourself and those for whom you stand guard as a faithful, prayerful watchman (Isaiah 62:6-7).

"LORD, Your gifts and calling are irrevocable.
From You and through You and to You are all things.
Let _____ and I live
the rest of our lives for Your glory forever.
Amen."

Please read Romans 12.

Meditate on verse 1.

> *Therefore I urge you, brethren, by the mercies of God,*
> *to present your bodies a living and holy*
> *sacrifice, acceptable to God,*
> *which is your spiritual service of worship.*

Chapter 12 is the pinnacle of Romans. Up to this point, Paul stated the facts about God and salvation. He answered questions about who God is, why He hates sin, what God does about sin, and how He saves. He explained how God chooses you to be in a saving relationship with Him through Jesus Christ and how He keeps you from sinning.

Romans 12:1 begins with the word, "therefore." *Therefore* refers you back to everything you know about God and yourself from Romans 1-11. Because of who God is and everything you have and are in Him, give yourself completely and sacrificially to the LORD. Giving yourself to God is the only thing that makes sense in light of everything He has done for you.

The rest of the chapter is a list of about 40 actions and attributes that typify those who have offered themselves as a holy sacrifice to God. You could take a phrase or two a day and ask the LORD to make it more evident in your life. For example, "LORD, help me to abhor what is evil and cling to what is good" (Romans 12:9).

The remaining chapters of Romans will teach you practical ways to live your life as a follower of the LORD Jesus Christ.

Pray Romans 12:1-2 over yourself and those for whom you stand guard as a faithful, prayerful watchman (Isaiah 62:6-7).

"LORD, help _____ and me to present
our bodies as living and holy sacrifices acceptable to
You, which is our spiritual service of worship.
Do not let us be conformed to this world,
but let us be transformed
by the renewing of our minds,
so that we may prove what Your will is, God,
that which is good and acceptable and perfect.
In Your name, Jesus~"

JUNE 13

Please read Romans 13.

Meditate on verse 14.

But put on the LORD Jesus Christ,
and make no provision for the flesh in regard to its lusts.

You probably spend at least a few moments each day deciding what to wear. Depending on the occasion, you may even spend hours deciding; shopping for just the right outfit, trying it on for the approval of others, adorning yourself for the perfect appearance.

How much time do you spend each day ensuring you have laid aside the deeds of darkness and have put on the LORD Jesus Christ? Who do people see when they look at you? What do they observe and hear? What does the LORD see and hear when only He is in the room with you?

Pray Romans 13:11-14 over yourself and those for whom you stand guard as a faithful, prayerful watchman.

"LORD, it is time for _____ and me to wake up!
Salvation is nearer to us than when we believed.
The night is almost gone, and the day is near.
Therefore, let us lay aside the deeds of darkness,
and put on the armor of light.
Let us behave properly as in the day,
not in carousing and drunkenness,
not in sexual promiscuity and sensuality,
not in strife and jealousy.
Let us put on You, LORD Jesus Christ,
and make no provision for the flesh in regard to its lusts.
In Your name, Jesus~"

JUNE 14

Please read Romans 14.

Meditate on verses 16-17.

> *Therefore do not let what is for you a*
> *good thing be spoken of as evil;*
> *for the kingdom of God is not eating and drinking,*
> *but righteousness and peace and joy in the Holy Spirit.*

Romans 14 gives you God's perspective on religious legalism. Are you doing certain things because somebody said you had to do that to be right with God? Are you teaching others they must not eat or drink certain things or go to church on a certain day in order to really be right with God? God's Word says to stop judging one another, but rather determine that you are not putting an obstacle in a brother's way (Romans 14:13).

When you serve Christ out of righteousness, peace, and joy in the Holy Spirit, then you are acceptable to God (Romans 14:17-18). Think about your life and the way you treat others. Is your life characterized by righteousness, joy, and peace?

Pray Romans 14:17-21 over yourself and those for whom you stand guard as a faithful, prayerful watchman (Isaiah 62:6-7).

> *"LORD, help _____ and me remember that*
> *Your Kingdom is not about eating and drinking.*
> *Help us to live for Your Kingdom which is:*
> *righteousness and peace and joy in the Holy Spirit.*
> *Help us serve You, Christ.*
> *Make us acceptable to God and approved by men.*
> *May we pursue the things which make for peace*
> *and the building up of one another.*
> *Do not let us tear down Your work, God, for the sake of food.*
> *LORD, help us not to do anything*
> *that makes a brother stumble.*
> *In Your name, Jesus~"*

JUNE 15

Please read Romans 15.

Meditate on verse 13.

Now may the God of hope fill you with
all joy and peace in believing,
so that you will abound in hope by the power of the Holy Spirit.

Paul prayed for the believers at Rome to be of the same mind with one another, so with one accord and one voice they could glorify God (Romans 15:5-6). *One accord* means having the same passion, running together in unison. It is also a musical picture of different notes harmonizing with each other.

Does your family and church have the same passion for Jesus Christ? Are you running together the race God has set before you (Hebrews 12:1)? Do you harmonize with each other in order to glorify God?

Pray Romans 15:5-6 and 13 over yourself and those for whom you stand guard as a faithful, prayerful watchman (Isaiah 62:6-7).

"God, who gives perseverance and encouragement,
please grant that _____ and I be of the same mind
with one another according to Christ Jesus,
so that with one accord we may with one voice
glorify You, God and Father of our LORD Jesus Christ.
Now, God of hope, fill us with all joy and peace in believing,
so that we will abound in hope by the power of the Holy Spirit.
In Your name, Jesus~"

JUNE 16

Please read Romans 16.

Meditate on verse 19.

> *For the report of your obedience has reached to all;*
> *therefore, I am rejoicing over you,*
> *but I want you to be wise in what is good*
> *and innocent in what is evil.*

You have come to the last chapter in Romans, the chapter you might be tempted to skip because it contains 35 names of people you may have never heard of. It is like those Old Testament genealogy chapters which are sometimes described as boring. Remember, "all Scripture is inspired by God and profitable for teaching, for reproof, for correction, for training in righteousness" (2 Timothy 3:16). Romans 16 is no exception.

First, the names are fascinating. For example, Rufus, in verse 13, is the son of Simon of Cyrene, who was "pressed into service" by the Roman soldiers to carry the cross of Christ (Mark 15:21). Imagine how that moment changed for eternity the life of Simon's family, so much so, his boy, Rufus, would later be described by Paul as "a choice man in the LORD" (Romans 16:13).

The descriptions that accompany the 35 names are great phrases to pray over yourself and others. Pray for these to characterize you and those you love.

- A helper of many
- Risked their own necks for my life
- Worked hard for you
- Outstanding among the apostles
- Fellow worker in Christ
- The approved in Christ

- In the LORD
- Workers in the LORD
- Worked hard in the LORD
- A choice man in the LORD
- Host to me and to the whole church

Also pray Romans 16:19 over those for whom you stand guard as a faithful, prayerful watchman (Isaiah 62:6-7).

"LORD, let the report
of _____ obedience reach to all,
so that I am rejoicing over them.
Let them be wise in what is good
and innocent in what is evil.
In Your name, Jesus~"

JUNE 17

Please read 1 Corinthians 1.

Meditate on verses 30-31.

> *But by His (God's) doing you are in Christ Jesus,*
> *who became to us wisdom from God,*
> *and righteousness and sanctification and redemption,*
> *so that just as it is written,*
> *"Let him who boasts, boast in the LORD."*

Paul started his letter to the church in Corinth by reminding them about who Jesus is. Jesus is wisdom from God. The Corinthians were Greeks. They lived in a world captivated by Greek philosophy and the wisdom of men. God wanted them to know Jesus is the power and wisdom of God, and the foolishness of God is wiser than men, and the weakness of God is stronger than men (1 Corinthians 1:24-25).

You live in a world still captivated by man's knowledge and power. Do not be deceived! Filter everything you read and hear through the truth of God's Word. Your life's goal as a Christian is to know God. God says, "the world through its wisdom did not come to know God" (1 Corinthians 1:21). You know God by knowing the Bible.

Pray 1 Corinthians 1:4-9 over yourself and those for whom you stand guard as a faithful, prayerful watchman (Isaiah 62:6-7).

> *"LORD, give grace to _____ and me in Christ Jesus,*
> *that in everything we will be enriched in You,*
> *in all speech and all knowledge.*
> *Jesus, confirm Your testimony in us,*
> *so that we are not lacking any gift*
> *as we eagerly await the revelation of You.*

LORD Jesus Christ, You will confirm us to the end,
blameless in Your day.
God, You are faithful.
Thank You for calling us into fellowship
with Your Son, Jesus Christ our LORD."

Please read 1 Corinthians 2.

Meditate on verse 16b.

We have the mind of Christ.

Sear that sentence into your conscious and subconscious mind. You can think like Jesus thinks because the Spirit of God lives in you. The Spirit gives you the mind of Jesus. Since you have His mind, you can speak with His wisdom. You can spiritually discern and determine things because God's Spirit is inside you.

When Paul went to Corinth, he determined to know nothing among the Corinthians except Jesus Christ and Him crucified (1 Corinthians 2:2). Paul was a learned man. He could have impressed them with his knowledge of philosophy or Jewish laws, but the Spirit of God told him to speak about Jesus and the crucifixion. Paul's obedience demonstrated the power of the Holy Spirit, and as a result, many Corinthians became Christians.

You have the mind of Christ. Let that sentence rule every thought you have, every word that comes out of your mouth, and every step you take. Your obedience will have eternal results.

Pray 1 Corinthians 2:12-13 and 16 over yourself and those for whom you stand guard as a faithful, prayerful watchman (Isaiah 62:6-7).

"God, _____ and I have received Your Spirit.
Let us know the things freely given to us by You.
Let us speak things taught by the Spirit.
Help us combine spiritual thoughts with spiritual words.
May we never forget that we can know Your mind, LORD,
because we have Your mind.
In Your name, Jesus~"

Please read 1 Corinthians 3.

Meditate on verse 19a.

For the wisdom of this world is foolishness before God.

Paul wanted the Corinthians to change their minds. They lived in a society that idolized Greek philosophy. Paul wanted them to know the wisdom of God. They were impressed with and wanted to impress people. Paul wanted them to please the LORD. They thought they were so wise, yet Paul could figuratively give them only milk to drink and not solid food as he taught them because they were fleshly, infants in Christ, not growing up in the LORD (1 Corinthians 3:1-3).

Examine your life. Where are you on the spiritual growth chart? What do you love, this present world or Jesus Christ? Who do you desire to please, your selfish desires or the LORD? It is time to do away with childish things and grow up in all aspects into Christ (1 Corinthians 13:11; Ephesians 4:15).

Pray 1 Corinthians 3:1-3 over yourself and those for whom you stand guard as a faithful, prayerful watchman (Isaiah 62:6-7).

"LORD, please help _____ and me
stop being people of flesh, infants in Christ.
Give us the desire to receive
not only the milk of Your Word but solid food.
Take away our desire to be fleshly.
Let us cease from jealousy and strife.
Let us walk as followers of You,
In Your name, Jesus~"

Please read 1 Corinthians 4.

Meditate on verse 4.

For I am conscious of nothing against myself,
yet I am not by this acquitted;
but the one who examines me is the LORD.

The church at Corinth had members who were not growing up in Christ. They judged their behavior by comparing themselves to others and deciding they were doing nothing wrong. Paul, their father in Christ Jesus (1 Corinthians 4:15), was not pleased with their attitudes and behaviors. They were arrogant and thought they were doing just fine in their Christianity. Paul reminded them it did not matter what they thought about their behavior; the LORD was the one examining them.

God knows everything. He knows what you do in the dark that you think no one sees. He knows the motives of your heart. Compared to others your behavior may appear golden; however, a day is coming when God will pass judgment, and your opinion of yourself will not matter. The only thing that matters then and now is what God thinks.

Pray 1 Corinthians 4:1-2 and 5 over yourself and those for whom you stand guard as a faithful, prayerful watchman (Isaiah 62:6-7).

"LORD, make _____ and me servants of You
and stewards of Your mysteries.
Make us trustworthy.
Let us not forget that You will come
and bring to light the things hidden in the darkness
and disclose the motives of our hearts.
May our praise come from You, God.
For the glory of Your name, Jesus~"

Please read 1 Corinthians 5.
Meditate on verse 2.

You have become arrogant and have not mourned instead,
so that the one who had done this deed would
be removed from your midst.

There was sin in the church at Corinth, and the people did nothing about it. Paul said it was because of their arrogance and lack of grief over sin that they would not remove the sinner from their midst in order to discipline him in hope of repentance.

What is your attitude toward sin? Are you grieved by sin in your life and the life of others? Or in your pride, do you ignore it and rationalize: "This is no big deal; everyone does it, and I am not as bad as most"?

God hates sin! Do not trivialize it! Sin always ends in death; it is not to be toyed with. Sin destroys lives. Paul commanded the church at Corinth to "remove the wicked man from among yourselves" (1 Corinthians 5:13). God says the same to you: "Remove the wickedness from your life!"

Pray 1 Corinthians 5:2 over yourself and those for whom you stand guard as a faithful, prayerful watchman (Isaiah 62:6-7).

"LORD, may _____ and I not be arrogant.
Let us mourn over sin.
Help us remove sin from our midst.
In Your name, Jesus~"

Please read 1 Corinthians 6.

Meditate on verses 9 and 10.

> *Or do you not know that the unrighteous*
> *will not inherit the kingdom of God?*
> *Do not be deceived; neither fornicators,*
> *nor idolaters, nor adulterers, nor effeminate,*
> *nor homosexuals, nor thieves, nor the covetous,*
> *nor drunkards, nor revilers, nor swindlers,*
> *will inherit the kingdom of God.*

There, God said it. He has given you the politically incorrect list of people who will not inherit His Kingdom. And He warns you not to be deceived because you will be tempted to say: "Did God really say, 'The covetous will not inherit His Kingdom; the fornicators will not inherit His Kingdom; homosexuals will not inherit His Kingdom?'" Yes, God really said that.

"Did God really say?" were the first recorded words from the lips of Satan (Genesis 3:1). He still says the same thing. Do not fall for his lie!

There is great news in 1 Corinthians 6 because all of us fit into at least one of the categories in verses 9 and 10. God washes, sanctifies, and justifies you in the name of the LORD Jesus Christ and in His Spirit from everything on the list when you choose to flee immorality and join yourself to the LORD (1 Corinthians 6:11, 17-18).

Pray 1 Corinthians 6:18-20 over yourself and those for whom you stand guard as a faithful, prayerful watchman (Isaiah 62:6-7).

> *"LORD, help _____ and me to flee immorality.*
> *Let us not forget that our bodies are a temple of the Holy Spirit*
> *who is in us, and we are not our own.*
> *We have been bought with a price.*
> *God, may we glorify You in our body.*
> *In Your name, Jesus~"*

Please read 1 Corinthians 7.

Meditate on verse 24.

> *Brethren, each one is to remain with God*
> *in that condition in which he was called.*

1 Corinthians 7 addressed various relationships people were in: married, single, divorced, and widowed. The point being made was no matter what condition or situation you are in, be holy.

The lie of Satan is God wants you to be happy. The truth is God wants you to be holy; God expects you to be holy (1 Peter 1:15-16). People will give this as their reason for divorcing their husband or wife: "God wants me to be happy."

Know with certainty; God cares more about your holiness than your happiness. Your concern should be whether or not the decision you are about to make will make your holy God happy. The only way to be truly happy is to be holy because God is holy.

God taught in this chapter that marriage pleases Him and being single pleases Him. You have to seek God's will for your life, and as you do, you will grow closer to Him, which is the real goal, anyway.

Pray 1 Corinthians 7:17 and 24 over yourself and those for whom you stand guard as a faithful, prayerful watchman (Isaiah 62:6-7).

> *"LORD, let _____ and me walk in what*
> *You have assigned and called us to do.*
> *Let us remain with You as*
> *we remain in Your calling.*
> *In Your name, Jesus~"*

Additional insight: 1 Corinthians 7:36-38 is addressed to fathers who were required to give permission for their daughters to marry. If a father chose to let his daughter remain unmarried for the purpose of devotion to Christ, it was his responsibility to continue his financial care of her. It was an important decision the father had to make; one that required much wisdom from God. Fathers should heed this instruction today in helping their children decide whom to marry or if they should marry.

Please read 1 Corinthians 8.

Meditate on verse 9.

But take care that this liberty of yours
does not somehow become a stumbling block to the weak.

Paul wrote this letter to the church in Corinth to address problems and to answer questions and concerns the Corinthians had. They were concerned about relationships, so Paul wrote about being single, married, and divorced in 1 Corinthians 7.

In chapter 8, Paul answered a question concerning things sacrificed to idols by saying, "knowledge makes arrogant, but love edifies" (v. 1). It seems like an odd answer, but not if you keep it in the context of relationships. Paul wanted the Christians in Corinth to take the things they were learning about God and apply them with love to the people around them. For example, the believers were taught that in Christ they had freedom to eat anything. However, with that freedom came the responsibility not to cause someone else to stumble in their walk with Christ or in their opportunity to know Christ as Savior. If eating a steak that has been sacrificed to an idol, even though an idol is nothing, hurts another's spiritual growth, then don't eat the steak. Be motivated by love for others rather than the pride of knowing you have the freedom in Christ to do certain things.

Pray 1 Corinthians 8:1 and 9 over yourself and those for whom you stand guard as a faithful, prayerful watchman (Isaiah 62:6-7).

"LORD, may _____ and I not become
arrogant in our knowledge.
In love, help us edify others.
May we take care that the liberty we have
not become a stumbling block to the weak.
For the sake of Your name, Jesus~"

Please read 1 Corinthians 9.
Meditate on verse 23.

I do all things for the sake of the Gospel,
so that I may become a fellow partaker of it.

Paul addressed purpose in chapter 9. Paul's purpose was the Gospel of Christ. Everything Paul did was motivated by how he could tell others about the salvation and grace of God through Christ Jesus. Paul's purpose determined his behavior, his relationships, his occupation, and his disciplines.

What is your purpose? What motivates you to get up in the morning? Are you a partaker of the salvation and grace of Jesus Christ? Has it so impacted your life that you are living the rest of your life in such a way others see, hear, feel, taste, and smell Jesus emanating from you? Can you say, like Paul, "I do all things for the sake of the Gospel"?

Pray 1 Corinthians 9:23-27 over yourself and those for whom you stand guard as a faithful, prayerful watchman (Isaiah 62:6-7).

"LORD, may _____ and I do all things
for the sake of Your Gospel,
so that we may become fellow partakers of it.
Help us run this race in such a way that we may win.
Help us exercise self-control in all things
to receive an imperishable wreath.
Help us run with aim and box without beating the air.
LORD, help us discipline our bodies and make them Your slaves,
so that, after we have preached to others,
we will not be disqualified.
Because of Your name, Jesus~"

Please read 1 Corinthians 10.

Meditate on verse 31.

> *Whether, then, you eat or drink or whatever you do,*
> *do all to the glory of God.*

1 Corinthians 10 is rich with truth. Here are some of the fascinating facts.

The Rock in the wilderness from which the Israelites drank water was Jesus (1 Corinthians 10:4; Exodus 17:6; Numbers 20:11-12). Ponder that fact as it will give you new insight as to why God did not let Moses enter the Promised Land after he struck the Rock, Jesus, twice. The Rock had been stricken once (Exodus 17:6); He was not to be struck again.

The Old Testament, filled with examples of what makes God angry, was written for your instruction, so you do not crave evil things (1 Corinthians 10:6-11). God creates a way of escape especially for you in every temptation (1 Corinthians 10:13). Fix your eyes on Jesus and His righteous path of escape. Flee from sin!

These are just a few of the precious, life-changing truths. Reread the chapter and ask God to reveal other treasures.

Pray 1 Corinthians 10:24, 31, and 33 over yourself and those for whom you stand guard as a faithful, prayerful watchman (Isaiah 62:6-7).

> *"LORD, help _____ and me not to seek our own good,*
> *but that of others. Whether, then, we eat or drink*
> *or whatever we do, let us do all to the glory of You, God.*
> *Let us do things to please others, not seeking our own profit,*
> *but the profit of the many, so they may be saved.*
> *For the sake of Your name, Jesus~"*

Please read 1 Corinthians 11.

Meditate on verse 1.

Be imitators of me, just as I also am of Christ.

Wow! Paul is bold in his exhortations. At first glance, his command sounds arrogant. But think about what he is saying. His command is to imitate Christ. Paul took his own command so seriously that he, too, was imitating Christ; therefore, these young Christians in Corinth who were surrounded by idolatrous paganism, could look to Paul as an example of how to live in Christ.

What about your life? Do you behave and speak in such a way that you could encourage another to come alongside you, and by imitating you, actually learn how to imitate Jesus? It is a convicting thought, and as a follower of Jesus Christ, should be what you would not hesitate to tell a less mature believer.

Spend the next 24 hours examining every moment of your day. Is there even a second when you would be embarrassed to have another Christian observing you?

Live for the LORD in such a way that your family and friends can imitate you and actually be imitating Jesus.

Pray 1 Corinthians 11:1 over yourself and those for whom you are discipling and standing guard as a faithful, prayerful watchman (Isaiah 62:6-7).

"LORD, make me an imitator of You.
When _____ imitates me,
may it actually be imitating You.
In Your name, Jesus~"

Please read 1 Corinthians 12.

Meditate on verses 14 and 20.

For the body is not one member, but many.
But now there are many members, but one body.

This is an important chapter for church doctrine. The church is the body of Christ made up of many members. God uses the analogy of a human body to help you understand. Just as a human body has many parts: hands, feet, lungs, etc., and they are all vitally important, so does the body of Christ have many members, and they are all vitally important. In a human body, some of the parts are visible; some are less visible, yet for a human body to function properly, every single part, even the tiniest cell is important. In Christ's body, the church, every single member is important for the church to function the way God intended.

You may feel like a tiny, invisible cell in your church, but you know that in your own body if one cell becomes diseased, it can sicken your entire body. Do not be a sick cell. Practice your spiritual gifts in a local body of believers, a local church. It will keep you spiritually and even physically healthy, and it will keep the church healthy. It is God's plan and purpose for those who call themselves Christians to be part of the body of Christ, His church.

Pray 1 Corinthians 12:11 and 18 over yourself and those for whom you stand guard as a faithful, prayerful watchman (Isaiah 62:6-7).

"Holy Spirit, make _____ and me mindful of Your work
and how You have distributed gifts to us
individually just as You will.
God, You have placed us in Your body as You desired.
Help us to use our gifts faithfully in the church where you put us.
For the sake of Your name, Jesus~"

JUNE 29

Please read 1 Corinthians 13.

Meditate on verse 11.

When I was a child, I used to speak like a child,
think like a child, reason like a child;
when I became a man, I did away with childish things.

As Paul wrote this letter to Christians in Corinth, he was burdened by their lack of maturity in Christ (1 Corinthians 3:1-2). God is concerned about the same thing in your life. Are you putting away childish behaviors and speaking and acting like Christ?

It was not by accident that God had Paul write about love and maturity in the same section of this letter. When you let the love of Christ rule your life, you will grow up in Him.

Pray 1 Corinthians 13:4-8a over yourself and those for whom you stand guard as a faithful, prayerful watchman (Isaiah 62:6-7). Insert your names in the place of the word *love*.

"LORD, may this describe _____ and me.
_____ is patient;
_____ is kind and is not jealous;
_____ does not brag and is not arrogant,
does not act unbecomingly;
_____ does not seek our own,
is not provoked,
does not take into account a wrong suffered,
does not rejoice in unrighteousness, but rejoices with the truth;
bears all things, believes all things,
hopes all things, endures all things.
_____ never fails.
Because of You, Jesus~"

JUNE 30

Please read 1 Corinthians 14.

Meditate on verses 33 and 40.

> *For God is not a God of confusion but of peace,*
> *as in all the churches of the saints.*
> *But all things must be done properly*
> *and in an orderly manner.*

1 Corinthians 14 is one of those chapters in the Bible that can create controversy among Christians to the delight of nonbelievers. So when God wanted Paul to write about concerns that were causing division in the church, He had him remind the believers about who God is. God is a God of peace, and church should be a place where things are done properly and in an orderly manner. It should not be confusing to go to church. (If your church is confusing, do not quit attending. As a member of the body, teach your church this truth from God's Word.)

God is a God of peace. When you are controlled by the God of peace, your home, your church, and your life should be functioning in an orderly, proper manner.

Pray about areas where you need the God of peace to take control. Be obedient to His instruction and pray 1 Corinthians 14:20 over yourself and those for whom you stand guard as a faithful, prayerful watchman (Isaiah 62:6-7).

> *"LORD, help _____ and me*
> *not be children in our thinking;*
> *yet in evil let us be infants,*
> *but in our thinking make us mature.*
> *In Your name, Jesus~"*

On your walls, O Jerusalem,
I have appointed watchmen;
All day and all night they
will never keep silent.
You who remind the LORD,
take no rest for yourselves;
And give Him no rest
until He establishes
And makes Jerusalem a
praise in the earth.
ISAIAH 62:6-7, NASB

JULY 1

Please read 1 Corinthians 15.

Meditate on verses 3-4.

> *For I delivered to you as of first importance what I also received,*
> *that Christ died for our sins according to the Scriptures, and that*
> *He was buried, and that He was raised on the third day according*
> *to the Scriptures.*

Paul stayed in Corinth for a year and a half getting this church started (Acts 18:1-11). After he left, he wrote this letter reminding the Corinthians of the Gospel message saying it is the most important message: Christ died; Christ was buried; Christ rose from the dead.

The Corinthian church had lost their focus on these doctrinal truths about who Jesus is and were arguing about whether or not there was resurrection of the dead.

Paul admonished them for engaging in this foolish argument because Christ proved there is resurrection from the dead. The reason the Christian church exists is because there is resurrection from the dead.

Knowing the doctrine of God stops foolish controversies. You learn that doctrine by studying the Bible. Be diligent to know God through His Word then be willing to teach the truth of God to others, so your family and church can be established in Christ.

Pray 1 Corinthians 15:58 over yourself and those for whom you stand guard as a faithful, prayerful watchman (Isaiah 62:6-7).

> *"LORD, make _____ and me steadfast, immovable,*
> *and always abounding in Your work.*
> *May we never forget that our toil is not in vain when it is in You.*
> *For the sake of Your name, Jesus~"*

JULY 2

Please read 1 Corinthians 16.

Meditate on verse 14.

Let all that you do be done in love.

Paul concluded his letter to the church in Corinth by addressing their concern about collecting money to meet the needs of others and giving them five exhortations which would help them grow up more in Christ (1 Corinthians 16:13-14). They are:

1. Be on the alert.
2. Stand firm in the faith.
3. Act like men.
4. Be strong.
5. Let all that you do be done in love.

These exhortations will help you in your spiritual growth as well. Memorize verse 14 today. Say it over and over a hundred times. You may want to change the "you" to "I." "Let all that I do be done in love." It will be fun to see your attitudes and actions change for the better. Like Stephanas, Fortunatus, and Achaicus, refresh the spirit of others today by letting everything you do be done in the love of Christ (1 Corinthians 16:17-18).

Pray 1 Corinthians 16:14 and 18 over yourself and those for whom you stand guard as a faithful, prayerful watchman (Isaiah 62:6-7).

"LORD, let all that _____ and I do be done in love.
May we refresh the spirit of others.
In Your name, Jesus~"

As you finish reading 1 Corinthians, remember that Paul was writing to immature believers in Jesus Christ (1 Corinthians 3:1). They lived in an important Greek city with the temple of Aphrodite (the goddess of love) on top of its acropolis. One thousand young boys and girls served as prostitutes to facilitate temple worship. In town, there were at least a dozen other heathen temples. Blatant immorality was rampant throughout Corinth.

Paul lived in Corinth for a year and a half telling the people about Jesus Christ who died to save sinners. The church started with immoral sinners made holy by the blood of Jesus. Paul addressed them as saints, holy ones (1 Corinthians 1:2).

Paul exhorted and admonished these saints to deal with problems and issues in their church and in their personal lives, even sexually immoral issues.

Despite who you were, remember who you are in Jesus. Remember that IN Christ you are sanctified (cleansed and purified); you are a saint.

Please read 2 Corinthians 1.

Are you in need of comfort today? Soak in the Words of your LORD.

Meditate on verses 2-4.

> *Grace to you and peace from God our Father*
> *and the LORD Jesus Christ.*
> *Blessed be the God and Father of our LORD Jesus Christ,*
> *the Father of mercies and God of all comfort,*
> *who comforts us in all our affliction*
> *so that we will be able to comfort those*
> *who are in any affliction with the comfort*
> *with which we ourselves are comforted by God.*

Jesus, the God of all comfort, comforts you, so you can comfort others. Emotionally and spiritually where are you today? Are you in a tough place? Are you allowing the Father of mercies to comfort you right now? As you experience His comfort, are you going to keep it to yourself, or will you deliberately comfort another today? Often the comfort and healing will truly begin when you stop being self-focused and focus on others and their needs.

Pray 2 Corinthians 1:12, 21-22, and 24 over yourself and those for whom you stand guard as a faithful, prayerful watchman (Isaiah 62:6-7).

> *"LORD, help us to have a good conscience by conducting ourselves*
> *in holiness, Godly sincerity, and Your grace.*
> *Establish us in You, Christ.*
> *Thank You that You anoint us, seal us,*
> *and give us Your Spirit in our hearts as a pledge.*
> *Help us to stand firm in our faith.*
> *In Your name, Jesus~"*

Please read 2 Corinthians 2.

Meditate on verse 14.

> *But thanks be to God,*
> *who always leads us in triumph in Christ,*
> *and manifests through us the sweet aroma*
> *of the knowledge of Him in every place.*

Paul continued to mentor these immature believers at Corinth. Paul instructed them in an earlier letter to deal with sin within their church (1 Corinthians 5:1). The church took Paul's admonition to heart and so punished the offending sinner that after he repented of his sin, the church did not forgive and comfort him. Paul urged the believers to reaffirm their love for him and not let unforgiveness cause Satan to take advantage of them.

This is an important principle for your personal discipleship. Sin must be stopped. After the sinner repents and asks forgiveness, you are to forgive, comfort, and reaffirm your love for them. By forgiving, comforting, and loving the repentant one, Satan will not get an advantage in your life. Such Christian maturity on your part causes the sweet aroma of Jesus to be evident in your life.

Pray 2 Corinthians 2:14-15 over yourself and those for whom you stand guard as a faithful, prayerful watchman (Isaiah 62:6-7).

> *"God, thank You for leading _____ and*
> *me in triumph in Christ.*
> *Manifest through us the sweet aroma*
> *of the knowledge of Jesus in every place we go.*
> *May we be the fragrance of Christ*
> *among those who are being saved*
> *and among those who are perishing.*
> *For the sake of Your name, Jesus~"*

Please read 2 Corinthians 3.

Meditate on verse 5.

Not that we are adequate in ourselves
to consider anything as coming from ourselves,
but our adequacy is from God.

You live in a world that is focused on "self." I looked up "self- __ " in the dictionary and started counting. When I got to 100, I was only in "self-e... "

Paul made the point in this chapter that he was not going to commend himself. His confidence was through Christ. His adequacy was from God. His image was of the glory of the LORD.

Do not be deceived. Worldly ideology focuses on self-confidence, self-adequacy, and self-image. You will waste the lifetime God has given you on earth if you focus on self. When you focus on Jesus and live for Him, the issues you have with yourself will "grow strangely dim in the light of His glory and grace" (Helen H. Lemmel).

Pray 2 Corinthians 3:4-5 and 18 over yourself and those for whom you stand guard as a faithful, prayerful watchman (Isaiah 62:6-7).

"Jesus, help _____ and me know
our confidence is through You
and toward God.
We are not adequate in ourselves
to consider anything as coming from ourselves.
God, You make us adequate.
May our image be transformed
to reflect the glory of You, LORD.
For the sake of Your name, Jesus~"

JULY 6

Please read 2 Corinthians 4.

Meditate on verse 7.

> *But we have this treasure in earthen vessels,*
> *so that the surpassing greatness of the power*
> *will be of God and not from ourselves.*

Chapter 4 starts, "Therefore, since we have this ministry, as we received mercy, we do not lose heart."

The ministry Paul was referring to is the ministry of the Spirit, the ministry of righteousness (2 Corinthians 3:8-9). God has given you the ministry of righteousness, and it can only be done in the power of the Holy Spirit.

You may be tired and discouraged today. You may feel overwhelmed. Say this phrase from verses 1 and 16 over and over.

> *We do not lose heart.*

God has put you in an earthly body, so you will rely on His strength and not become prideful thinking that anything good comes from yourself. You can serve the LORD today because of His great power in you.

Pray 2 Corinthians 4:5, 7, and 16 over yourself and those for whom you stand guard as a faithful, prayerful watchman (Isaiah 62:6-7).

> *"As your bond-servants, Jesus,*
> *may _____ and I preach that You are LORD.*
> *We do not want to preach ourselves.*
> *Let us not lose heart as we serve*
> *by the surpassing greatness of Your power.*
> *For the sake of Your name, Jesus~"*

JULY 7

Please read 2 Corinthians 5.

Meditate on these phrases from verses 14 and 20.

The love of Christ controls us.
We are ambassadors for Christ.

2 Corinthians 5 is rich with treasure verses to pray, and it gives you God's eternal perspective.

You are burdened by present circumstances. God encourages you, "what is mortal will be swallowed up by life" (v. 4).

You are scared. God saya, "always be of good courage" (v. 6).

You do not know where to go. God reminds you, "walk by faith, not by sight" (v. 7).

You lack ambition. God exhorts you, "have as your ambition to be pleasing to Me" (v. 9).

You are selfish. God tells you, "Christ died for you, so you will no longer live for yourself. Christ died for you; let His love control you" (v. 14-15).

You lack purpose. God gives you your job description: "You are an ambassador for Christ" (v. 20).

Let these truths sink in as you pray them over yourself and those for whom you stand guard as a faithful, prayerful watchman (Isaiah 62:6-7).

"Christ, let _____ and me not forget that in You,
we are being swallowed up by Life. Help us to be of
good courage as we walk by faith and not by sight.
May we have as our ambition to be pleasing to You.
Thank You for dying for us, so we can stop living for ourselves.
Let Your love control us. Make us pleasing ambassadors for You.
For the sake of Your name, Jesus~"

Please read 2 Corinthians 6.
Meditate on verses 1, 3, and 4a.

And working together with Him,
we also urge you not to receive the grace of God in vain—
giving no cause for offense in anything,
so that the ministry will not be discredited,
but in everything commending ourselves as servants of God.

God's Words in this chapter give you an opportunity for a Holy Spirit evaluation of your life. If you are a Christian, you are a recipient of God's grace—His merciful kindness that drew you to Him. God graced you with salvation. The rest of your life should not be lived in vain but as an offering to God of thanksgiving for all He has done for you.

Paul listed about two dozen circumstances that could be used as excuses to be offensive, yet as a servant of God, Paul chose not to discredit the ministry. The eternity of others was at stake.

Let the Holy Spirit examine you. Is anything in your life causing offense, and is the ministry God called you to being discredited? Earlier in this letter, God said you are called to the ministry of righteousness and reconciliation (2 Corinthians 3:9; 5:18). Are you serving in those ministries as a servant of God?

Pray 2 Corinthians 6:1, 3, and 4 over yourself and those for whom you stand guard as a faithful, prayerful watchman (Isaiah 62:6-7).

"Father, help _____ and me work with You.
Do not let us receive Your grace in vain.
May we give no cause for offense in anything,
so that the ministry will not be discredited.
In everything, may we commend ourselves as servants of You.
Because of Your name, Jesus-"

JULY 9

Please read 2 Corinthians 7.

Meditate on verse 1.

> *Therefore, having these promises, beloved,*
> *let us cleanse ourselves*
> *from all defilement of flesh and spirit,*
> *perfecting holiness in the fear of God.*

In Paul's first letter to the church at Corinth, he admonished them severely for allowing sin in the church that would not even be committed by the pagans outside their church (1 Corinthians 5:1). The Corinthian believers were saddened by Paul's reproof in a good way because the sin was acknowledged and stopped. Paul said in this second letter that such sorrow was according to the will of God; it brought repentance leading to salvation and repentance that frees people from regrets (2 Corinthians 7:10).

Sin should make you sad. Are you grieved when you see the results of sin in your life and in the lives of others? Does grief over sin bring you to repentance and a desire to not commit that sin again? Ask God to give you and those you love His perspective on sin.

Pray 2 Corinthians 7:1 over yourself and those for whom you stand guard as a faithful, prayerful watchman (Isaiah 62:6-7).

> *"LORD, since _____ and I have Your promises,*
> *let us cleanse ourselves from*
> *all defilement of flesh and spirit,*
> *perfecting holiness in the fear of You, God.*
> *In Your name, Jesus~"*

Please read 2 Corinthians 8.

Meditate on this phrase from verse 5.

They first gave themselves to the LORD.

The Christians in Corinth had areas in their lives where they needed to mature. Giving was one of those areas, so Paul told them about the churches in Macedonia. By comparison, the Corinthian believers were much wealthier than the believers in Macedonia, yet even in their deep poverty, the churches in Macedonia "overflowed in the wealth of their liberality" (2 Corinthians 8:1). The Macedonian believers gave beyond their ability because they first gave themselves to the LORD.

When you give yourself to the LORD, He enables you to do things beyond your ability. You do things by the will of God and not by your will. God causes you to abound in everything to do His will.

Pray 2 Corinthians 8:5 and 7 over yourself and those for whom you stand guard as a faithful, prayerful watchman (Isaiah 62:6-7).

"LORD, may _____ and I first give ourselves to You
then to others by Your will.
Make us abound in everything,
in faith and utterance and knowledge
and in all earnestness and in love,
so we can abound in Your gracious work.
For the sake of Your name, Jesus~"

JULY 11

Please read 2 Corinthians 9.

Meditate on verse 8.

> *And God is able to make all grace abound to you,*
> *so that always having all sufficiency in everything,*
> *you may have an abundance for every good deed.*

The church at Corinth promised to give an offering, and believers from Macedonia were coming to receive the offering. Paul wrote to the Corinthians to ensure they were going to keep their word. They promised a bountiful gift; Paul did not want them to be affected by covetousness and decide to give sparingly (2 Corinthians 9:5-6).

Examine your life. Is there a promise you need to keep? How do you give to your church and to others? Are you a bountiful believer or are you motivated by covetousness? This applies to time as well as money.

Pray 2 Corinthians 9:8 and 10-11 over yourself and those for whom you stand guard as a faithful, prayerful watchman (Isaiah 62:6-7).

> *"God, make all grace abound to _____ and me,*
> *so we will always have all sufficiency in everything.*
> *May we have an abundance for every good deed.*
> *You, who supply seed to the sower*
> *and bread for food will supply*
> *and multiply our seed for sowing*
> *and increase the harvest of our righteousness.*
> *Please enrich us in everything for all liberality,*
> *which through us is producing thanksgiving to You, God.*
> *For the sake of Your name, Jesus~"*

JULY 12

Please read 2 Corinthians 10.

Meditate on verses 3-5.

> *For though we walk in the flesh, we do not war according*
> *to the flesh, for the weapons of our warfare are not of the flesh,*
> *but divinely powerful for the destruction of fortresses.*
> *We are destroying speculations and every lofty thing*
> *raised up against the knowledge of God,*
> *and we are taking every thought captive to the obedience of Christ.*

What would you think if someone said about you, "your personal presence is unimpressive and your speech contemptible"? Can you imagine? Well, perhaps you can. If so, take heart because that is what people said about Paul (2 Corinthians 10:10).

I wonder if he wanted to punch them and tell them what he thought. I wonder if he had to repeat, "I am taking every thought captive to the obedience of Christ," so he wouldn't say something regrettable.

What fortresses are you up against today? Is it another person or a difficult situation? Is it a battle going on in the lives of people you love? Is it your vain imaginations you have thought about so much they have become your reality?

Paul knew that people's rudeness was actually spiritual warfare. He refused to war in the flesh. Almighty God was Paul's weapon.

Pray 2 Corinthians 10:3-5 over yourself and those for whom you stand guard as a faithful, prayerful watchman (Isaiah 62:6-7).

> *"LORD, I do not want to war according to my flesh,*
> *so I am depending You.*
> *You are divinely powerful for the destruction of fortresses.*
> *LORD, help _____ and me destroy speculations*
> *and every lofty thing raised up against the knowledge of You*
> *and take every thought captive to the obedience of You, Christ.*
> *In Your powerful name, Jesus~"*

JULY 13

Please read 2 Corinthians 11.

Meditate on verse 14.

No wonder, for even Satan
disguises himself as an angel of light.

The church had been in earthly existence approximately 22 years when Paul wrote this letter to the Christians in Corinth. In that short amount of time, there were already people preaching a different Jesus, a different spirit, and a different gospel. Times have not changed, and there are still plenty of cults and world religions that preach differently; often the preaching is based on revelations by an angel of light.

Do not be deceived! Satan disguises himself as an angel of light. He never was and never will be an angel of light. In fact the Bible does not mention an angel of light. Jesus is the Light. Satan pretends to be an angel of light, so he can trick people into false christs, false spirits, false scripture, and false teaching. Hundreds of thousands of people have believed the father of lies (John 8:44). Are you one of them? Do you know someone who has been led astray by the liar, Satan, who has no truth in him (John 8:44)?

Pray 2 Corinthians 11:3 over yourself and those for whom you stand guard as a faithful, prayerful watchman (Isaiah 62:6-7).

"LORD, do not let _____ and me be like Eve
who was deceived by the craftiness of the serpent.
May our minds not be led astray
from the simplicity and purity of devotion to You, Christ.
In Your name, Jesus~"

Please read 2 Corinthians 12.

Meditate on verse 9a.

> *And He has said to me,*
> *"My grace is sufficient for you,*
> *for power is perfected in weakness."*

The church in Corinth was a mess. Paul wanted to come visit these Christians, but he was afraid when he arrived, he would find strife, jealousy, angry tempers, disputes, slanders, gossip, arrogance, and disturbances (2 Corinthians 12:20). Paul said that many who had sinned in the past had not repented of their impurity, immorality, and sensuality. Their unrepentant hearts caused them to engage in other sins like strife, jealousy, and angry tempers.

What is going on in and around you? Are there disputes, gossip, and arrogance? Ask the Holy Spirit to convict you of unconfessed sins from your past that might be leading to disturbances in your present.

Pray 2 Corinthians 12:9 and 20-21 over yourself and those for whom you stand guard as a faithful, prayerful watchman.

> *"Christ, _____ and I need Your power to dwell in us.*
> *LORD, I repent of the impurity, immorality, and sensuality*
> *I practiced in the past.*
> *Please convict _____ to do the same.*
> *Let the strife, jealousy, angry tempers, disputes,*
> *slanders, gossip, arrogance, and disturbances cease.*
> *In Your name, Jesus~"*

JULY 15

Please read 2 Corinthians 13.

Meditate on verse 5.

Test yourselves to see if you are in the faith;
examine yourselves!
Or do you not recognize this about yourselves,
that Jesus Christ is in you—unless indeed you fail the test?

Paul planned to visit the church at Corinth for a third time. They needed to grow up in Christ. Paul did not want to use severity when he came to Corinth, but he would spare no one if sin continued to abound in this church (2 Corinthians 13:2, 10). Paul commanded each member to examine themself to make sure they were really believers. They should not be abiding in sin if they were abiding in Christ.

Proof of being a Christian is Christ in you. As a believer, you abide in Christ rather than remaining in the sins of your old life. God exhorts you. Examine yourself! Is Christ in you? Does Jesus define who you are or does sin define you?

Pray 2 Corinthians 13:11 over yourself and those for whom you stand guard as a faithful, prayerful watchman (Isaiah 62:6-7).

"LORD, let _____ and me rejoice, be made complete,
be comforted, be like-minded, and live in peace.
God of love and peace be with us.
In Your name, Jesus~"

JULY 16

Please read Galatians 1.
Meditate on verses 15-16a.

> *But when God, who had set me apart*
> *even from my mother's womb*
> *and called me through His grace*
> *was pleased to reveal His Son in me*
> *so that I might preach Him …*

As Paul preached salvation by grace, Judaizers (Jews who embraced Christianity yet taught that some of the Law, including circumcision, still must be observed to really be saved) followed him preaching a gospel contrary to the truth (Galatians 1:9). Paul wrote this letter to the church in Galatia to counter false teaching and to proclaim righteous freedom through faith in Christ.

Paul knew God freed him from sin so he could live the rest of his life for Christ. Paul was confident of God's call in his life: to tell others about the grace of God and the freedom from sin through Jesus Christ.

God set you apart from your mother's womb for the same purpose. His plan for you is to be rescued from sin, to be saved to Christ, and to tell others about the amazing life God has for them.

Pray Galatians 1:3-5 over someone you stand guard as a faithful, prayerful watchman (Isaiah 62:6-7).

> *"God, my Father, and my LORD Jesus Christ,*
> *extend Your grace and peace to _____ .*
> *You gave Yourself for their sins.*
> *According to Your will and for Your glory,*
> *rescue them from this present evil age.*
> *For the sake of Your name, Jesus~"*

JULY 17

Please read Galatians 2.

Meditate on verse 20.

I have been crucified with Christ; and it is no longer I who live,
but Christ lives in me; and the life which I now live in the flesh
I live by faith in the Son of God, who loved
me and gave Himself up for me.

Oh the challenges of Jews and Gentiles in one body. Early church leaders such as: Paul, James (the brother of Christ), Peter (also called Cephas), and Barnabas had their hands full!

Paul wrote that Peter had been eating with Gentiles until men from the Jerusalem church showed up. Peter feared what these Jewish Christians would think of him for this. He was aloof to the Gentiles so he could impress the Jews. Paul called him out on his hypocrisy and reminded his readers that salvation is through faith in Christ alone and not through keeping the Law.

This is an encouraging chapter from Scripture because you, like Peter, make foolish decisions that you later regret. Yet you, like Peter, are still loved and able to be used by God. The early Christian church struggled to integrate Jews and Gentiles, yet God of the impossible made it work. Your church may be struggling with groups that are not getting along. Bring your difficulties to Jesus. He wants His bride to be unified.

Pray Galatians 2:20 over yourself and those for whom you stand guard as a faithful, prayerful watchman (Isaiah 62:6-7).

"LORD, please let _____ and me have this attitude:
We have been crucified with Christ;
and it is no longer we who live, but Christ lives in us;
and the life we now live in the flesh
we live by faith in the Son of God,
who loved us and gave Himself up for us.
For the sake of Your name, Jesus~"

Please read Galatians 3.

Meditate on verses 6 and 9.

Even so Abraham believed God, and it was reckoned to him
as righteousness. So then those who are of faith
are blessed with Abraham the believer.

There was one time in the Bible when Abraham was declared righteous. Abraham was 76 years old, and God made promises to him. After God declared His promises, Abraham "believed in the LORD, and He reckoned it to him as righteousness" (Genesis 15:6). God declared Abraham to be right with God because Abraham believed God.

Approximately 40 years later, Abraham showed great faith in God by being willing to sacrifice Isaac. Interestingly, God did not credit him with righteousness for such a noble deed because Abraham was already righteous. Abraham was righteous because God is righteous. Paul wanted the Galatian Christians to understand that truth about salvation. God wants you to understand it, too. Salvation is begun and completed by the Spirit of God. You must believe God in order to be saved, to be declared righteous. You are a child of God through faith in Christ Jesus (Galatians 3:26). What the Spirit started in you is perfected by the Spirit living inside you (Galatians 3:3).

Pray Galatians 3:6, 9, and 27 over someone for whom you stand guard as a faithful, prayerful watchman (Isaiah 62:6-7).

"LORD, may _____ be blessed like Abraham the believer.
Let them believe You, so they can be declared righteous.
May they be baptized (immersed and identified) into You.
Let them clothe themselves with You, Christ.
In Your name, Jesus~"

Please read Galatians 4.

Meditate on verse 9.

> *But now that you have come to know God,*
> *or rather to be known by God,*
> *how is it that you turn back to the weak*
> *and worthless elemental things,*
> *to which you desire to be enslaved all over again?*

If you are in Christ, you are known by God. Let that truth soak in for a moment. Now think about the most important person alive today. Can you imagine knowing and being known by that person?

As a believer, you are known intimately by God Almighty. This kind of *knowing* means knowing intimately like a husband and wife know each other. This is amazingly freeing truth!

Paul wanted the believers in Galatia to know they were loved and known by God; adhering to religious ritual and the commands of men would not make God know or love them any better. There were people in the Galatian churches who said Christians had to keep parts of the Old Testament law to be right with God.

Paul wrote this letter to continue discipling the believers who were still children in their faith. They needed to grow and mature in Christ.

Pray Galatians 4:19 over those for whom you are laboring as a faithful, prayerful watchman (Isaiah 62:6-7).

> *"LORD, I continue to labor on behalf of _____*
> *until You are formed in them.*
> *For the sake of Your name, Jesus~*

Please read Galatians 5.

Meditate on verse 16.

Walk by the Spirit,
and you will not carry out the desire of the flesh.

The Christians in Galatia were deceived. There were people in their churches who wanted to subject them to the yoke of slavery of keeping the Law (Galatians 5:1). Paul wanted them to know without a doubt that in Christ they were free; free from the Law and free from sin. He also warned them not to turn their freedom into an opportunity for the flesh.

The result of Christ formed in you is you are led by the Holy Spirit (Galatians 4:19; 5:18). You will stop being led by fleshly desires.

Galatians 5:19 says, "Now the deeds of the flesh are evident." Paul lists 15 things that are desires set against the Spirit:

1. Immorality
2. Impurity
3. Sensuality
4. Idolatry
5. Sorcery
6. Hostilities
7. Strife
8. Jealousy
9. Fits of anger
10. Selfish ambitions
11. Dissensions
12. Selfish rivalries

13. Envying

14. Drunkenness

15. Carousing

Are you doing things in opposition to the Holy Spirit? Or is your life so full of the evidence of the Holy Spirit there is no more room for that junk?

Pray Galatians 5:16, 22-23, and 25 over yourself and those for whom you stand guard as a faithful, prayerful watchman (Isaiah 62:6-7).

"LORD, help _____ and me walk by Your Spirit,
so we do not carry out the desire of the flesh.
May Your fruit be evident in our lives:
love, joy, peace, patience, kindness, goodness,
faithfulness, gentleness, and self-control.
May we live by Your Spirit.
In Your name, Jesus~"

Please read Galatians 6.

Meditate on verse 3.

> *For if anyone thinks he is something when he is nothing,*
> *he deceives himself.*

Some people in the Galatian churches were proud when they compelled Gentile believers to be circumcised or keep other parts of the Law. They desired to be influential even if it meant influencing others into the slavery that was life apart from Christ.

What do you take pride in, and do you use your influence to feed your pride? Do you influence people to even join you in sin to justify your behavior?

Paul was proud of the cross of Christ. All that mattered was being a new creation as a result of what Christ did on that cross (Galatians 6:14-15). Paul used his influence to establish others in that truth.

Pray Galatians 6:14 over yourself and those for whom you stand guard as a faithful, prayerful watchman (Isaiah 62:6-7).

> *"Jesus Christ, through Your cross,*
> *let _____ and me be crucified to the world*
> *and the world to us.*
> *May we boast only in You and Your cross.*
> *For the sake of Your name, LORD Jesus Christ~"*

Please read Ephesians 1.

Meditate on verses 4-5.

> *Just as He chose us in Him before the foundation of the world,*
> *that we would be holy and blameless before Him.*
> *In love He predestined us to adoption as sons*
> *through Jesus Christ to Himself,*
> *according to the kind intention of His will.*

God chose you before He said, "Let there be light." He set you apart to be faultless and blameless in Christ. He did it because He loves you, and it is what He wanted to do. In Christ, you are a chosen, holy, unblemished, loved child of God. Walk confidently in Christ as you meditate on those truths.

Paul wanted the believers in Ephesus to know those truths as well. He had heard about their faith in the LORD and their love for all the saints. Paul could not cease giving thanks for them and praying for them (Ephesians 1:15-16).

Ephesians 1:17-21 is the prayer he prayed. Pray that prayer over yourself and those for whom you stand guard as a faithful, prayerful watchman (Isaiah 62:6-7).

> *"God of our LORD Jesus Christ,*
> *the Father of glory,*
> *give _____ and me*
> *a spirit of wisdom and revelation*
> *in the knowledge of You.*
> *Let the eyes of our heart be enlightened,*
> *so that we will know what is the hope of Your calling,*
> *what are the riches of the glory of Your inheritance in the saints,*

and what is the surpassing greatness of Your
power toward us who believe.
Your power toward us is in accordance
with the working of the strength of Your might
which You brought about in Christ when
You raised Him from the dead
and seated Him at Your right hand in the heavenly places,
far above all rule and authority and power and dominion,
and every name that is named,
not only in this age but also in the one to come.
In that name, Jesus~"

JULY 23

Please read Ephesians 2.

Meditate on verses 4-5.

> *But God, being rich in mercy,*
> *because of His great love with which He loved us,*
> *even when we were dead in our transgressions,*
> *made us alive together with Christ.*
> *By grace you have been saved.*

If you are a Christian, your life's story is recorded in Ephesians 2.

Before believing in Jesus, you were dead in your sins. You walked a worldly course in accordance with Satan's purposes. You lived in the lust of your flesh, indulging the desires of your flesh and mind. You were by nature a child of wrath.

But God ... because of His great mercy and love for you, when you were dead in your transgressions, made you alive together with Christ, raised you up with Christ, and seated you with Christ in the heavenly places.

Now you are God's workmanship created in Christ Jesus for good works, which God prepared beforehand for you to walk in. "Prepared beforehand" has the same connotation as "before the foundation of the world" in Ephesians 1:4. Before God said, "Let there be light," He planned your purpose here on earth. He prepared the good works He desires you to walk in today before He started creating the universe. Ask God to reveal the good things He pre-planned for you to do.

Pray Ephesians 2:10 over yourself and those for whom you stand guard as a faithful, prayerful watchman (Isaiah 62:6-7).

> *"Christ Jesus, You created _____ and me in You*
> *as Your workmanship. Help us to walk in the good works*
> *which You prepared beforehand for us to walk in.*
> *For the sake of Your name, Jesus~"*

JULY 24

Please read Ephesians 3.
Meditate on verses 20-21.

Now to Him who is able to do far more abundantly
beyond all that we ask or think,
according to the power that works within us,
to Him be the glory in the church
and in Christ Jesus to all generations forever and ever. Amen.

Do you love a good mystery? Do you like to know how a mystery ends?

God gave Paul insight into the mystery of Christ. Since the beginning of time, God gave the promise of Messiah. There were mysteries surrounding Messiah. Who was He? When would He come? Would He be a Messiah only for Israel or the whole world? Generations had waited in anticipation of the mystery being revealed.

Paul revealed the mystery in Ephesians 3:6. To be specific, that the Gentiles are fellow heirs and fellow members of the body, and fellow partakers of the promise in Christ Jesus through the Gospel.

Not only was the mystery revealed to Paul, he was made a minister to bring the mystery to light and to preach to the Gentiles the unfathomable riches of Christ (Ephesians 3:7-9).

Paul knew the mystery, and He knew he had confident access to God through Jesus Christ. For that reason he prayed a bold prayer on behalf of the Christians at Ephesus.

Pray Paul's prayer (Ephesians 3:14-21) over yourself and those for whom you stand guard as a faithful, prayerful watchman (Isaiah 62:6-7).

"For this reason I bow my knees before You, Father,
from whom every family in heaven and on earth derives its name,
that You would grant _____ and me,
according to the riches of Your glory,
to be strengthened with power through
Your Spirit in our inner man,
so that You, Christ, will dwell in our hearts through faith.
Let us be rooted and grounded in love and
be able to comprehend with all the saints
what is the breadth and length and height and depth,
and to know Your love, Christ, which surpasses knowledge,
that we may be filled up to all the fullness of You.
Now to You, Father, who is able to do far more abundantly
beyond all that we ask or think,
according to the power that works within us,
to You be the glory in the church and in Christ Jesus
to all generations for ever and ever. Amen."

Please read Ephesians 4.

Meditate on verse 5.

> *But speaking the truth in love, we are to grow up in all*
> *aspects into Him who is the head, even Christ.*

Paul wanted the Christians at Ephesus to grow up. He lived in Ephesus for two years sharing the Gospel of Christ and teaching and training the new believers (Acts 19). Eight to ten years passed; these followers of Jesus should have been more mature in Christ. Why hadn't they matured? They walked just as the non-Christians walked in the futility of their mind. They were excluded from the life God purposed for them because of the hardness of their hearts. They were callous because they gave themselves over to sensuality for the practice of every kind of impurity with greediness (Ephesians 4:17-19).

You can hear Paul's next words scream off the page.

"You did not learn Christ in this way!"

Is God saying the same thing to you? "Grow up! The way you are living is not how you learned Jesus."

Ask God to help you live for Christ today.

Pray Ephesians 4:22-24 over yourself and those for whom you stand guard as a faithful, prayerful watchman (Isaiah 62:6-7).

> *"LORD, in reference to _____ and my former manner of life,*
> *help us lay aside the old self,*
> *which is being corrupted in accordance with the lusts of deceit,*
> *and let us be renewed in the spirit of our mind.*
> *Help us put on the new self,*
> *which in the likeness of You, God,*
> *has been created in righteousness and holiness of the truth.*
> *In Your name, Jesus~"*

Please read Ephesians 5.

Meditate on verse 10.

Learn what is pleasing to the LORD.

Paul wrote this letter to people who claimed to be followers of Jesus Christ yet walked just as the Gentiles, nonbelievers (Ephesians 4:17). Paul exhorted them to stop partaking with the sons of disobedience and walk as children of Light (Ephesians 5:6-8). After all, God's wrath comes upon the sons of disobedience; why would a Christian participate in their immorality, impurity, and greed?

Hear the truth from God's Word to you, today. Before you gave your life to Christ, you were called a son of disobedience. In Christ, you are Light in the LORD (Ephesians 5:6, 8). Learn what is pleasing to the LORD and walk in those things.

Pray Ephesians 5:15-17 over yourself and those for whom you stand guard as a faithful, prayerful watchman (Isaiah 62:6-7).

"LORD, help _____ and me be careful how we walk,
not as unwise men but as wise.
Let us make the most of our time because the days are evil.
May we not be foolish
but let us understand what Your will is, LORD.
In Your name, Jesus~"

Please read Ephesians 6.

Meditate on verse 10.

Finally be strong in the LORD
and in the strength of His might.

Paul wrote this letter to believers who had re-engaged in sinful behaviors from their lives before Christ. Paul commanded them to grow up in Jesus, walk in a manner worthy of their calling in Christ Jesus, and be strong in the LORD and the strength of His might (Ephesians 4:1, 15; 6:10). The Christians at Ephesus could overcome sin in the strength of the LORD. Without Christ, it was a losing battle. "Put on the full armor of God, so you will be able to stand firm against the schemes of the devil (Ephesians 6:11)."

By putting on truth, righteousness, faith, salvation, the Word of God, and praying at all times in the Spirit, you will not be participating in the unfruitful deeds of darkness (Ephesians 5:11). As you put on this armor, be aware you are actually putting on what God wears (Isaiah 59:17).

Pray Ephesians 6:10-18 over yourself and those for whom you stand guard as a faithful, prayerful watchman (Isaiah 62:6-7).

"LORD, make _____ and me strong in You
and in the strength of Your might.
Let us put on Your full armor,
so we will be able to stand firm
against the schemes of the devil,
for our struggle is not against flesh and blood,
but against the rulers, powers, world forces of darkness,
and the spiritual forces of wickedness.
Therefore, let us take up Your full armor, God,

so we will be able to resist in the evil day
and having done everything, to stand firm.
May we stand firm having girded our loins with truth,
and having put on the breastplate of righteousness,
and having shod our feet with the
preparation of the Gospel of Peace;
in addition let us take up the shield of
faith with which we will be able
to extinguish all the flaming arrows of the evil one.
Let us take the helmet of salvation
and the sword of the Spirit, which is the Word of God.
With all prayer and petition,
help us pray at all times in the Spirit.
Let us be on the alert
with all perseverance and petition for all the saints.
Because of Your name, Jesus~"

Please read Philippians 1.

Meditate on verse 9.

And this I pray that your love
may abound still more and more
in real knowledge and all discernment.

This is one of the verses the LORD will bring to my remembrance when a husband and wife or other family relationship needs prayer for love to abound. This is also a great verse to pray when someone needs to know God's will for their life.

It is God's will for your family to abound in love for each other. It is God's will for you to have His knowledge and discernment, so you can distinguish between things that are excellent and things that are not. It is God's will for you to be sincere and blameless for the day of Christ.

Pray Philippians 1:3-6 and 9-11 over those for whom you stand guard as a faithful, prayerful watchman (Isaiah 62:6-7).

"LORD, thank You for _____.
I offer prayer for them with joy as I see their participation
in Your Gospel from the first day until now.
I am confident of this very thing,
that You who began a good work in them
will perfect it until the day of Christ Jesus.
Let their love abound still more and more
in real knowledge and all discernment,
so that they may approve the things that are excellent,
in order to be sincere and blameless until the day of Christ.
Fill them with the fruit of righteousness
which comes through You, Jesus Christ,
to the glory and praise of You, God.
In Your name, Jesus~"

Please read Philippians 1.

Meditate on this phrase from verse 19.

Prayers and the provision of the Spirit of Jesus Christ

I have been praying Philippians 1:3-6 and 9-11 over my family for more than twenty-five years. They were the verses you prayed yesterday. Today, you have read Philippians 1 again because there are more treasures to pray.

"The provision of the Spirit of Jesus Christ" is a captivating phrase in verse 19. Keeping the phrase in context, you read that Paul knew he would be delivered, and deliverance would come through the prayers of the believers at Philippi and the provision of the Spirit of Jesus Christ.

Paul was imprisoned in Rome when he wrote this letter, and he needed help. He never mentioned hiring the best lawyer in Italy to come to his defense. He knew God would defend and provide for him. Paul knew that the prayers of the faithful were key to unlocking that provision of the Spirit.

DO NOT be lazy in your prayer life! Like Paul, your loved ones need help, and they need a faithful, prayerful watchman, someone who will remind the LORD day and night of their needs. Take no rest for yourself and give Him no rest until He establishes those you love (Isaiah 62:6-7).

Pray Philippians 1:19, 22, and 27 over yourself and those for whom you stand guard as a faithful, prayerful watchman (Isaiah 62:6-7).

> *"LORD, please give _____ and me*
> *the provision of the Spirit of Jesus Christ,*
> *so we will be involved in fruitful labor.*
> *Christ, help us conduct ourselves*
> *in a manner worthy of Your Gospel.*
> *In Your name, Jesus~"*

Please read Philippians 2.

Meditate on verse 3.

> *Do nothing from selfishness or empty conceit,*
> *but with humility of mind regard one another*
> *as more important than yourselves.*

Paul lived in a world ruled by Rome. The Roman empire was characterized by wealth, luxury, and lack of virtue and decency. Paul described the generation he lived in as "crooked and perverse" (Philippians 2:15).

You live in a world that could be described the same way: crooked, perverse, lacking virtue and decency, a world where attaining luxury and wealth is the goal of many. Paul's exhortation to the Christians at Philippi is God's exhortation to you: "Hold fast the Word of Life" (Philippians 2:16).

Hold fast to God's Word. Filter everything you read and hear through the Truth, the Bible. Even seemingly good ideas are not necessarily God's ideas. For example, for decades people have been concerned about their self-esteem. Everyone should have a good self-esteem, right?

Interestingly, there is only one place in the Bible where self and esteem are used in the same verse, Philippians 2:3. The King James translation says it this way, "Let each esteem others better than themselves." Immediately following that command, Jesus Christ is given as the example of how He esteemed you better than Himself and died for you.

Do you esteem yourself or do you esteem others? Caring about the needs of others will fix "self-esteem" issues you may have.

Know God's Word and do not be taken captive by the wisdom of the world.

Pray Philippians 2:13-16 over yourself and those for whom you stand guard as a faithful, prayerful watchman (Isaiah 62:6-7).

"God, you are at work in _____ and me,
both to will and to work for Your good pleasure.
Help us to do all things without grumbling and disputing,
so we will prove ourselves to be blameless and innocent.
May we be Your children who are above reproach
in the midst of a crooked and perverse generation.
Let us appear as lights in the world, holding fast the Word of Life,
so that in Your day, Christ, we will have reason to glory
because we did not run or toil in vain.
For the sake of Your name, Jesus~"

Please read Philippians 3.

Meditate on verse 14.

I press on toward the goal for the prize
of the upward call of God in Christ Jesus.

Paul's addressed the attitude of the Philippians in this letter. He exhorted them to have the attitude of Christ Jesus and regard others as more important than themselves (Philippians 2:3-5). Paul challenged the mature believers to press on in the call of God in Christ Jesus for their lives. God would reveal their wrong attitudes (Philippians 3:14-15).

It is time to check your attitude. Your attitude is the foundation for your behavior. God knows your attitude; you cannot hide it from Him. Pride, rebellion, and dishonesty are a few of the attitudes God hates (Proverbs 6:16-18). You do not want an attitude that God opposes (James 4:6). Ask God to reveal attitudes within you that are not pleasing to Him. Then pray Philippians 3:12-15 over yourself and those for whom you stand guard as faithful, prayerful watchman (Isaiah 62:6-7).

"LORD, reveal to _____ and me
attitudes that are different from Yours.
Make us mature with the attitude of Christ.
Jesus, You have laid hold of us;
for that reason, help us to press on.
Let us forget what lies behind
and reach forward to what lies ahead.
Help us press on toward the goal
for the prize of Your upward call, God.
In Christ Jesus~"

On your walls, O Jerusalem,
I have appointed watchmen;
All day and all night they
will never keep silent.
You who remind the LORD,
take no rest for yourselves;
And give Him no rest
until He establishes
And makes Jerusalem a
praise in the earth.
ISAIAH 62:6-7, NASB

Please read Philippians 4.

Meditate on verse 8.

Finally, brethren, whatever is true,
whatever is honorable, whatever is right,
whatever is pure, whatever is lovely,
whatever is of good repute, if there is any excellence
and if anything worthy of praise,
dwell on these things.

God wants this letter to change your attitude and make you mature in Christ. The LORD's goal for you is to stand firm in Him (Philippians 4:1). In order to stand firm, you need to think like Christ. God does not leave you guessing how He thinks. He gives you the mind of Christ in a list and commands you to dwell there.

The word "dwell" has the connotation of not just something you think about doing, but something you are actually living.

Do you live in truth, honor, righteousness, purity, loveliness, a good reputation, excellence, and things worthy of praise? Do those eight characteristics describe your attitudes and actions? Do they describe your life?

Pray Philippians 4:8 over yourself and those for whom you stand guard as a faithful, prayerful watchman (Isaiah 62:6-7).

"LORD, let _____ and me dwell
on and in whatever is
true, honorable, right,
pure, lovely, of good reputation,
excellent, and worthy of praise.
For the sake of Your name, Jesus~"

AUGUST 2

Please read Colossians 1.

Meditate on verse 17.

> He (Jesus) is before all things,
> and in Him all things hold together.

God had Paul write this letter to the Christians in Colossae because they needed to know they were complete in Christ (Colossians 1:28). They needed to know they were not going to fall apart because Jesus held them together.

God's Word is timeless. When God had Paul pen this letter 2,000 years ago, He knew you would be reading it today. God wanted you to know you are complete in Christ, and you are not going to fall apart because Jesus is holding you together.

There are at least 70 actions and attributes of Jesus in this letter. There are also at least 70 things that you are if you are IN Christ. Treasure hunt this letter and see how many attributes you can find about Jesus and you. Write them on a piece of paper and keep it in a place where you can read it anytime the enemy lies to you about your identity.

Colossians also contains powerful prayers. One of those is a prayer Paul prayed over those for whom he stood guard as a faithful, prayerful watchman (Isaiah 62:6-7).

Pray Colossians 1:9-14 over those you are guarding.

> *"LORD, I do not cease to pray for _____*
> *asking You to fill them with the knowledge of Your will*
> *in all spiritual wisdom and understanding,*
> *so that they will walk in a manner worthy of You,*
> *to please You in all respects,*
> *bearing fruit in every good work*

and increasing in the knowledge of You, God.
Strengthen them with all power
according to Your glorious might
for the attaining of all steadfastness and patience.
I joyously give thanks to You, Father, who has qualified
us to share in the inheritance of the saints in Light.
Rescue _____ from the domain of darkness,
and transfer them to Your kingdom.
In You, Jesus, we have redemption, the forgiveness of sins.
For the sake of Your name-"

Please read Colossians 2.

Meditate on verses 6 and 10a.

> *Therefore as you have received Christ Jesus*
> *the LORD, so walk in Him.*
> *In Him you have been made complete.*

What are you striving for in order to feel complete? God tells you in Colossians 2 to make sure no one takes you captive or deceives you with worldly principles (v. 8). The world tries to convince you to own, dress, act, and achieve certain things in order to feel complete. God's Word says you are already complete if you are in Christ Jesus.

Remember Colossians contains at least 70 characteristics of who you are if you are in Christ. What do you learn about Jesus and you from this chapter? Verses 13 and 14 tell you that you were dead in your transgressions, but God made you alive together with Christ because He forgave ALL your transgressions. He even cancelled your certificate of debt by nailing it to the cross. Knowing those truths brings completion to your life.

Let the truth of God's Word be established in your heart and mind, so you can walk and live in Christ. Pray Colossians 2:5-7 over yourself and those for whom you stand guard as a faithful, prayerful watchman (Isaiah 62:6-7).

> *"LORD, let me rejoice to see _____*
> *good discipline and stability of faith in You.*
> *As we have received You,*
> *let us walk in You firmly rooted and built up*
> *and established in our faith just as we were instructed.*
> *Let us overflow with gratitude.*
> *In Your name, Jesus~"*

Please read Colossians 3.

Meditate on verse 3.

For you have died and your life is hidden with Christ in God.

Colossians 3 is rich with truths about who you are in Christ. Please memorize these facts about yourself.

∽ **Christ is your life** (v. 4). If you are a Christian, then Jesus is NOT part of your life. Jesus is NOT the top priority in your life. Jesus IS your life. Jesus is not a priority. Priorities can be rearranged. Jesus is the Arranger of your priorities because He is your life.

There are things you are dead to when Christ is your life (v. 5). Imagine a dead body in a coffin. Can a dead body even wiggle? No! These are things you cannot be moving in because they no longer live in you. Christ lives in you!

∽ **You are dead to**:

1. Immorality
2. Impurity
3. Passion

4. Evil desire
5. Greed

∽ **Lay aside**:

1. Anger
2. Wrath
3. Malice

4. Slander
5. Abusive Speech
6. Lying (vs. 8-9)

✆ Put on a heart of:

1. Compassion
2. Kindness
3. Humility
4. Gentleness
5. Patience
6. Bearing with one another
7. Forgiving others just as the LORD forgave you
8. Love (vs. 12-14)

Pray Colossians 3:15-17 over yourself and those for whom you stand guard as a faithful, prayerful watchman (Isaiah 62:6-7).

"LORD, please let the peace of Christ rule
in _____ and my hearts.
Let Your Word dwell in us richly with all wisdom.
May whatever we do in word or deed be
done in Your name, LORD Jesus.
We give thanks through You to God the Father~

Please read Colossians 4.

Meditate on verse 2.

> *Devote yourselves to prayer,*
> *keeping alert in it with an attitude of thanksgiving.*

How is your prayer life? Would you describe yourself as devoted to prayer? Are you alert in prayer? Do you pray with an attitude of thanksgiving? Do you desire to be an Epaphras, a bondslave of Jesus Christ, who labors earnestly in prayer so those you pray for "may stand perfect and fully assured in all the will of God" (Colossians 4:12)?

Prayer is a big deal! You will not completely understand its impact on eternity until you get to heaven. In the meantime, do not grow weary and lose heart in praying. The ones you are praying for need to be mature in Christ and confident in the will of God for their lives. Your prayers help accomplish that goal.

Pray Colossians 4:3-6 over yourself and those for whom you stand guard as a faithful, prayerful watchman (Isaiah 62:6-7).

> *"LORD, open up the door for Your Word,*
> *so _____ and I may speak forth Your mystery, Jesus.*
> *Please make it clear in the way we ought to speak.*
> *May we conduct ourselves with wisdom.*
> *Let our speech always be with grace, as though seasoned with salt,*
> *so we will know how to respond to each person.*
> *For the sake of Your name, Jesus~"*

Please read 1 Thessalonians 1.

Meditate on verse 2.

We give thanks to God always for all of you,
making mention of you in our prayers.

Paul established the church at Thessalonica amid much persecution. The believers were falsely accused, and physical violence was used against them. Paul was sent away from the city, and after going to Berea and Athens, arrived in Corinth (Acts 17). The Thessalonian Christians were still on his mind and heart. He wrote this letter to find out how they were holding up under tremendous opposition and to encourage them that they were not forgotten. He told them he was always thanking God for them and praying for them. His words were a healing balm to spiritual, emotional, and even physical wounds.

More than 2,000 years later, Christians are still under severe opposition. Who do you know that is going through a difficult situation? Who needs an encouraging word and a reminder that they are not forgotten but being mentioned in prayer?

Pray 1 Thessalonians 1:2-4 and 6-7 over them as a faithful, prayerful watchman (Isaiah 62:6-7) then tell them that you did.

"LORD, thank You for _____ .
Thank You for their work of faith,
labor of love, and steadfastness of hope in You, Jesus.
Thank You for loving them and for choosing them.
Even in the midst of much tribulation,
let them continue to receive Your Word
with the joy of the Holy Spirit,
so they will be an example to all the believers.
For the sake of Your name, Jesus~"

Please read 1 Thessalonians 2.

Meditate on verse 12.

> *Walk in a manner worthy of the God*
> *who calls you into His own kingdom and glory.*

Prior to coming to Thessalonica to share the Gospel of God, Paul and Silas were beaten and put in prison at Philippi for sharing the truth of God's Word (Acts 16:11-24). After they were miraculously released from jail, they made their way to Thessalonica. Paul reasoned with the Thessalonians from the Scriptures explaining that Jesus is the Christ. The result was the same as at Philippi; some people were persuaded to follow Christ, and some persecuted Paul and Silas (Acts 17:1-9).

Why would these men persevere for the cause of Christ amid such opposition? Why did beatings not silence them? There was no doubt in their mind that the Word of God was exactly that—the Word of Almighty God and not the word of men. Paul knew God's Word would perform its work in those who believed. The Gospel of God working in the lives of others was worth dying for.

Paul walked in a manner worthy of God who called him into His kingdom and glory. Examine your behavior. Do you please the One who died for you? Do you walk in obedience to the Word of God?

Pray 1 Thessalonians 2:12-13 over yourself and those for whom you stand guard as a faithful, prayerful watchman (Isaiah 62:6-7).

> *"LORD, please help _____ and me*
> *walk in a manner worthy of You.*
> *Thank You for calling us into Your own kingdom and glory.*
> *May we receive Your Word for what it really is,*
> *the Word of God, not the word of man.*
> *Let Your Word perform its work in us.*
> *In Your name, Jesus-"*

Please read 1 Thessalonians 3.

Meditate on verse 8.

For now we really live, if you stand firm in the LORD.

Paul was concerned about the Christians in Thessalonica. He wanted to ensure they were not discouraged in their faith and the deciever had not tempted them. Paul had to know how they were doing, so he sent Timothy. Paul was relieved when Timothy returned with good news about their faith and love (1 Thessalonians 3:1-6).

One of the greatest joys in life is to know that those whom you are helping grow up in Christ are standing firm in Him. As a faithful, prayerful watchman, do not grow weary in praying for those God has put in your care. Ask them how they and the LORD are doing. You will REALLY live when you hear and see those you love standing firm in Jesus.

Pray 1 Thessalonians 3:8 and 12-13 over yourself and those for whom you stand guard as a faithful, prayerful watchman (Isaiah 62:6-7).

"LORD, please let _____ and me stand firm in You.
Cause us to increase and abound in love
for one another and for all people.
Let our hearts be established without blame
in holiness before You, God and Father,
at the coming of our LORD Jesus.
In Your name, Jesus~"

Please read 1 Thessalonians 4.

Meditate on verse 3.

> *For this is the will of God, your sanctification, that is,*
> *you abstain from sexual immorality.*

Paul was concerned about the sanctification of the Thessalonian Christians. The 1828 Webster's Dictionary defines *sanctification* as "the act of God's grace by which the affections of men are purified from sin and the world and exalted to a supreme love to God."

It is God's will for you to be sanctified. In order to be in God's will, you cannot be living in sin. God commands you in 1 Thessalonians 4:4-5 to control your body in holiness and honor, not in lustful passion.

How is your sanctification coming? Are you allowing sinful lusts to possess you, or are you allowing the Holy Spirit to possess you for the purpose of becoming more and more like Christ? This letter to the Thessalonians is also a letter written to you. God exhorts you to excel still more as you live to please Him (1 Thessalonians 4:1, 10).

Pray 1 Thessalonians 4:1, 3-5, and 7 over yourself and those for whom you stand guard as a faithful, prayerful watchman (Isaiah 62:6-7).

> *"LORD, please let _____ and me walk and please You.*
> *Help us to excel still more in pleasing You.*
> *Let us abstain from sexual immorality.*
> *May we possess our bodies for*
> *sanctification and honor.*
> *Do not let us allow lustful passion to possess us.*
> *God, You have not called us for the purpose*
> *of impurity but for holiness.*
> *Help us live in Your calling.*
> *For the sake of Your name, Jesus~*

Please read 1 Thessalonians 5.

Meditate on verses 16-18.

> *Rejoice always;*
> *pray without ceasing;*
> *in everything give thanks,*
> *for this is God's will for you in Christ Jesus.*

Do you want to know God's will for your life? God specifically tells you three things to do in 1 Thessalonians 5:16-18. It is God's will for you to always rejoice, to unceasingly pray, and to give thanks in everything. You learned in 1 Thessalonians 4:3 that your sanctification is also God's will for your life. Obeying the commands to rejoice, pray, and give thanks will expedite your process of becoming more and more pure and holy, more and more like Jesus.

Pray 1 Thessalonians 5:23-24 over yourself and those for whom you stand guard as a faithful, prayerful watchman (Isaiah 62:6-7).

> *"God of peace, sanctify* _____ and me entirely.*
> *May our spirit, soul, and body be preserved complete,*
> *without blame at Your coming, LORD Jesus Christ.*
> *Father, You are faithful; You have called us,*
> *and You will bring it to pass.*
> *In Your name, Jesus~"*

*Sanctify means to separate from profane things and dedicate to God.

Please read 2 Thessalonians 1.

Meditate on verse 4.

We ourselves speak proudly of you
among the churches of God
for your perseverance and faith
in the midst of all your persecutions
and afflictions which you endure.

Persecution did not let up for the believers in Thessalonica, but their perseverance was unwavering, for which Paul was thankful. In the midst of affliction, their faith and love became greater. Paul handwrote this second letter to exhort and encourage them to not grow weary in doing good.

God's Word is timeless and eternally preserved, so you can be encouraged in your faith. In the midst of suffering, remember these truths (2 Thessalonians 1:5-10):

- God's righteous judgment will prove you worthy of His Kingdom.
- God will repay with affliction those who afflict you.
- God will give relief to you who are afflicted.
- The LORD Jesus will be revealed from heaven with His mighty angels in flaming fire.
- The LORD Jesus will deal out retribution to those who do not obey His Gospel.
- The LORD Jesus will be marveled at among all who have believed.

Aren't you thankful God wrote to remind you of these things? When you are in the midst of trials, you need to know how the story ends.

Pray 2 Thessalonians 1:11-12 over yourself and those for whom you stand guard as a faithful, prayerful watchman (Isaiah 62:6-7).

"God, count _____and me worthy of our calling,
and fulfill every desire for goodness
and the work of faith with power,
so that Your name, LORD Jesus,
will be glorified in us and us in You.
According to Your grace, God and LORD Jesus Christ~"

Please read 2 Thessalonians 2.

Meditate on verse 13.

God has chosen you from the beginning for salvation.

The believers in Thessalonica needed reassurance. There were false rumors that the day of the LORD (events that will occur at the end of time) had come. Paul reassured them of what must occur prior to that day, about their assurance of salvation, and that God chose them and loved them.

These are reassuring words for you, too. If you are in Christ, you are much loved by the LORD; God has chosen you for salvation, and you will gain the glory of your LORD Jesus Christ (2 Thessalonians 2:13-14). Stand firm in these truths and do not allow the deception of wickedness into your thoughts (2 Thessalonians 2:10, 15).

Pray 2 Thessalonians 2:16-17 over yourself and those for whom you stand guard as a faithful, prayerful watchman (Isaiah 62:6-7).

"LORD Jesus Christ and God our Father,
You have loved _____ and me
and given us eternal comfort
and good hope by grace.
Comfort and strengthen our hearts
in every good work and word.
In Your name, Jesus~"

Please read 2 Thessalonians 3.

Meditate on verse 3.

> *The LORD is faithful,*
> *and He will strengthen and protect*
> *you from the evil one.*

Paul prayed for the Thessalonian Christians, and he needed them to pray for him. His prayer request was for the Word of the LORD to spread rapidly and be glorified and that Silas, Timothy, and he be rescued from perverse and evil men. Paul knew the LORD was faithful, and he wanted the believers to trust God by praying for His strength and protection.

God is faithful, and He is able to make those you love stable and constant in Him. Do not grow weary in your prayer life. The LORD wants you to ask Him for His strength and protection.

Pray 2 Thessalonians 3:1-5 and 16 over yourself and those for whom you stand guard as a faithful, prayerful watchman (Isaiah 62:6-7).

> *"LORD, let Your Word spread rapidly and be glorified*
> *in the life of _____ and me.*
> *Rescue us from perverse and evil men;*
> *for not all have faith.*
> *But You are faithful, LORD,*
> *and You will strengthen and protect*
> *us from the evil one.*
> *Help us do what You command.*
> *God, direct our hearts into*
> *Your love and steadfastness.*
> *LORD of peace, continually grant us*
> *peace in every circumstance.*
> *LORD, be with us.*
> *In Your name, Jesus~"*

Please read 1 Timothy 1.

Meditate on verse 12.

I thank Christ Jesus our LORD, who has strengthened me
because He considered me faithful, putting me into service.

Paul left Timothy in Ephesus to teach the believers how to function as a church (1 Timothy 1:3; 3:15). Before Paul gave Timothy guidelines for church administration, Paul thanked Jesus for giving him strength, mercy, grace, faith, love, and patience. Paul acknowledged his past life as a blasphemer, persecutor, violent aggressor, and the foremost of sinners. If Jesus Christ saved Paul and put him into service, then no one in Ephesus was hopeless for eternal life and serving the LORD.

This letter is for you and those for whom you are praying. Are you standing guard over someone who appears will never follow Christ? Be encouraged by blasphemous, violently aggressive, persecuting, sinful Paul, who because of the LORD Jesus Christ, became a faithful servant to eternal, immortal, invisible King Jesus. If God can save Paul, He can save anyone!

Pray 1 Timothy 1:12-19 over yourself and those for whom you stand guard as a faithful, prayerful watchman (Isaiah 62:6-7).

"LORD Jesus Christ, strengthen _____ and me.
Please consider us faithful and put us into service.
Show us Your mercy, grace, faith, and love.
Thank You for coming into the world to save sinners.
Please let _____ believe in You for eternal life.
Help us fight the good fight, keep the faith, and keep a good
conscience. Now to You, King eternal, immortal, invisible,
the only God, be honor and glory forever and ever. Amen~"

Please read 1 Timothy 2.

Meditate on verses 1-4.

> *First of all, then,*
> *I urge that entreaties and prayers,*
> *petitions and thanksgivings,*
> *be made on behalf of all men,*
> *for kings and all who are in authority,*
> *so that we may lead a tranquil and quiet life*
> *in all Godliness and dignity.*
> *This is good and acceptable in the sight of God our Savior,*
> *who desires all men to be saved*
> *and to come to the knowledge of the truth.*

Paul commanded Timothy to fight the good fight, keep the faith, and keep a good conscience. Some people in the church rejected doing those things, and their faith suffered shipwreck (1 Timothy 1:18-20). How could the shipwreck of one's faith be averted? Pray! Pray for yourself and pray for everyone else. The way to fight the good fight is with prayer. It was the first thing God told the Ephesian Christians to do, and He commands you to do the same. Your faith and the faith of others is at stake. God wants all people to be saved, and He wants you to pray for their salvation.

Pray 1 Timothy 2:4 over those for whom you stand guard as a faithful, prayerful watchman (Isaiah 62:6-7).

> *"LORD, You say in Your Word*
> *You desire for all people to be saved*
> *and come to the knowledge of the truth.*
> *Please save _____ .*
> *For the sake of Your name, Jesus~"*

Please read 1 Timothy 3.
Meditate on verse 15.

*But in case I am delayed, I write so that you will know
how one ought to conduct himself in the household
of God, which is the church of the living God,
the pillar and support of the truth.*

1 Timothy 3:15 contains the definition of church. The church of the living God is the household of God and the pillar and support of the truth. Does your church fit that description? Does it take a stand for the truth of God's Word, or does it capitulate to worldly ideology because the members are more afraid of offending people than offending God? Pray for your church to be a pillar of truth and for the members to possess the 25 Godly characteristics listed in this chapter.

Pray 1 Timothy 3:2-11 and 15 over yourself and your church as a faithful, prayerful watchman (Isaiah 62:6-7).

*"Living God, let Your church, Your household, be the pillar
and support of the truth. Establish these characteristics
in me and the other members of Your church:*

- *above reproach*
- *husband of one wife*
- *temperate*
- *prudent*
- *respectable*
- *hospitable*
- *able to teach*
- *not addicted to wine*

- ✍ not pugnacious
- ✍ gentle
- ✍ peaceable
- ✍ free from the love of money
- ✍ able to manage our own household well
- ✍ able to keep our children under control with dignity
- ✍ not conceited
- ✍ able to take care of the church of God
- ✍ not falling into the condemnation of the devil
- ✍ good reputation outside of church
- ✍ not falling into the snare of the devil
- ✍ dignified
- ✍ not double-tongued
- ✍ not fond of sordid gain
- ✍ holding to the mystery of the faith with a clear conscience
- ✍ not malicious gossips
- ✍ faithful in all things

For Your sake, Jesus~"

Please read 1 Timothy 4.

Meditate on verse 7b.

Discipline yourself for the purpose of Godliness.

Paul warned Timothy that in later times some will fall away from the truth because they are paying attention to and being deceived by spirits and doctrines of demons. Today, witches, zombies, vampires, and walking dead things fascinate many. These topics are not merely adult entertainment, but are in children's books, movies, and television shows.

God says in 1 Timothy 4:2 that doctrines of demons are propagated by the hypocrisy of liars and will sear your conscience as with a branding iron when you choose to pay attention to them. Do not be deceived! If you are a Christian, you are part of the church of the living God, and you are to be a pillar and support of the truth (1 Timothy 3:15). Are you disciplining yourself for the purpose of Godliness, or are you allowing yourself to be disciplined by the demonic? Do you spend any moment of the day in the doctrines of demons? Do you allow your children to read, watch, or in any way be involved in things that are part of the deceit of Satan?

Paul told Timothy to keep on commanding and teaching the Word of God. God is telling you to be absorbed in Scripture, to teach and exhort the Bible. The world is absorbed in lies; you must live and speak the Truth of God.

Pray 1 Timothy 4:7 and 11-16 over yourself and those for whom you stand guard as a faithful, prayerful watchman (Isaiah 62:6-7).

"LORD, let _____ and me have
nothing to do with worldly fables.
Instead, help us discipline ourselves for the purpose of Godliness.
Let us fix our hope on You, the living God and Savior of all men.
In our speech, conduct, love, faith, and purity,
may we show ourselves an example of those who believe.
Help us give attention to the reading of Scripture,
to the exhortation and teaching of the Word.
Do not let us neglect the spiritual gift within us.
Help us practice and immerse ourselves in the things of You, God,
so that our progress will be evident to all.
Help us pay close attention to ourselves
and persevere in Your things, LORD.
In Your name, Jesus~"

Please read 1 Timothy 5.
Meditate on verse 22b.

Keep yourself free from sin.

God's Word is so practical. In this part of Paul's letter to Timothy, specific principles were given for men and women of all ages and in various life situations: married, widowed, leading a church, dealing with sin, and working with others. Paul even addressed stomach ailments. God cares about every detail of your life, and He wants you to live the plans and purposes He has for you.

Most of God's will for your life is contained in the Bible. Remain faithful to study and live His Word.

Pray 1 Timothy 5:21-22 over yourself and those for whom you stand guard as a faithful, prayerful watchman (Isaiah 62:6-7).

"God, may _____ and I maintain Your principles.
Let us do nothing in a spirit of partiality.
Do not let us share in the sins of others;
keep us free from sin.
In Your name, Jesus~"

Please read 1 Timothy 6.

Meditate on verses 20-21.

> *O Timothy, guard what has been entrusted to you,*
> *avoiding worldly and empty chatter*
> *and the opposing arguments of what is falsely called "knowledge"—*
> *which some have professed and thus gone astray from the faith.*
> *Grace be with you.*

Paul closed his letter to Timothy with a plea to guard the truth entrusted to him. Paul knew that believing ideas in opposition to God's Word caused people to stray from true faith in God.

Insert your name in place of Timothy in the verses above.

> *"O _____ , guard what has been entrusted to you…"*

God is begging you to avoid what the world calls "knowledge." If what you are reading and learning is in opposition to the Bible, it is a lie. God's Word is timeless truth; hold fast the Word of Life, so you will not be deceived by the liar and father of lies (Philippians 2:16; John 8:44).

Pray 1 Timothy 6:4-5 and 11-12 over yourself and those for whom you stand guard as a faithful, prayerful watchman (Isaiah 62:6-7).

> *"LORD, let _____ and me flee from controversial questions,*
> *disputes about words, envy, strife, abusive language, evil suspicions,*
> *and constant friction between men of depraved*
> *mind deprived of the truth.*
> *Help us flee from those who oppose Godliness as a means of gain.*
> *Let us pursue righteousness, Godliness,*
> *faith, love, perseverance, and gentleness.*
> *Let us fight the good fight of faith*
> *and take hold of the eternal life to which we were called.*
> *Because of Your name, Jesus~"*

AUGUST 20

Please read 2 Timothy 1.

Meditate on verse 7.

> *God has not given us a spirit of timidity,*
> *but of power and love and discipline.*

Paul's first letter to Timothy was filled with instructions for leading the church in Ephesus. A few years passed since Timothy received that letter; now Paul's beloved son in the faith needed a letter of personal encouragement.

Even a faithful bond-servant of Christ gets discouraged at times. So although Paul was close to death, imprisoned as a criminal in Rome because of Jesus, and rejected by many of his friends, he wrote this letter to exhort and encourage Timothy.

There are at least 30 exhortations from Paul to Timothy in this letter, commands to be strong and diligent, to remember Jesus, to do certain things and to avoid doing other things. They are wise words from a concerned spiritual father, and they are words from a loving Heavenly Father to you.

No matter what is happening to you right now, remember God has saved you and given you a holy calling for His purposes (2 Timothy 1:9). Read this letter in its entirety, as if it were a letter written personally to you, because it truly is. Be encouraged by your LORD, today.

Pray 2 Timothy 1:6-9 and 14 over yourself and those for whom you stand guard as a faithful, prayerful watchman (Isaiah 62:6-7).

"LORD, help _____ and me to kindle
afresh Your gift within us.
Thank You for not giving us a spirit of timidity,
but of power and love and discipline.
Let us not be ashamed of Your testimony, LORD.
Let us not forget that You have saved us
and called us with a holy calling,
not according to our works,
but according to Your own purpose and grace
which was granted us in You, Christ Jesus, from all eternity.
Holy Spirit, who dwells in us,
guard the treasure which has been entrusted to us.
Because of Your name, Jesus~"

Please read 2 Timothy 2.

Meditate on verse 1.

You therefore, my son, be strong in the grace that is in Christ Jesus.

Timothy needed to consider the Truth of God. He needed to remember Jesus Christ and remind others of Godly things (2 Timothy 2:7, 8, 14).

What are you pondering today? What occupies your thoughts? Is it the Word of Truth, the Bible, or is it the worries and cares of life? Pondering your worries will not change your circumstances or the circumstances of others. Considering, sharing, and praying the Word of God will change life situations. There are many treasure verses to pray over your loved ones from 2 Timothy 2. Find the ones you need to pray and occupy yourself with those verses today.

Pray 2 Timothy 2:15-16 and 22-25 over yourself and those for whom you stand guard as a faithful, prayerful watchman (Isaiah 62:6-7).

"LORD, help _____ and me to be diligent to present ourselves
approved unto You as workmen who do not need to be ashamed.
Help us accurately handle the Word of Truth.
Let us avoid worldly and empty chatter,
for it will lead to further ungodliness.
Let us flee youthful lusts and pursue
righteousness, faith, love, and peace
with those who call on You from a pure heart.
Help us refuse foolish and ignorant speculations,
knowing that they produce quarrels.
Make us Your bond-servants who are not quarrelsome,
but kind to all, able to teach, patient when wronged,
gently correcting those who are in opposition.
For the sake of Your name, Jesus~"

AUGUST 22

Please read 2 Timothy 3.

Meditate on verse 1.

But realize this, that in the last days difficult times will come.

The last days started after Christ's ascension (Acts 1). Timothy and Paul were living in the last days and so are you. The last days are the days being lived as you await the return of Christ. Over 2,000 years ago, Paul wrote the description of people who do not know Christ during the last days and commands Timothy to avoid them (2 Timothy 3:2-5). In the last days people will be:

- lovers of self
- lovers of money
- boastful
- arrogant
- revilers
- disobedient to parents
- ungrateful
- unholy
- unloving
- irreconcilable
- malicious gossips
- without self-control
- brutal
- haters of good
- treacherous

- reckless
- conceited
- lovers of pleasure rather than lovers of God
- holding to a form of godliness, although they have denied its power

People have not changed in 2,000 years and still need God and His Word to change their lives for good. Paul exhorted Timothy to continue in the things he had learned from the sacred writings (God's Word) because Scripture gave him the wisdom leading to salvation in Christ Jesus (2 Timothy 3:14-15). Unless the truth of God's Word changes you, you are the nineteen things listed above. Pray for Scripture to impact you and those you love.

Pray 2 Timothy 3:16-17 over yourself and those for whom you stand guard as a faithful, prayerful watchman (Isaiah 62:6-7).

"All Scripture is inspired by You, God.
Let it teach, reprove, correct, and train
_____ and me in righteousness.
Make us Your people, adequate and equipped for every good work.
In Your name, Jesus~"

Please read 2 Timothy 4.

Meditate on verse 3.

For the time will come when they will not endure sound doctrine;
but wanting to have their ears tickled,
they will accumulate for themselves teachers
in accordance to their own desires.

The list of the ungodly in 2 Timothy 3:2-5 accurately describes people today. Amazingly, God had Paul write the list long, long ago. Today's verse from 2 Timothy 4 also sounds like it was recently written, yet Paul penned it nearly 2,000 years ago. God's Word is eternal and still remains profitable for teaching, reproof, correction, and training in righteousness (2 Timothy 3:16).

Does 2 Timothy 4:3 reprove you? What teachings do you surround yourself with? Do you merely want your ears tickled, or do you really want to know truth? Are you attending a church where the Bible is preached and taught as the inerrant Word of God, the supreme and final authority for faith and life? Or does your church capitulate to pop-culture and political correctness, ignoring the truth of God's Word?

Pray 2 Timothy 4:2 and 5 over yourself and those for whom you stand guard as a faithful, prayerful watchman (Isaiah 62:6-7).

"LORD, in these last days, let _____ and me
preach the Word; be ready in season and out of season;
reprove, rebuke, and exhort with great patience and instruction.
Let us be sober in all things, endure hardship,
do the work of an evangelist, and fulfill our ministry.
In Your name, Jesus~"

Please read Titus 1.

Meditate on verse 10.

> *For there are many rebellious men, empty talkers and deceivers,*
> *especially those of the circumcision.*

Paul left Titus in Crete to set the churches in order and appoint elders in every city on the island (Titus 1:5). There were people in the Cretan churches who contradicted sound doctrine and taught things upsetting entire families. Strong leadership was needed to exhort in sound doctrine and refute the contradictors. Paul gave Titus a list of 18 qualifications to be a church elder or overseer. He must be:

- above reproach
- the husband of one wife
- have children who are believers and are not rebellious

He must have these first three qualifications because he has to be:

- above reproach as God's steward (An elder cannot be a good steward of the church if his own family is not obediently following Christ.)
- not self-willed
- not quick-tempered
- not addicted to wine
- not pugnacious
- not fond of sordid gain
- hospitable
- loving what is good
- sensible

- just
- devout
- self-controlled
- holding fast the faithful Word
- able to exhort in sound doctrine
- able to refute those who contradict sound doctrine

This describes a man of God, a leader who guides his family to faith and obedience in Christ and who leads those in his church as well. This is the list of Godly attributes that should describe every Christian man.

If you are an unmarried woman, this is your list for what you want in a husband. If you are a married woman, this is the list to pray every day over your husband. Men, pray this list over yourself. Mothers and fathers, pray for your sons and grandsons to be established in the LORD with these 18 attributes characterizing their lives.

Our churches desperately need men in leadership positions with ALL 18 characteristics because there are many rebellious men in our churches, empty talkers and deceivers who must be silenced because they are upsetting whole families by teaching things they should not teach for the sake of sordid gain (Titus 1:10-11).

Pray Titus 1:6-9 over the men in your life as a faithful, prayerful watchman (Isaiah 62:6-7).

"LORD, make _____ above reproach,
the husband of one wife.
Let his children be believers and not accused
of dissipation or rebellion.
Make _____ above reproach as Your steward.

Do not let him be self-willed, quick-tempered,
addicted to wine, pugnacious,
or fond of sordid gain.
Let him be hospitable, loving what is good,
sensible, just, devout, and self-controlled.
Let him hold fast the faithful Word, which
is in accordance with the teaching,
so that he will be able both to exhort in sound doctrine
and refute those who contradict.
For the sake of Your name, Jesus~"

AUGUST 25

Please read Titus 2.

Meditate on verse 10b.

> *Showing all good faith so that they will adorn*
> *the doctrine of God our Savior in every respect.*

The churches on the island of Crete needed Godly leaders and Godly members. Paul gave the characteristics, the LORD's expectations, for men and women, young and old, from all walks of life. These attributes are listed in Titus 2. When believers exhibit these characteristics, they show all good faith and adorn the doctrine of God in every respect (Titus 2:10).

Examine your life. How do you adorn the doctrine of God your Savior? Does your behavior beautifully give credence to the doctrine of God, or does it portray things of God as being ridiculous? The way you speak and act tells the world what you believe about God. Evaluate your words and actions in light of Titus 2. God said in Titus 1:16 that those who profess to know God but deny Him by their deeds are detestable, disobedient, and worthless for any good deed. What would the LORD say about you?

Pray Titus 2:1-8 over yourself and those for whom you stand guard as a faithful, prayerful watchman (Isaiah 62:6-7). [I prayed these verses over my son and his wife everyday for 256 days prior to their wedding, so God would establish them in these Godly characteristics. I continue to pray them over my husband, children, and grandchildren.]

> *"LORD, let _____ and me speak*
> *things fitting for sound doctrine.*
> *Let _____ be temperate, dignified, sensible,*
> *sound in faith, sound in love, sound in perseverance.*

Let _____ be reverent in her behavior,
not a malicious gossip nor enslaved to much wine.
May she teach what is good,
so she can encourage _____ to love her husband,
to love her children, to be sensible, pure, a stayer at home,
kind, subject to her own husband
so that Your Word will not be dishonored.
Likewise let _____ be sensible.
In all things let _____ and me show ourselves
to be an example of good deeds with purity in doctrine,
dignified, sound in speech which is beyond reproach,
so that the opponent will be put to shame
and have nothing bad to say about us.
In Your name, Jesus-"

Please read Titus 3.

Meditate on verses 4 -6.

> *But when the kindness of God our Savior*
> *and His love for mankind appeared,*
> *He saved us, not on the basis of deeds*
> *which we have done in righteousness,*
> *but according to His mercy,*
> *by the washing of regeneration and renewing by the Holy Spirit,*
> *whom He poured out upon us richly*
> *through Jesus Christ our Savior.*

Apart from Jesus, you are a mess. Before being saved, you were foolish, disobedient, deceived, and enslaved to sin. There was not one righteous deed you could do to save yourself. But when the kindness of God your Savior and His love for you appeared, He saved you according to His mercy, by the washing and renewing of the Holy Spirit whom He poured out upon you richly through Jesus Christ your Savior (Titus 3:3-6).

Salvation is such a great news story. Why would God be so kind to you? Why would He pour out His mercy on despicable mankind? Because God loves people, and He wants to save them from their mess. Behave in a Godly way so others will be drawn to the kindness and love of your Savior.

Pray Titus 3:1-2 over yourself and those for whom you stand guard as a faithful, prayerful watchman (Isaiah 62:6-7).

> *"LORD, help _____ and me to be*
> *subject to rulers, to authorities,*
> *to be obedient, to be ready for every good deed.*
> *Let us malign no one;*
> *let us be peaceable, gentle,*
> *and show every consideration for all men.*
> *For Your cause, Jesus~"*

Please read Philemon 1.

Meditate on verse 7.

For I have come to have much joy and comfort in your love,
because the hearts of the saints have been
refreshed through you, brother.

Philemon had a decision to make. His runaway slave, Onesimus, became a Christian while he was with Paul. Paul sent Onesimus back to his master with this letter appealing to Philemon to receive Onesimus as a brother in Christ rather than punishing him as a runaway slave.

By law, Philemon could have killed Onesimus for his crime. Yet Philemon was a follower of Jesus Christ who even had a church meeting in his home. Paul had confidence in Jesus that Philemon would do what was proper.

What would you do? You have the legal right to do _____, but because of the love and grace you have received from the LORD, will you extend that mercy to another, even if they do not deserve it?

Read Colossians 4:7-9 to find out the rest of Onesimus' story. Philemon's decision refreshed the heart of Paul (Philemon 1:20).

Pray Philemon 1:4-7 over someone for whom you stand guard as a faithful, prayerful watchman (Isaiah 62:6-7).

"Thank You, God, for _____. May I always hear of their love
and faith toward You and all the saints. Let the sharing
of their faith be effective for the knowledge of every good thing
that is in us for Your sake, Christ. Let the hearts of
the saints be refreshed through _____.
Thank You for the joy and comfort I have in their love.
In Your name, Jesus~"

Please read Hebrews 1.

Meditate on verses 1-2.

> *God, after He spoke long ago to the fathers in the prophets*
> *in many portions and in many ways, in these last day has*
> *spoken to us in His Son, whom He appointed heir of all things,*
> *through whom also He made the world.*

Hebrews is a masterpiece crafted by God to tell you who Jesus is. A theme of the letter is "fix your eyes on Jesus" (Hebrews 12:2). God ensures you focus only on Christ because He does not name the earthly writer. Do not waste time speculating about the scribe; Jesus Christ is the focus of this letter.

Hebrews 1 tells you God made the world through Jesus, and Jesus is the radiance of God's glory, the exact representation of God's nature. Christ upholds all things by the Word of His power. He is also superior to angels.

These are truths about who God is. You live in a world that denies there is a Creator of the universe and the deity of Christ. The writer of Hebrews tells you God created the world through Jesus Christ who is the expression of the glory of God.

Enjoy getting to know your Savior as you read and study this amazing letter.

Pray Hebrews 1:2-3 over yourself and those for whom you stand guard as a faithful, prayerful watchman (Isaiah 62:6-7).

> *"Jesus, in these last days You have spoken to _____ and me.*
> *Jesus, You made the world and are the radiance of God's glory*
> *and the exact representation of God's nature. Please form*
> *Your nature in us and uphold us by the Word of Your power.*
> *Thank You that You have made purification of our sins.*
> *For the sake of Your name, Jesus~"*

Please read Hebrews 2.

Meditate on verse 1.

For this reason we must pay
much closer attention to what we have heard,
so that we do not drift away from it.

In these last days God has spoken to you in His son (Hebrews 1:2); therefore, you must pay much closer attention to what you have heard (Hebrews 2:1).

Pick up your Bible. You are holding in your hand the very Words of Jesus Christ! The Bible is the way God chose to reveal Himself to you and communicate with you. Do you pay attention to it?

Hebrews 2 tells you truth about Jesus you must pay attention to:

- Your "so great a salvation" was spoken through the LORD; do not neglect it (vs. 2-3).

- Jesus rendered the devil powerless who had the power of death; therefore, you are free from the fear of death (v.15).

- Jesus had to become a human like you, so He would be your merciful and faithful high priest and your sacrifice to appease the wrath of God against your sin (v.17).

- When Jesus became a human, He was tempted like you are; therefore, He is able to come to your aid when you are tempted (v.18).

What a relief to know these truths about God! Pay close attention to what you have learned and pray Hebrews 2:1 and 3 over yourself and those for whom you stand guard as a faithful, prayerful watchman (Isaiah 62:6-7).

"LORD, help _____ and me to pay much closer attention
to what we have heard from You,
so we do not drift away from it.
Do not let us neglect our so great a salvation.
In Your name, Jesus-"

Please read Hebrews 3.

Meditate on verse 1.

> *Therefore, holy brethren,*
> *partakers of a heavenly calling,*
> *consider Jesus, the Apostle and High Priest of our confession.*

Consider Jesus! Fix your mind on Him. Observe Him carefully in the book of Hebrews. He is superior to Moses. He is the builder of all things. He is the living God. You are a partaker of Jesus if you hold fast to Him and are not hardened by sin's deceitfulness. Christ builds you up as you hold fast your confidence in Him. People who are disobedient and do not believe in Jesus do not dwell with Him.

There are warnings for you in Hebrews 3. "Today, if you hear His voice, do not harden your hearts. Take care that none of you has an evil, unbelieving heart that forsakes the living God (vs. 7-8, 12)."

Examine yourself. What do you believe about Jesus? Do you allow Him to build your life? Do you hold fast to Him? Do not harden your heart towards your LORD.

Pray Hebrews 3:12-14 over yourself and those for whom you stand guard as a faithful, prayerful watchman (Isaiah 62:6-7).

> *"Living God, do not let _____ and me*
> *have an evil, unbelieving heart that falls away from You.*
> *Help us encourage one another day after day,*
> *so we will not be hardened by the deceitfulness of sin.*
> *May we be partakers of You, Christ,*
> *and let us hold fast the beginning of our*
> *assurance firm until the end.*
> *In Your name, Jesus~"*

Please read Hebrews 4.

Meditate on verses 15-16.

> *For we do not have a high priest who cannot sympathize with*
> *our weaknesses, but One who has been tempted*
> *in all things as we are, yet without sin.*
> *Therefore let us draw near with confidence to the throne of grace,*
> *so that we may receive mercy and find grace to help in time of need.*

Are you tired and worn out? Do the struggles of life have you feeling exhausted? God mentioned *rest* fourteen times in Hebrews 3 and 4. God wants you to enter His rest. Hearing the Word of God and by faith, believing the Good News, results in God's rest for your life. Doing good works will not bring God's rest. Works make you tired. There is nothing good enough to get you to God except Jesus Christ.

Reread Hebrews 3 and 4. Ask God to give you insight with understanding into His Word. The LORD wants you to be able to experience His rest here on earth as well as in heaven. Jesus gives you favor with God. Jesus is the High Priest who gives you mercy and grace. Draw near with confidence to God, today. You will find rest for your weary soul.

Pray Hebrews 4:6-7 and 12-13 over yourself and those for whom you stand guard as a faithful, prayerful watchman (Isaiah 62:6-7).

> *"LORD, do not let _____ and me fail to enter Your rest*
> *because of disobedience. Let us hear Your voice and not*
> *harden our hearts. Your Word is living and active and sharper*
> *than any two-edged sword. Let it pierce our soul and spirit and*
> *divide our joints and marrow. Judge the thoughts and intentions*
> *of our hearts. Let us hold fast our confession of You,*
> *Jesus, the Son of God, our Great High Priest.*
> *In whose name I pray~"*

SEPTEMBER

On your walls, O Jerusalem,
I have appointed watchmen;
All day and all night they
will never keep silent.
You who remind the LORD
take no rest for yourselves;
And give Him no rest
until He establishes
And makes Jerusalem a
praise in the earth.
ISAIAH 62:6-7, NASB

SEPTEMBER 1

Please read Hebrews 5.

Meditate on verse 12.

For though by this time you ought to be teachers, you have need
again for someone to teach you the elementary principles of the
Oracles of God, and you have come to need milk and not solid food.

Hebrews is a meaty book. It contains many doctrines (truths) of God. Hebrews was originally written to Jewish Christians to teach that they no longer needed an earthly priest to offer sacrifices for their sins. Jesus fulfilled the Old Covenant laws; He became to everyone who obeys Him the source of eternal salvation (Hebrews 5:9).

The writer of Hebrews wanted to explain to his readers many deep things about the Oracles of God, but they could not stomach such rich teaching. They were not accustomed to the Word of Righteousness (Hebrews 5:12-13).

Are you accustomed to the Word of God? Because of use, are you familiar with the Bible? Or is God addressing you when He says, "You ought to be teaching My Word by now, but instead, you need someone teaching you My elementary principles. You have come to need the milk of My Word"?

Pray Hebrews 5:13-14 over yourself and those for whom you stand guard as a faithful, prayerful watchman (Isaiah 62:6-7).

"LORD, help _____ and me stop being infants,
partaking only of the milk of Your Word.
May we become accustomed to Your Word of Righteousness.
Make us mature in You, so we can eat solid food.
Help us practice eating the solid food of Your Word.
Train our senses to discern good and evil.
In Your name, Jesus~"

Please read Hebrews 6.

Meditate on verses 19-20a.

This hope we have as an anchor of the soul,
a hope both sure and steadfast and one which enters within the veil,
where Jesus has entered as a forerunner for us …

When rain falls, it waters an entire piece of land. The land uses the water and either produces useful vegetation or worthless thorns and thistles. God used this comparison to explain the work of the Holy Spirit. Every person on earth partakes of the blessings of the Holy Spirit and tastes the good Word of God. Like rain-watered ground, each individual chooses what to do with those blessings. Every person must choose to either receive the blessings of God resulting in salvation or to fall away from the truth. Refusing the Holy Spirit results in no repentance; then, like thorns and thistles, that life is worthless, cursed, and will end up being burned.

BUT, if your life gives evidence of salvation, then you have full assurance of hope until the end. The hope you have in Christ is the anchor of your soul; it is a sure and steadfast hope because Jesus runs before you to God the Father announcing your arrival into the presence of the LORD forever. This is truth from the Word of God, and it is impossible for God to lie (Hebrews 6:18).

Pray Hebrews 6:11-12 over yourself and those for whom you stand guard as a faithful, prayerful watchman (Isaiah 62:6-7).

"LORD, help _____ and me show diligence in our salvation
so as to realize the full assurance of hope until the end.
Do not let us be sluggish, but help us be imitators of those
who through faith and patience inherit the promises.
In Your name, Jesus-"

Please read Hebrews 7.

Meditate on verse 25.

> *Therefore He (Jesus) is able also to save forever*
> *those who draw near to God through Him,*
> *since He always lives to make intercession for them.*

Notice the doctrines of God in Hebrews 7:26-28. Jesus is:

- high priest
- holy
- innocent
- undefiled
- separated from sinners
- exalted above the heavens
- does not need to daily offer sacrifices because He offered up Himself once for all for your sins
- perfect forever

Amazingly, your perfect, holy, undefiled Savior lives to intercede for you. Jesus is compared to Melchizedek, a priest and king in the days of Abraham (Genesis 14:18-20). Melchizedek was a priest before God established the Jewish law or the priestly system. He had no recorded genealogy in the Bible and no record of his birth or death. He was a picture for the Israelites of Messiah. Melchizedek even brought bread and wine to Abraham. God was giving His people a picture of Christ 2,000 years before Jesus came to earth.

The writer of Hebrews wanted to teach his readers about Melchizedek in chapter 5, but stopped because they were dull of hearing. He decided to explain Melchizedek in chapter 7 anyway. God knew you would have ears to hear.

Jesus, who is a priest forever according to the order of Melchizedek, is constantly putting in a good word for you. Satan wants to condemn you, but when you are in Christ, he cannot because Jesus always lives to intercede on your behalf. When you belong to Christ, you can boldly run to the Father because the Son of God is talking favorably about you to Him.

Pray Hebrews 7:25 over someone for whom you stand guard as a faithful, prayerful watchman (Isaiah 62:6-7).

"Jesus, please let _____ draw near to God through You.
Save them forever.
Thank You for always living to make intercession for us.
In Your name, Jesus~"

Please read Hebrews 8.

Meditate on verse 12.

> *For I will be merciful to their iniquities,*
> *and I will remember their sins no more.*

The writer of Hebrews sums up the first seven chapters of this letter in Hebrews 8:1-2:

> *Now the main point in what has been said is this:*
> *we have such a high priest, who has taken His seat*
> *at the right hand of the throne of the Majesty in the heavens,*
> *a minister in the sanctuary and in the true tabernacle,*
> *which the LORD pitched, not man.*

God wanted the Jewish believers to know that in Christ they were in a better covenant relationship than what they had under the Old Covenant. Jesus was their high priest; He was in the position of authority on the throne of God, and He was ministering on their behalf in the true tabernacle built by God instead of their earthly tabernacle that was about to be destroyed by the Romans in 70 A.D. and has yet to be rebuilt.

God wants you to know these truths as well. The Old Covenant consists of 613 laws that are impossible to perfectly keep. In the New Covenant of Christ Jesus, God's laws are written on your mind and heart, and you are able to know God and be His people. Under the New Covenant, God is merciful to your iniquities and remembers your sins no more. What an amazing salvation God offers you!

God warns you at the beginning of this letter not to neglect so great a salvation (Hebrews 2:3). Jesus has mediated a better covenant with better promises on your behalf. Why would anyone not want to be part of this covenant of salvation in Christ Jesus?

Pray Hebrews 8:10-12 over someone for whom you stand guard as a faithful, prayerful watchman (Isaiah 62:6-7).

"LORD, put Your laws into the mind of _____ .
Write them on their heart.
Please become their God,
and let them become your people.
Let them know You.
Be merciful to their iniquities
and remember their sins no more.
For the sake of Your name, Jesus~"

Please read Hebrews 9.

Meditate on verse 28.

So Christ also, having been offered once to bear the sins of many,
will appear a second time for salvation without reference to sin,
to those who eagerly await Him.

Well, the news about this covenant in Jesus Christ gets better and better. Not only is God merciful to your iniquities remembering them no more; when He returns to take you out of this world, He will make no reference to your sin. His blood so completely covers your sins that Jesus refuses to remember your very sins that killed Him. If that is not enough, His blood even cleanses your conscience from dead works so you can serve Him (Hebrews 9:14).

Jesus does not remember your sins, so do not allow the guilt and shame of your past to paralyze you and keep you from serving the Living God. Let God cleanse your conscience of all the dead junk from your past, so you can serve your Savior for the rest of eternity. Do not neglect your so great a salvation (Hebrews 2:3)!

Pray Hebrews 9:14 and 28 over yourself and those for whom you stand guard as a faithful, prayerful watchman (Isaiah 62:6-7).

"Christ, by Your blood,
through Your eternal Spirit,
cleanse _____ and my conscience
from dead works to serve You, our living God.
Thank You for bearing our sins.
Thank You that when You appear a second time for salvation,
You will not reference our sin,
if we eagerly await You.
God, please cause _____ to eagerly await You.
In Your name, Jesus~"

Please read Hebrews 10.

Meditate on verses 19-23.

> *Therefore, brethren, since we have confidence*
> *to enter the holy place by the blood of Jesus,*
> *by a new and living way which He inaugurated*
> *for us through the veil, that is, His flesh,*
> *and since we have a great high priest over the house of God,*
> *let us draw near with a sincere heart in full assurance of faith,*
> *having our hearts sprinkled clean from an evil conscience*
> *and our bodies washed with pure water.*
> *Let us hold fast the confession of our hope without wavering,*
> *for He who promised is faithful.*

The Old Covenant law was only a shadow of the New Covenant salvation found in Jesus Christ. For 1,500 years, imperfect Jewish priests offered sacrifices over and over for the cleansing of sins. Daily offering the blood of bulls and goats did not take away sins, and it did not perfect the people. God instituted this seemingly futile sacrificial system to show people their need for a Savior. Trying time after time to do something to please God to save yourself is futilely exhausting. You desperately need a Savior; you need Jesus.

The sacrifice of Jesus Christ did amazing things for you:

1. You get forgiveness of all your sins and lawless deeds.
2. You have confidence to enter the Holy Place (the presence of God).
3. You have a great Priest (Jesus).
4. You can draw near to God with a sincere heart in full assurance of faith.
5. Your heart has been sprinkled clean from an evil conscience.

6. Your body has been washed with pure water.

7. You can hold fast to your confession of hope in Jesus Christ without wavering.

JESUS—WHO MADE THESE PROMISES TO YOU—IS FAITHFUL!

Jesus did everything for you. All you have to do is have faith in the Faithful One.

Pray Hebrews 10:35-36 and 38-39 over yourself and those for whom you stand guard as a faithful, prayerful watchman (Isaiah 62:6-7).

> *"LORD, help _____ and me not throw*
> *away our confidence in You*
> *because it has a great reward.*
> *Give us endurance in doing Your will,*
> *so we may receive the promise.*
> *Make us righteous. May we live by faith.*
> *Do not let us shrink back. We want Your*
> *soul to find pleasure in us.*
> *LORD, do not let us be like those who shrink back to destruction.*
> *Make us like those who have faith to the preserving of the soul.*
> *Because of Your faithfulness, Jesus~"*

Please read Hebrews 11.

Meditate on verses 1 and 6.

Now faith is the assurance of things hoped for,
the conviction of things not seen.
And without faith it is impossible to please Him,
for he who comes to God must believe that He is
and that He is a rewarder of those who seek Him.

Hebrews 11 is the Hall of Faith, a list of 20 Old Testament saints who believed God plus a list of 25 faithful actions by unnamed believers. God had their names and stories eternally written, so you could have examples of faith pleasing to the LORD.

These 45 individuals believed God's promise of Messiah. They did not actually see Messiah before their earthly death, but they did not waver in unbelief because they knew God who promised is faithful (Hebrews 10:23; 11:11).

What about you? Do you believe that God is? Are you a person of faith? Could you be Hebrews 11:41? By faith _____, ... Would God write your name in that blank?

Pray Hebrews 11:6 over yourself and those for whom you stand guard as a faithful, prayerful watchman (Isaiah 62:6-7).

"LORD, may _____ and I please You.
Make us people of faith.
May we come to You, God, and believe that You are.
We want to be rewarded by You
because we are people who seek You.
Because of Your name, Jesus~"

SEPTEMBER 8

Please read Hebrews 12.
Meditate on verses 1-2.

Therefore, since we have so great a cloud
of witnesses surrounding us,
let us also lay aside every encumbrance and
the sin which so easily entangles us,
and let us run with endurance the race that is set before us,
fixing our eyes on Jesus, the author and perfecter of faith,
who for the joy set before Him endured the cross,
despising the shame, and has sat down at the
right hand of the throne of God.

Hebrews 12:1-2 tells you how to live your life successfully. Get rid of every weight and sin that clings to you and run, without being swerved, the race God has set before you. Fix your eyes on Jesus. Permanently place your eyes on Christ; do not let them wander. He is the One who started you on this race, and He is the One who will finish it for you. Do not take your eyes off of your LORD even for a second.

Pray Hebrews 12:1-2 and 25a over yourself and those for whom you stand guard as a faithful, prayerful watchman (Isaiah 62:6-7).

"LORD, let _____ and me lay aside every encumbrance
and the sin which so easily entangles us.
Let us run with endurance the race that is set before us.
Keep our eyes fixed on You, Jesus,
the author and perfecter of our faith.
Because of the joy set before You,
You endured the cross, despising the shame.
Thank You for doing that for us.
Now You have sat down at the right hand of the throne of God.
May we never refuse You, Jesus.
Because of Your name~"

SEPTEMBER 9

Please read Hebrews 13.
Meditate on verse 18.

*Pray for us, for we are sure that we have a good conscience,
desiring to conduct ourselves honorably in all things.*

God wrote this letter called *Hebrews* to prove Jesus is superior to angels, superior to the Law of Moses, superior to earthly priests, and superior to the sacrificial system. He is superior because He is God, your Great High Priest, and your perfect sacrifice.

Every human must consider Jesus, and no one will escape the fiery judgment should they choose to refuse Christ and neglect the so great a salvation found only in Him. The only way to please God is by faith, believing Him and His promises. Laying aside your sin and fixing your eyes on Jesus will prove your life of faith in Christ.

Because Jesus did everything to cleanse you from sin and an evil conscience, it only makes sense to desire to conduct yourself honorably in all things. The Writer urges you to pay attention to this Word of exhortation (Hebrews 13:22).

Pray the prayer that the scribe of Hebrews prayed over the readers (Hebrews 13:20-21). Pray it over those for whom you stand guard as a faithful, prayerful watchman (Isaiah 62:6-7).

*"Now God of peace, who brought up from the dead
the great Shepherd of the sheep,
through the blood of the eternal covenant,
Jesus our LORD,
equip _____ in every good thing to do Your will,
working in them that which is pleasing in Your sight,
through Jesus Christ, to whom be the
glory forever and ever. Amen-"*

Please read James 1.

Meditate on verse 1a.

James, a bond-servant of God and of the LORD Jesus Christ …

James is a letter written by the half-brother of Jesus Christ. Before the resurrection of Christ, James was a mocking younger brother who thought Jesus was crazy (John 7:1-9; Mark 3:20-21). A risen LORD so changed his skeptical life, he not only became a Christian, he became the head of the church at Jerusalem and a mentor to Paul (Acts 1; 15; 21; Galatians 1:15-19).

James laid no claim to the fame of being Christ's brother, rather he said he was a bond-servant, and Jesus Christ was his LORD. A resurrected Savior changes a person for eternity.

This letter is crucial for your walk as a disciple of Jesus Christ. From his salutation, James described true discipleship. If you are a follower of Christ, you will be His bond-servant—one who chooses to stay with a benevolent master rather than leaving to live on their own. The bond-servant gives their master their ear to have an awl pierce the lobe, permanently marking the person as belonging to another. Are you a bond-servant of Jesus Christ? Does He have your ear? Are His the Words you hear and obey? Is He LORD? Is He your Master, the One possessing supreme power and authority in your life?

Pray James 1:1 and 21-22 over yourself and those for whom you stand guard as a faithful, prayerful watchman (Isaiah 62:6-7).

"LORD Jesus Christ,
make _____ and me Your bond-servants.
Help us put aside all filthiness and all that remains of wickedness.
In humility let us receive the Word implanted,
which is able to save our souls.
Let us prove ourselves doers of the Word
and not merely hearers who delude ourselves.
In Your name, Jesus~"

Please read James 2.

Meditate on verses 12-13.

So speak and so act as those who are to be
judged by the law of liberty.
For judgment will be merciless to one who has shown no mercy;
mercy triumphs over judgment.

If you are in Christ, then His mercy has trumped the judgment you deserve for your sins. Because of mercy, Jesus will not make reference to your sins when He returns to judge the rest of the world that does not know Him as Savior (Hebrews 9:28). When Christ returns, you will be judged by the law of freedom; non-believers will be judged according to their lawless deeds. In Christ you receive amazing mercy!

As a recipient of God's mercy, what should be the obvious proof of your salvation? You ought to be a merciful person. If you have received the mercy of Jesus Christ, you cannot help but extend mercy to others. So speak and so act as someone living in the mercy of Jesus Christ. If you are a merciless person, then you need to evaluate your salvation. Are you truly a child of God?

Pray James 2:1 and 12-13 over yourself and those for whom you stand guard as a faithful, prayerful watchman (Isaiah 62:6-7).

"Glorious LORD Jesus Christ, do not let _____ and me
hold our faith in You with an attitude of personal favoritism.
Help us speak and act as those who are to
be judged by Your law of liberty.
Help us show mercy to others.
We do not want Your judgment that
will be merciless to those who show no mercy.
In Your name, Jesus-"

Please read James 3.

Meditate on verse 17.

> *But the wisdom from above is first pure,*
> *then peaceable, gentle, reasonable,*
> *full of mercy and good fruits, unwavering, without hypocrisy.*

James will grow you up in Jesus. He teaches you how to handle trials, temptations, favoritism, and proof of salvation. Chapter 3 of his letter disciples you in the use of your tongue. Jesus needs to pilot your tongue; otherwise you are in possession of an instrument full of deadly poison and capable of setting an entire forest on fire (James 3:4-8).

This chapter also addresses wisdom, which is key to the control of your tongue. Be aware there are two types of wisdom. There is God's wisdom, and there is demonic wisdom. Demonic wisdom is characterized by bitter jealousy, selfish ambition, arrogance, and lies. It is earthly and unspiritual. Demonic is a strong adjective; God wants to grab your attention and make you think about what you believe. Does the wisdom you advocate come from God or Satan?

God's wisdom is:

1. Pure
2. Peaceable
3. Gentle
4. Reasonable

5. Full of mercy
6. Full of good fruits
7. Unwavering
8. Without hypocrisy

Examine your thoughts, words, and actions by the wisdom of God. Whose wisdom is governing your life?

Pray James 3:13-18 over yourself and those for whom you stand guard as a faithful, prayerful watchman (Isaiah 62:6-7).

"LORD, please make _____ and me wise and understanding.
Let us show our good behavior in the gentleness of wisdom.
Remove bitter jealousy and selfish ambition from our hearts.
Do not let us be arrogant and lie against the truth.
Let us have nothing to do with
earthly, natural, and demonic wisdom
that does not come from above.
Let us have Your wisdom which is:
pure, peaceable, gentle, reasonable, full of mercy,
full of good fruits, unwavering, and without hypocrisy.
May we bear the fruit of righteousness as makers of peace.
In Your name, Jesus~"

Please read James 4.

Meditate on verse 6.

But He gives greater grace. Therefore it says,
"God is opposed to the proud, but gives grace to the humble."

As if God's grace to save you from eternity in hell isn't enough, He gives greater grace to forgive you when you fall back into the sins listed in James 4:1-4. James wrote to Christians. These believers were fighting, quarreling, lusting, envying, murdering, being friends with the world, and being enemies of God. James calls them adulteresses for engaging in such hostile behaviors.

God jealously desires the Holy Spirit He caused to dwell in you to be allowed to live in you. You have a choice to make. In appreciation of God's greater grace will you submit to God, resist the devil, draw near to God, purify your heart and mind, be miserable and mourn over your sin, and humble yourself in the presence of the LORD?

Pray James 4:6-10 over yourself and those for whom you stand guard as a faithful, prayerful watchman (Isaiah 62:6-7).

"LORD, You are opposed to the proud.
May _____ and I be humble;
we need Your greater grace.
Help us to submit to You and resist the devil.
Make the devil flee from us.
Draw near to us, LORD, as we draw to You.
Cleanse our hands and our double-minded hearts.
Let us be miserable, mourn, and weep over sin.
Let us never laugh and be joyful about sin.
LORD, may we humble ourselves in Your presence.
You be exalted, Jesus,
For Your name's sake~"

Please read James 5.

Meditate on verse 16b.

The effective prayer of a righteous man can accomplish much.

Do not grow weary and lose heart in your prayer life. God heard and answered Elijah's prayers, and he was a person just like you. Even Elijah had a sinful nature.

Do not believe Satan when he says your prayers will not make a difference, or the sins of your past disqualify you to ask the LORD to work in your life and the lives of others.

God says you must pray. You must pray when you are suffering; you must pray when you are cheerful. You must pray for others and yourself. James compares human lives to soil that needs early and late rains in order to produce a crop. Pray for God's truth to rain on those you love in order to produce a bountiful harvest of righteousness.

Pray James 5:19-20 over those for whom you stand guard as a faithful, prayerful watchman (Isaiah 62:6-7).

"LORD, _____ has strayed from Your truth.
Turn them back. Turn them from the error of their ways.
Save their soul from death and cover a multitude of their sins.
In Your name, Jesus~"

Please read 1 Peter 1.

Meditate on verse 25.

But the Word of the LORD endures forever.
And this is the Word which was preached to you.

Peter was the disciple who denied knowing Jesus three times the night before Christ was crucified. Peter was part of Jesus' inner circle of friends, but that night, Peter was more motivated by fear than love for his LORD. However, rather than killing himself in his shame like Judas did, Peter let Jesus forgive and restore him. After the resurrection, Christ graciously came to Peter, asked him if he loved Him, and exhorted him three times to shepherd His sheep (John 21:15-19). Peter wrote two letters as part of obeying his LORD's command to tend His lambs. Thankfully, as a lamb of God, you have these shepherding letters to tend your heart and the hearts of those God has called you to shepherd.

Peter's enduring letter explains how you are saved and protected by the power of God. It says that your faith is more precious than gold, so do not be distressed by trials because God uses trials to prove your faith.

Based on these and the many other truths found in 1 Peter 1, pray 1 Peter 1:13-16 over yourself and those for whom you stand guard as a faithful, prayerful watchman (Isaiah 62:6-7).

"LORD, let _____ and me prepare our minds for action,
keep sober in spirit, and fix our hope completely on the grace
to be brought to us at the revelation of You, Jesus Christ.
As obedient children, do not let us be conformed to the former
lusts which were ours in our ignorance. But like You, Holy One,
who called us, let us be holy in all our behavior.
We can be holy because You are holy.
In Your name, Jesus~"

Please read 1 Peter 2.

Meditate on verse 2.

*Like newborn babies, long for the pure milk of the Word,
so that by it you may grow in respect to salvation,
if you have tasted the kindness of the LORD.*

A good shepherd makes sure his sheep are fed. Jesus commanded Peter to feed His sheep (John 21:15). Peter took his sheep to the enduring Word of God for nourishment.

God's Word lasts forever (1 Peter 1:25). God commands you in 1 Peter 2:2 to long for that Word like a newborn baby longs for his mama's milk. The word *long* means to intensely crave and pursue something. Does that describe your pursuit of God's Word everyday? As a child of God, your spiritual nourishment comes from the Word of God. What would happen to a newborn baby who was not given any milk for an entire day? What would happen if that newborn were given only a drop of milk, just a small taste each day? You understand why God used this comparison; now spend time in the Word of God as if your life depends on it because it most certainly does.

Pray 1 Peter 2:1-3 over yourself and those for whom you stand guard as a faithful, prayerful watchman (Isaiah 62:6-7).

*"LORD, may _____ and I put aside all malice, all deceit,
hypocrisy, envy, and all slander.
Like newborn babies,
may we long for the pure milk of Your Word,
so that by it we may grow in respect to salvation.
Thank You that we have tasted of Your kindness, LORD.
In Your name, Jesus~"*

Please read 1 Peter 3.

Meditate on verse 8.

To sum up, all of you be harmonious,
sympathetic, brotherly,
kindhearted, and humble in spirit.

Peter shepherded wives, husbands, and everyone in 1 Peter 3. Wives were exhorted to submit to their own husbands in the same way Jesus submitted to God the Father. Husbands were exhorted to understand and honor their wives. And everybody was to bless others.

Remember the Word of God is enduring (1 Peter 1:23), and it is the wisdom of God versus demonic wisdom (James 3:15). The exhortations in 1 Peter 3 have not changed or become old-fashioned. God still says, "Wives submit to your own husbands. Your gentle and quiet spirit is precious in My sight. Husbands live with your wives in an understanding way and honor her as a fellow heir of My grace, so I will hear your prayers."

This is timeless truth that improves marriage relationships. Pray 1 Peter 3:8-9 over the relationships you guard as a faithful, prayerful watchman (Isaiah 62:6-7).

"LORD, please help _____ and me
be harmonious, sympathetic,
brotherly, kindhearted, and humble in spirit.
Do not let us return evil for evil or insult for insult,
but let us give a blessing instead
because we were called for that very purpose
so that we might inherit a blessing.
In Your name, Jesus–"

SEPTEMBER 18

Please read 1 Peter 4.

Meditate on verse 7.

The end of all things is near; therefore, be of sound judgment
and sober spirit for the purpose of prayer.

Instead of living for the lusts of men, it is time to live for the will of God. Before you became a Christian, you had time to live like an unbeliever, pursuing sensuality, lusts, drunkenness, carousing, drinking parties, and abominable idolatries (1 Peter 4:3). As a follower of Jesus Christ, you should not be wasting your time doing those activities. Even if old friends make fun of you for not running with them in ungodly pleasures, do not be swayed from the abundant life God desires for you. If you are consumed in the pursuit of the things of this world, the things of God will not consume you. Ask God to give you an eternal perspective. Time is short; God wants you to focus on things that will positively impact His Kingdom.

Pray 1 Peter 4:7-11 over yourself and those for whom you stand guard as a faithful, prayerful watchman (Isaiah 62:6-7).

"LORD, the end of all things is near,
so give _____ and me sound judgment
and a sober spirit for the purpose of prayer.
Help us keep fervent in our love for one another
because love covers a multitude of sins.
Let us be hospitable to one another without complaint.
With the gifts You have given us,
let us serve one another as good stewards of Your grace.
May we speak Your utterances, God.
May we serve by the strength You supply,
so that in all things You will be glorified through Jesus Christ.
To You, Jesus, belongs the glory and dominion
forever and ever. Amen~"

Please read 1 Peter 5.

Meditate on verse 2a.

Shepherd the flock of God among you.

Peter took Jesus seriously when commanded three times to shepherd His sheep (John 21:15-19). Peter's obedience is seen in this letter that still tends the LORD's flock. Learning from Jesus' example, Peter concluded his letter by exhorting his readers to shepherd the flock God had placed in their care.

Who has the LORD placed in your realm of influence to shepherd? There is at least one person Christ trusts you to feed and tend. He wants you to shepherd His flock voluntarily, eagerly, and by setting an example for them. The Chief Shepherd promises you a reward for being a good shepherd, the unfading crown of glory (1 Peter 5:4).

As you shepherd the flock God has entrusted to you, pray 1 Peter 5:6-11 over them as their faithful, prayerful watchman (Isaiah 62:6-7).

"LORD, help _____ humble themselves under Your mighty hand,
so You may exalt them at the proper time.
Let them cast all their anxiety upon You
because You care for them.
Give them a sober spirit;
keep them on the alert, so their adversary,
the devil, will not devour them.
Help them resist the devil.
Make them firm in their faith.
God of all grace, call _____ to Your eternal glory in Christ.
Perfect, confirm, strengthen, and establish them.
To You, Jesus, be dominion forever and ever. Amen~"

September 20

Please read 2 Peter 1.

Meditate on verse 3.

> *Seeing that His divine power has granted*
> *to us everything pertaining to life and Godliness,*
> *through the true knowledge of Him*
> *who called us by His own glory and excellence.*

Peter was about to die, and the sheep entrusted to him by the LORD were on his mind. He wrote another letter to remind them of things they already knew. Once he departed this earthly dwelling, Peter did not want the sheep to forget the truth established in them. His letter is eternal Scripture, so you need not forget either.

As you shepherd the flock God has given you, remember that His divine power gives you everything you need to tend them with Godliness. Be like Peter and remind them of the truths of God. Be diligent to make sure they can recall those truths at any time.

Beware it is demonic wisdom that advises you to let children decide for themselves what they will believe about God. It is a lie of Satan that says truth is relative. Truth is according to Godliness, and all of God's Word is truth (Titus 1:1; Psalm 119:160).

Pray 2 Peter 1:4-8 over yourself and those for whom you stand guard as a faithful, prayerful watchman (Isaiah 62:6-7).

> *"LORD, let _____ and me become partakers of Your divine*
> *nature. Help us escape the corruption that in in the world by lust.*
> *May we apply all diligence in our faith. Supply us with moral*
> *excellence, knowledge, self-control, perseverance, Godliness,*
> *brotherly kindness, and love. Let these qualities be increasingly*
> *ours, so we will be neither useless nor unfruitful in the true*
> *knowledge of You, LORD Jesus Christ~"*

Please read 2 Peter 2.

Meditate on verse 2.

Many will follow their sensuality,
and because of them the way of the truth will be maligned.

Peter warned his readers there were false teachers among them. These teachers introduced destructive heresies, followed their sensuality, and maligned the truth. Their eyes were full of adultery, never ceasing from sin.

More than 2,000 years have passed, but your world is similar to Peter's. There are false teachers, even in churches, teaching heresy as if it was truth. God's Word does not change; He still hates sin. God hates sin because it destroys lives. Just because the world legalizes and condones sin does not change what God thinks about it. Sin will still ruin your life and the lives of your loved ones even when it is legalized. What God said was immoral and wrong in the Old Testament was immoral and wrong in the New Testament and is immoral and wrong today. If God did not spare angels when they sinned, but cast them into hell, He will keep the unrighteous under punishment for the Day of Judgment (2 Peter 2:4, 9).

Do not be swayed from the truth of the Bible. Do not let a preacher, teacher, family member, or friend convince you that God or His Word has changed. Stand firm! Live to please the LORD rather than men.

Pray 2 Peter 2:9a over yourself and those for whom you stand guard as a faithful, prayerful watchman (Isaiah 62:6-7).

"LORD, You know how to rescue the Godly from temptation.
Rescue _____ and me, today.
For Your sake, Jesus~"

Please read 2 Peter 3.

Meditate on verse 2.

> *You should remember the Words spoken beforehand by the holy*
> *prophets and the commandment of the LORD and Savior*
> *spoken by your apostles.*

People forget the world was created by the Word of God. People forget the world was destroyed by water. People forget what God spoke about a future judgment. People forget the Word of God; they make fun of the Word of God, and they distort the Word of God to their own destruction.

Peter knew people had a tendency to forget, so he wanted to stir up the minds of his readers by way of reminder. When God had Peter pen these words, He knew you would be reading them today and your mind would be stirred. Take God's Word to heart, and do not be disheartened by the mockers and false teachers of your day. Their destruction is coming; therefore, what sort of person ought you to be in holy conduct and Godliness (2 Peter 3:11)?

Pray 2 Peter 3:14 and 17-18 over yourself and those for whom you stand guard as a faithful, prayerful watchman (Isaiah 62:6-7).

> *"LORD, make _____ and me diligent*
> *to be found by You in peace, spotless and blameless.*
> *Help us to be on our guard not to be carried away*
> *by the error of unprincipled men.*
> *Do not let us fall away from our steadfastness.*
> *Let us grow in the grace and knowledge of You,*
> *our LORD and Savior Jesus Christ.*
> *To You, Jesus, be the glory, both now and to*
> *the day of eternity. Amen~"*

Please read 1 John 1.

Meditate on verse 5b.

God is Light, and in Him is no darkness at all.

John knew Jesus. He had seen, touched, and heard Him. John wrote these truths, so his joy would be made complete. John fellowshipped with the Word of Life; He wanted fellowship with other followers of Jesus. These followers must know the truth of Christ; otherwise, they walked in darkness, and John could not fellowship with someone walking in darkness.

John's letter teaches you doctrines of God, truths about who God is and who you in Christ. If you say you have fellowship with Jesus Christ, yet you walk in darkness, you are lying about fellowshipping with Jesus. It is impossible to be living in darkness and Light at the same time.

Examine yourself. What are you living in? Do you live and practice the truth of the Word of God, or do you live and practice the darkness of Satan and the world? And be careful, the world will call dark, demonic things good and appropriate; however, if God's Word calls it sin; that is what it is, and you need the blood of Jesus to cleanse you from all of it (1 John 1:7).

Pray 1 John 1:7 and 9 over yourself and those for whom you stand guard as a faithful, prayerful watchman (Isaiah 62:6-7).

"LORD, please help _____ and me to walk in the Light
as You are in the Light. Let us fellowship with people of Light.
Jesus, let Your blood cleanse us from all sin. May we always
confess our sins. Thank You, Father, for being faithful
and righteous to forgive us our sins and cleanse
us from all unrighteousness.
Because of Your name, Jesus~"

Please read 1 John 2.

Meditate on verse 6.

The one who says he abides in Him
ought himself to walk in the same manner as He walked.

Jesus Christ the Righteous advocates on your behalf with the Father because He is your appeasement for sins. Your sins offend God. It is incredible that Jesus Christ, God's perfectly righteous Son would become your sin, so you could become His righteousness (2 Corinthians 5:21). After dying, Jesus Christ the Righteous now always lives for your sake to advocate on your behalf, constantly reminding God the Father that you can be in His presence because you belong to Him (Hebrews 7:25).

Since Jesus does all this for you, obey Him. If you say you know Jesus, yet you refuse to obey Him, then you are a liar (1 John 2:4). Jesus even asked, "Why do you call Me, 'LORD, LORD,' and do not do what I say?" (Luke 6:46). Obedience is proof of your salvation.

John knew that he knew Jesus. God had John write this letter so you can know that you know Jesus.

Pray 1 John 2:3, 5-6, 15, and 28-29 over yourself and those for whom you stand guard as a faithful, prayerful watchman (Isaiah 62:6-7).

"LORD, help _____ and me to keep Your commandments.
As we keep Your Word, let Your love be truly perfected in us.
As we abide in You, help us to walk in the same manner as
You walked. Help us to not love the world or the things in
the world. Father, we want Your love in us. Let us abide in You,
so we will not shrink in shame at Your coming.
Jesus, You are righteous. May we practice righteousness because
we are born of You.
For Your name's sake~"

Please read 1 John 3.

Meditate on verse 7.

> *Little children, make sure no one deceives you;*
> *the one who practices righteousness is*
> *righteous, just as He is righteous.*

There is an old saying, "Practice makes perfect." That saying is false. Practice makes permanent. Practicing perfectly makes perfect.

What are you making permanent in your life? John said that what people practice depends on to whom they belong. Children of the devil practice sin, and children of God practice righteousness. If you call yourself a child of God, what are your habits of life; what are you making permanent? Do you make sin permanent in your life, or do you make righteousness permanent?

The Son of God appeared to destroy the works of the devil (1 John 3:8). See to it that you are not practicing things Christ came to destroy.

If you abide in Christ, these things will be evident:

- You will be purifying yourself just as Jesus is pure (1 John 3:3).
- You will not be practicing sin (1 John 3:4-6).
- You will practice righteousness, just as Jesus is righteous (1 John 3:7).

Pray 1 John 3:3 and 7 over yourself and those for whom you stand guard as a faithful, prayerful watchman (Isaiah 62:6-7).

> *"LORD, purify _____ and me just as You are pure.*
> *Help us practice righteousness just as You are righteous.*
> *In Your name, Jesus~"*

Please read 1 John 4.

Meditate on verse 4.

> *You are from God, little children, and have overcome them;*
> *because greater is He who is in you than he who is in the world.*

If you are from God, then whom have you overcome? Who is God greater than? 1 John 4:1-3 says there are spirits of false prophets and the spirit of the antichrist in the world. If you are a child of God, you have overcome those spirits because the Holy Spirit in you is greater than the spirit of the antichrist. Knowing these doctrines strengthens your faith in Christ.

John also wrote about the spirit of truth and the spirit of error (1 John 4:6). If you are talking to someone who knows God, they will listen to you; if they are not from God, they will not listen to you. Do not be surprised when the world ignores the truth you want to tell them. Do not fear the spirit of error or the spirits of false prophets. They cannot harm you if you are in Christ because He is greater than any other spirit. Test the spirits to see whether they are from God and stand firm in God's love and truth.

As a faithful, prayerful watchman (Isaiah 62:6-7), pray 1 John 4:6, 13, 15, and 17 over someone who needs the love of Christ.

> *"LORD, please let _____ listen to the spirit of truth,*
> *so they can receive Your Spirit.*
> *May they confess You, Jesus, as the Son of God,*
> *so You will abide in them and they in You.*
> *Let Your love be perfected in them,*
> *so they may have confidence in the day of judgment.*
> *In Your name, Jesus~"*

Please read 1 John 5.

Meditate on verse 19.

We know that we are of God,
and that the whole world lies in the power of the evil one.

John wrote many truths in his letter for building your faith. You need these truths because your faith in God is what overcomes the world (1 John 5:4).

These truths also comfort you as you live in a world where people call good "evil" and evil "good." It helps to know that such insanity is not a surprise to God. The words penned by John 2,000 years ago, describe the world today.

Take heart. Through John God wrote to "you who believe in the name of the Son of God, so that you may know that you have eternal life" (1 John 5:13). Remain strong because "the Word of God abides in you, and you have overcome the evil one" (1 John 2:14). Do not doubt what you know about God because God has given you understanding to know Him who is true. If you are in Jesus Christ then you are in Him who is true. Jesus is the true God and eternal life (1 John 5:20).

These are doctrines to build your life on. Take a moment to reread the letter of 1 John. It is a letter written to you. Ask God to show you the truths you need for your life today.

Pray 1 John 5:18 over yourself and those for whom you stand guard as a faithful, prayerful watchman (Isaiah 62:6-7).

"LORD, as those born of You,
let _____ and me not keep on sinning.
God, keep us in You.
Do not let the evil one touch us.
For the sake of Your promises, Jesus~"

Please read 2 John.

Meditate on verse 9.

> *Anyone who goes too far and does not*
> *abide in the teaching of Christ,*
> *does not have God; the one who abides in the teaching,*
> *he has both the Father and the Son.*

John wrote a second letter for the sake of the truth. He loved the children of God and wanted to be sure they were walking in the truth. John commanded his readers not to greet or receive into their homes people who did not abide in the teaching of Christ (2 John 1:9-10). Greeting or joyfully receiving a deceiver is participating in his evil deeds (2 John 1:11).

God wants you to take this letter seriously. Who and what do you receive into your home? Think about the friends, movies, shows, music, internet sites, entertainers, magazines, and books that are in your home. How do they compare to the truth of God? God says do not greet or receive into your house anyone or anything contradictory to the teaching of Christ. Remember you are the temple of God and the Spirit of God dwells in you (1 Corinthians 3:16). Do not allow deception into your mind or the minds of those God has placed in your care. You are commanded by the Father to walk in truth (2 John 1:4).

Pray 2 John 1:4 and 8 over those for whom you stand guard as a faithful, prayerful watchman (Isaiah 62:6-7).

> *"LORD, let me find _____ walking in Your truth.*
> *Father, help them obey Your commandment to do so.*
> *May they watch themselves*
> *not to lose what You have accomplished in them.*
> *Let them receive Your full reward.*
> *For the sake of Your Kingdom, Jesus~"*

Please read 3 John.

Meditate on verse 4.

I have no greater joy than this,
to hear of my children walking in the truth.

In all three of John's letters, *truth* is a key repeated word. He wanted his readers to be walking in *truth*, to be fellow workers with the *truth*, to have a good testimony based on the *truth*.

The world today wages war on truth. A secular pop singer said, "I am telling you a lie in a vicious effort to get you to repeat my lie until it becomes the truth." With an estimated 125 million singles sold, the lies propagated by this one singer are repeated over and over and over.

John exhorted his readers, "Beloved, do not imitate what is evil, but what is good. The one who does good is of God; the one who does evil has not seen God" (3 John 1:11).

John knew his testimony was true because he knew the Word of God (3 John 1:12).

What is your testimony? Is it based on truth or lies? What and who do you imitate? Would God call you evil or good?

Pray 3 John 1:2-4 over those for whom you stand guard as a faithful, prayerful watchman (Isaiah 62:6-7).

"LORD, I pray in all respects that _____
may prosper and be in good
health just as their soul prospers.
Let brethren come and testify
to how they are walking in the truth.
I have no greater joy than this,
to hear of my children walking in the truth.
In Your name, Jesus~"

Please read Jude.

Meditate on verse 3b.

Contend earnestly for the faith
which was once for all handed down to the saints.

Jude, like James, was also a half-brother of Jesus Christ who made no claim to this fact. Like James he referred to himself as a bond-servant of Jesus Christ. A risen Savior turned a skeptical, scoffing brother into a faithful follower (John 7:1-9; Mark 3:20-21).

Jude wrote his letter because people in the church had to be warned. There were mockers in church who followed after their own ungodly lusts. They caused divisions; they were worldly-minded and devoid of the Spirit (Jude 1:18-19). These were people in church, even partaking of the LORD's Supper as if they were believers in Jesus Christ, yet they were doubly dead, uprooted, and the black darkness had been reserved for them forever (Jude 1:12-13).

God included this letter in the Bible as a letter of warning to you. Attending church and taking communion does not make a person a Christian. Examine people's behavior; examine your own behavior.

Pray Jude 1:20-21 and 24-25 over yourself and those for whom you stand guard as a faithful, prayerful watchman (Isaiah 62:6-7).

"LORD, build _____ and me on our most holy faith.
Keep us praying in the Holy Spirit.
Keep us in Your love, God, as we wait anxiously for the mercy
of our LORD Jesus Christ to eternal life.
You are able to keep us from stumbling.
Make us stand in the presence of Your
glory blameless with great joy.
To You, the only God our Savior, through Jesus Christ our LORD,
be glory, majesty, dominion, and authority,
before all time and now and forever. Amen-"

On your walls, O Jerusalem,
I have appointed watchmen;
All day and all night they
will never keep silent.
You who remind the LORD,
take no rest for yourselves;
And give Him no rest
until He establishes
And makes Jerusalem a
praise in the earth.
Isaiah 62:6-7, NASB

Please read Hosea 1.

Meditate on verses 1-2.

> *The word of the LORD which came to Hosea the*
> *son of Beeri, during the days of Uzziah, Jotham,*
> *Ahaz, and Hezekiah, Kings of Judah,*
> *and during the days of Jeroboam the son of Joash, king of Israel.*
> *When the LORD first spoke through*
> *Hosea, the LORD said to Hosea,*
> *"Go, take to yourself a wife of harlotry*
> *and have children of harlotry;*
> *for the land commits flagrant harlotry, forsaking the LORD.*

The book of Hosea divinely reveals God's compassionate nature and love for you. In order to better understand this prophetic writing from 2750 years ago, it is helpful to set the background of the letter in the history of Israel. In 1445 BC, Moses led the children of Israel out of Egypt. In 1405 BC, they entered the promised land of Canaan. The Period of the Judges followed. During this 350-year period, the 12 tribes cooperated together and were led by judges during times of crisis. The tribes united in 1050 BC and formed a monarchy led by Saul, David, and Solomon. Following Solomon's reign, the nation divided. The northern tribes formed the kingdom known as Israel in 922 BC. It is sometimes called Ephraim. The southern kingdom was called Judah.

Hosea established his tenure of ministry by listing the kings of Judah. An Israelite himself, Hosea listed his own king, Jeroboam II. Jeroboam was the great-grandson of King Jehu. God promised King Jehu He would delay His judgment on the idolatrous northern kingdom for four generations. When Jeroboam II died around 750 BC, the judgment on Israel began. God wanted Israel to know He was judging them for their spiritual adultery of idol worship, yet His undying love would always offer them the opportunity to return to Him.

God said in Exodus 20:3-6:

You shall have no other gods before Me. You
shall not make for yourself an idol,
or any likeness of what is in heaven above or on the earth beneath
or in the water under the earth. You shall
not worship them or serve them;
for I, the LORD your God, am a jealous God, visiting the
iniquity of the fathers on the children, on the third and the fourth
generations of those who hate Me, but showing lovingkindness to
thousands, to those who love Me and keep My commandments.

As a faithful, prayerful watchman (Isaiah 62:6-7), pray Hosea 1:2 as a prayer of confession to your LORD.

"Forgive _____ and me when we commit flagrant harlotry,
forsaking You, LORD!
Forgive my country because the land commits flagrant harlotry,
forsaking You, LORD!
May we have no other gods before You.
In Your name, Jesus~"

Please read Hosea 1 again.

Meditate on verses 10.

> *Yet the number of the sons of Israel will be like the sand of the sea,*
> *which cannot be measured or numbered;*
> *and in the place where it was said to*
> *them, "You are not My people,"*
> *it will be said to them, "You are the sons of the living God."*

There can be little doubt that life was not turning out the way Hosea had planned. He must have felt like Moses at the burning bush, "I'm supposed to do what?!" or Peter asking, "Did You really say we can eat this stuff?" (Exodus 3-4; Acts 10).

Hosea was told to do the unspeakable for an upright Jew and prophet of God. God commanded him to marry a prostitute and have children of prostitution as an illustration of Israel's adulterous behavior toward Him. Hosea obeyed; he married a prostitute named Gomer.

As living illustrations, their children were named to reveal God's judgments:

- The firstborn was a son named *Jezreel*. God will destroy Israel in the valley of Jezreel (Hosea 1:4-5).

- The second was a daughter named *Lo-Ruhamah* meaning, "not pitied or no compassion." God will not have compassion on Israel (Hosea 1:6).

- The third child was a son named *Lo-Ammi* meaning, "not My people." God said to Israel, "You are not My people, and I am not your God" (Hosea 1:9).

Because idol worship was rampant in Israel and the worship of the true God was corrupted or non-existent, God was going to have no pity and totally destroy Israel. Yet verse 10 begins the theme of the remnant. The remnant was a group of people who survived the judgment by God's divine will and reformed with His blessings. Believers in Christ understand what it means to be saved from a judgment of death to life as "sons of the living God" (Hosea 1:10).

Pray Hosea 1:10-11b over Israel and those for whom you stand guard as faithful, prayerful watchman (Isaiah 62:6-7).

"LORD thank You that the number of the sons of Israel
will be like the sand of the sea, which
cannot be measured or numbered.
And in the place where it was said to
them, "You are not My people,
It will be said to them, "You are the sons of the living God."
Thank you that the sons of Judah and the sons
of Israel will be gathered together,
and they will appoint for themselves one leader, Jesus.
Jesus, cause _____ to appoint You as their leader.
LORD, please make them Your sons.
In Your name, Jesus~"

Please read Hosea 2.

Meditate on verses 19-20.

> *"I will betroth you to Me forever.*
> *Yes, I will betroth you to Me in righteousness and in justice,*
> *in lovingkindness and in compassion,*
> *and I will betroth you to Me in faithfulness.*
> *Then you will know the LORD."*

Baal worship came from Phoenicia and was based upon the agricultural seasons and rain cycles. Baal worshippers believed he was the fertility god. He sent rain, made the crops grow, and caused animals and humans to be born. When the rains stopped, his followers believed he had been killed. In order to bring Baal back to life, the followers needed to create enough positive energy for his mistress, Anath, to love him and resuscitate him so he would send rain and bring more fertility.

These beliefs made great business at the local Baal worship centers with many priests and temple prostitutes on staff. In Israel, the locals took worship of Yahweh and made it the worship of Baal. They credited Baal for what God gave them. Notice God's sorrowful response in Hosea 2:13: "I will punish her for the days of the Baals when she used to offer sacrifices to them and adorn herself with her earrings and jewelry, and follow her lovers, so that she forgot Me."

In spite of Israel's adulteries, God shows endless compassion and undying love for her. He allures her and speaks kindly to her. He wants her to call Him *Ishi* which means "my husband." He promises to make the heavens and the earth respond so there is food, wine, and oil. Only God can meet Israel's needs!

God extends that same compassion and love to you. He desires to draw you to Himself. God wants to bring life to you. No other person, job, status, or measure of security can take care of you. He wants to eternally provide for you as His bride. No one else can be God but God.

Pray Isaiah 2:19-20 and 23 over yourself and those for whom you stand guard as a faithful, prayerful watchman (Isaiah 62:6-7).

"LORD let _____ and me be betrothed to You forever.
Betroth us in righteousness and in justice,
in lovingkindness and in compassion.
Betroth us to You in faithfulness.
Then we will know You, LORD.
Sow us for Yourself in the land.
Have compassion on _____ who has not obtained compassion.
Say to those who were not Your people,
'You are My people!'
For the sake of Your name, Jesus~"

Please read Hosea 3.

Meditate on verses 1 and 5.

> *Then the LORD said to me, "Go again, love a*
> *woman who is loved by her husband,*
> *yet an adulteress, even as the LORD loves the sons of Israel,*
> *though they turn to other gods and love raisin cakes."*
> *Afterward the sons of Israel will return*
> *and seek the LORD their God and David their king;*
> *and they will come trembling to the LORD*
> *and to His goodness in the last days.*

Chapter 3 is a heart wrenching passage of Scripture. Gomer left Hosea to live with her lover. Her lover failed her, and she became a slave.

God told Hosea to go again and love her. She was unfaithful and brought destruction on herself, but Hosea was to love her again. Hosea bought her for the minimum price to redeem a human, 30 pieces of silver. He only had 15 pieces, so he used barley to make up the other 15 pieces of silver.

Judas sold Jesus for 30 pieces of silver (Matthew 26:14-15). Can you imagine the audacity of this transaction compared to Gomer. Jesus is the Author of freedom, the Creator of the world, and the Redeemer of all. His life was so valuable it could buy spiritual freedom for everyone. Judas did not sell Jesus for 30 pieces of silver; he sold himself out for 30 pieces of silver.

Hosea was not Jesus. He could not offer himself to redeem the world. Yet he sacrificed greatly to redeem his wife. He not only spent all he had to pay for the lowest level of slave, but he risked sacrificing his heart to love her again. Are you willing to love again in a holy, Godly way someone you have stopped loving?

Gomer, like Israel, had to purge what she thought gave her life. Gomer was chaste from sexuality, even with Hosea, until she realized what true love and Godliness were.

Israel has lost their precious kings, worship sites, and idols. But they will return to God and His goodness. They will honor the lineage of King David. That lineage is now complete. The King's name is Jesus. Someday, Israel will return to Him, their Creator, Savior, and King.

Pray Hosea 3:1 and 5 over yourself and those for whom you stand guard as a faithful, prayerful watchman (Isaiah 62:6-7).

"LORD let _____ and me go again and love.
Let us love as You love Israel.
Help _____ to return and seek You,
LORD, as their God and their King.
Let them come trembling back to You and
Your goodness in these last days.
In Your name, Jesus~"

Please read Hosea 4.

Meditate on verses 1 and 6a.

> *Listen to the word of the LORD, O sons of Israel,*
> *for the LORD has a case against the inhabitants of the land,*
> *because there is not faithfulness or kindness*
> *or knowledge of God in the land.*
> *My people are destroyed for lack of knowledge.*

What is the spiritual and moral state of your country? Does Hosea 4:1b-2 describe your nation?

> *There is no faithfulness or kindness or*
> *knowledge of God in the land.*
> *There is swearing, deception, murder, stealing, and adultery.*
> *They employ violence, so that bloodshed follows bloodshed.*

God said the people stumbled and were being destroyed because they did not have a relationship with Him. They lacked the knowledge to know how to have a personal relationship with the LORD. God blamed the priests. The corrupted priesthood did not teach the people about God and how to know Him.

Think about the role of the ministers in your life. Do they help others have a relationship with God? What about those God has called you to minister to? Do you teach them how to have a personal relationship with the LORD?

When people lack knowledge of God, they become like the Israelites. Instead of walking with God, people talk to their wooden idols and their diviners' wands to figure out what to do. It is a ridiculous picture, yet many choose the absurd. God wants people to know they can talk to Him, their Maker, the LORD God Almighty, who died for them so they can have an intimate relationship with Him. God never intended for people to talk to a piece of wood that should have been burned as firewood.

Pray Hosea 4:1 and 6a over yourself and those for whom you stand guard as a faithful, prayerful watchman (Isaiah 62:6-7).

"LORD, help _____ and me listen to Your Word,
for You have a case against the inhabitants of the land.
Make us faithful, kind, and knowledgeable of You.
Spread these traits throughout the land.
Help _____ not be destroyed for lack of knowledge;
let them stop rejecting the knowledge of You.
In Your name, Jesus~"

Please read Hosea 5.

Meditate on verses 1a, 11, and 15.

> *Hear this, O priests!*
> *Give heed, O house of Israel!*
> *Listen, O house of the king!*
> *For the judgment applies to you.*
> *Ephraim is oppressed, crushed in judgment,*
> *because he was determined to follow man's command.*
> *I will go away and return to My place*
> *until they acknowledge their guilt and seek My face.*
> *In their affliction they will earnestly seek Me.*

Have you ever been at a Bible study or heard a sermon which you knew God was aiming the application at you? God opened Hosea 5 with a broad list of people as His sermon targets. All of the people who had the ability to shape a different outcome for those under their influence were included in His sermon focus.

The people of Israel were so deep into sin they did not know how to return to the LORD. They were so far into their spiritual harlotry they did not know right from wrong. They did not know the LORD or how to worship Him.

The people were in a crushed and oppressed state. They had determined to hear the voice of men rather than God, so God said He would send the people away. In their exile, they would realize their ways, repent, and seek God's face. In affliction they would recognize their need for God and turn to Him.

What about your life? Is God trying to get your attention to recognize your need for Him? What a great privilege to have a God who loves you and desires for you to seek His face and listen to His voice!

Pray Hosea 5:1, 11, and 15 over yourself and those for whom you stand guard as a faithful, prayerful watchman (Isaiah 62:6-7).

"LORD, let _____ and me hear, give heed, and listen to You,
for the judgment applies to us!
We are oppressed and crushed in judgment
because we have been determined to follow
man's command instead of Yours.
LORD, we acknowledge our guilt and seek Your face!
We earnestly seek You!
In Your name, Jesus~"

OCTOBER 7

Please read Hosea 6.
Meditate on verses 2b-3.

He will raise us up on the third day, that we may live before Him.
So let us know, let us press on to know the LORD.
His going forth is as certain as the dawn;
and He will come to us like the rain,
like the spring rain watering the earth.

The Old Testament is wonderful! It is so full of the LORD. It is God's testimony of His love, righteousness, and provision for salvation. God's love and forgiveness bookend this chapter, despite the sinfulness of the people found in the middle.

Hosea's description of Israel's unfaithfulness sounds similar to the world today.

- The people were not loyal to God. They did not have knowledge of Him (Hosea 6:6).

- The people dealt treacherously with God. Their city was filled with wrongdoers and tracked with bloody footprints (Hosea 6:8).

- The priests were like raiders. They were a murderous band attacking people going to worship (Hosea 6:9).

- Harlotry and idol worship was found throughout the land. The people had defiled themselves (Hosea 6:10).

Yet, God still had a harvest planned for His people. He would restore their fortunes (Hosea 6:11).

Pray Hosea 6:1-2 over yourself and those for whom you stand guard as a faithful, prayerful watchman (Isaiah 62:6-7).

"LORD, let _____ and me return to You.
You have torn us, but You will heal us.
You have wounded us, but You will bandage us.
Revive us, LORD!
You rose on the third day; we want to live before You.
We want to press on to know You, LORD.
Your going forth is as certain as the dawn.
Come to us like the rain, like the spring rain watering the earth.
For the sake of Your name, Jesus~"

Please read Hosea 7.

Meditate on verses 13-16a.

> *Woe to them, for they have strayed from Me!*
> *Destruction is theirs, for they have rebelled against Me!*
> *I would redeem them, but they speak lies against Me.*
> *And they do not cry to Me from their heart*
> *when they wail on their beds.*
> *For the sake of grain and new wine, they assemble themselves;*
> *they turn away from Me.*
> *Although I trained and strengthened their arms,*
> *yet they devise evil against Me.*
> *They turn, but not upward.*

Instead of trusting God, Israel made alliances. They foolishly sought refuge with nations who wanted to destroy them.

In their sinful behavior, they were reminded that God was watching them. He remembered all their wickedness and would hold them accountable for their behavior. He described Israel as an oven that consumed themselves and their rulers.

The people, unaware of their own destruction, did not turn to God; they turned away from Him. They refused to turn and look up to God. Their behavior was like that of a three-year-old who refuses to look at the camera because that would be the right thing to do.

Their sin was so deep it could be argued that they did not know right from wrong. They strayed from God, rebelled against God, and lied about Him.

You may have someone in your life with this kind of attitude toward God. They are prideful and rebellious. You have some great verses to pray over them to God who is trustworthy! He is wiser and more powerful than they are, and He wants to change their lives!

Pray Hosea 7:13-16a over those for whom you stand guard as a faithful, prayerful watchman (Isaiah 62:6-7).

LORD, _____ has strayed from You!
Destruction is theirs, for they have rebelled against You!
Please redeem them even though they speak lies against You.
Help them to cry out to You from their heart
when they wail on their beds.
Help them not to live for the sake of grain and new wine.
Don't let them assemble themselves with
those who turn away from You.
You have trained and strengthened their arms;
let them not devise evil against You.
Help them to turn upward to You."
In Your name, Jesus~"

Please read Hosea 8.

Meditate on verses 6-7a and 12.

For from Israel is even this! A craftsman made it, so it is not God.
Surely the calf of Samaria will be broken to pieces.
For they sow the wind, and they reap the whirlwind.
Though I wrote for him ten thousand precepts of My Law,
they are regarded as a strange thing.

It is interesting what happens to people when they abandon truth for thoughts and ways that are not true. They work with great effort to justify and validate belief systems that do not make sense at all. Idolatry is so obviously silly. If one makes something from wood, silver, or marble and claims it is God, then how does the crafted item become the creator of the craftsman? The Israelites created idols and sowed for themselves a harvest of disaster.

God abhorred idol worship because He knew humans would rather trust what they could see and touch than trust Him. Idolatry caused the people to stop worshipping the LORD in spirit and in truth (John 4:24).

This was certainly the case with Baal worship. The sacrifices were offered locally (no long road trip to Jerusalem), temple prostitution was a part of the celebration, and stone pillars and groves of trees contained the gods of their worship. Worship made easy!

In their idol worship, Israel lost track of God's Law and subsequently God Himself. God's precepts were strange to the Israelites. They wondered why their offerings were not accepted. They forgot their Maker and His Law.

It is important for you and those you love to learn to maneuver and operate in the spiritual realm of the Father, Son, and Holy Spirit.

Pray for your loved ones to develop a strong spiritual life. Continue to invest your life in the Word of God and prayer!

Pray Hosea 8:7a and 12 over yourself and those for whom you stand guard as a faithful, prayerful watchman (Isaiah 62:6-7).

> *"LORD, let _____ and me not sow the*
> *wind and reap the whirlwind.*
> *Thank You that You wrote and gave us ten*
> *thousand precepts of Your Word.*
> *Let them never be regarded as a strange thing in our lives.*
> *In Your name, Jesus~"*

Please read Hosea 9.

Meditate on verse 8.

> *"Ephraim was a watchman with my God, a prophet;*
> *yet the snare of a bird catcher is in all his ways,*
> *and there is only hostility in the house of his God."*

It does not matter how long the race is that God has called you to run, you must run it faithfully. A trained runner will be exhausted at the end of whatever race they run. Whether 100 meters or 26.2 miles, a good runner will give all they have and finish exhausted.

You do not know when you will die, but you are called to run faithfully to the end the course God has planned for you. God doesn't leave you to run the race alone. His Spirit is your pacesetter. Yoked to Christ, He is with you every step of the way preparing you for every adventure (Matthew 11:29-30).

Ephraim failed to stay close to God. They failed to stay as faithful watchmen and prophets of the LORD. The reason was simple; distractions from their holy duties resulted in hostilities in the house of God. They stopped listening to their Pacesetter, and they ensnared themselves in sin. God stripped them of their holy duty as prophets and watchmen; therefore, their nation, tribes, cities, and families lost the watchmen's voices of holiness to help them live as God's children. In the end they perished worshipping rocks and trees.

Pray Hosea 9:8 over yourself and those for whom you stand guard as faithful, prayerful watchman (Isaiah 62:6-7).

> *"LORD, make _____ and me watchmen with You, God.*
> *Make us faithful prophets.*
> *Prevent the snare of the bird catcher in all of our ways.*
> *Let not hostility enter into Your house, God.*
> *In Your name, Jesus~"*

Please read Hosea 10.

Meditate on verses 12.

Sow with a view to righteousness;
reap in accordance with kindness;
break up your fallow ground,
for it is time to seek the LORD
until He comes to rain righteousness on you.

Baal worship was taking its toll on the people. They had been prosperous, but they had not used their wealth to glorify God. Instead, they used it to produce more idol worship. God would destroy them and their worship; they would realize how foolish it was to trust in Baal.

In the middle of a chapter of warnings and judgments is the message of hope. "Break up your fallow ground, for it is time to seek the LORD..." (Hosea 10:12).

Fallow ground is land that is normally used for crops but has been left unplowed and unplanted. Breaking up the fallow ground means to plow the land, turn the soil, and remove the weeds. It means to prepare the land for planting. In Jeremiah 4:3, God told the people of Judah to break up the fallow ground and not rush to plant seeds among the thistles.

What a great message! Are there unused parts of your life that are fallow grounds, areas where God can change you and bear fruit through you? Are you practicing your spiritual gifts among the believers at a local church? Is there more of your money that God can use to further the Kingdom? Are there parts of your heart and mind that used to belong to the LORD, but have been given over to the thistles—the sins of this world? Break the fallow ground; ask God to help you change your life to be fruitful for His pleasure, His Kingdom's work, and His relationship with you.

Pray Hosea 10:12 over yourself and those for whom you stand guard as a faithful, prayerful watchman (Isaiah 62:6-7).

"LORD, help _____ and me to sow
with a view to Your righteousness.
Let us reap in accordance with Your kindness.
Break up our fallow ground! Help us to seek You, LORD!
Come and rain righteousness on us.
For the sake of Your name, Jesus~"

OCTOBER 12

Please read Hosea 11.

Meditate on verses 1 and 10-11.

> *"When Israel was a youth I loved him, and*
> *out of Egypt I called My son.*
> *They will walk after the LORD.*
> *He will roar like a lion;*
> *indeed He will roar, and His sons will*
> *come trembling from the west.*
> *They will come trembling like birds from Egypt*
> *and like doves from the land of Assyria;*
> *and I will settle them in their houses," declares the LORD.*

Chapter 11 is a very tender passage that gives you insight into the pain God was going through judging Israel, also called Ephraim.

- In verse 1, God revealed that He loved Israel when Israel was a youth in Egypt.

- In verse 3, God taught Israel to walk. He carried them in His arms and was their healer.

- In verse 4, God led Israel with bonds of love. He lifted the yoke from their mouth and bent down to feed them.

- In verses 8-9, God spoke with great sadness and passion:

> *How can I give you up, O Ephraim?*
> *How can I surrender you, O Israel?*
> *My heart is turned over within me.*
> *All my compassions are kindled.*
> *I will not execute My fierce anger.*
> *I will not destroy Ephraim again.*

Despite the sins of Israel and Judah, the Holy One is faithful (Hosea 11:12). Despite your unfaithfulness, God is faithful! He is faithful to forgive you of all unrighteousness and to finish the work He started in you. God is faithful!

Pray Hosea 11:1 and 3 over those for whom you stand guard as a faithful, prayerful watchman (Isaiah 62:6-7).

"LORD, you have loved _____ from their youth.
Call them out their slavery to sin.
Teach them how to walk with You.
Take them in Your arms.
Please heal them, LORD.
Because You are faithful, Holy One~"

Please read Hosea 12.

Meditate on verses 4b-6 and 11.

He found Him at Bethel, and there He spoke with us,
even the LORD, the God of hosts, the LORD is His name.
Therefore, return to your God, observe kindness and justice,
and wait for your God continually.

Is there iniquity in Gilead? Surely they are worthless.
In Gilgal they sacrifice bulls.
Yes, their altars are like stone heaps beside the furrows of the field.

Israel's relationship with God was broken. This brokenness resulted in their inability to perceive wrongdoing:

1. Israel made relationships with foreign countries for security rather than trusting in God for their salvation (Hosea 12:1).

2. Israel assumed that since they were a rich country, they had no sin (Hosea 12:8).

3. In Gilgal, holy sacrifices were being offered, not in the temple on an altar by legitimate priests. Their altars at Gilgal would become like worthless piles of stones near a field (Hosea 12:11).

The LORD called for Israel to:

1. Return to Him.

2. Behave like Him, in kindness and justice.

3. Wait for Him to deliver them (Hosea 12:6).

These verses capture how to be a follower of "the LORD, the God of Hosts, the LORD is His name" (Hosea 12:5). Orient your life to God, emulate His nature, and trust Him.

Pray Hosea 12:4-6 over yourself and those for whom you stand guard as a faithful, prayerful watchman (Isaiah 62:6-7).

"LORD, the God of hosts, _____ and I
are weeping seeking Your favor.
Find us and speak to us.
We return to You, God.
Help us to observe kindness and justice.
We wait continually for You.
In Your name, LORD~"

Please read Hosea 13.

Meditate on verses 14.

> *Shall I ransom them from the power of Sheol?*
> *Shall I redeem them from death?*
> *O Death, where are your thorns?*
> *O Sheol, where is your sting?*
> *Compassion will be hidden from My sight.*

Because the LORD is so loving and gracious, it is often hard to see Him imposing justice. As a New Testament believer, you function in a Kingdom marked by merciful and graceful forgiveness from God and a resulting relationship with Him. That relationship is the result of satisfied justice. The execution of Jesus on the altar of the cross became the sacrifice needed to justify believers before God.

Judgment is coming for those who are not in Christ. Their situation is dire. Their future is tied to a certain end—unless—unless—unless they turn from their sin and give their lives to Jesus as their Savior and LORD. If you do not know Jesus as your Savior and you would like to, then find a Christian who can help you. If you do not have anyone in your life to help, write to us at GodsGreaterGrace.com, and we will help you.

Paul quoted part of Hosea 13:14 in I Corinthians 15:55: "O Death, where is your victory? O Death where is your sting?" He was celebrating that the power of the Law and death are removed in Christ Jesus. This is the goal of your prayers, believers. Pray for God's victory in the life of those you love who do not know Jesus as their Savior.

Pray Hosea 13:14 over those for whom you stand guard as a faithful, prayerful watchman (Isaiah 62:6-7).

LORD, please ransom _____ from the power of Sheol.
Redeem them from death.
Help them to know You,
so they will not know the thorns of death and the sting of Sheol.
May they have compassion in Your sight.
In Your name, Jesus-"

Please read Hosea 14.

Meditate on verse 1-2a.

> *Return, O Israel, to the LORD your God,*
> *for you stumbled because of your iniquity.*
> *Take words with you and return to the LORD.*
> *Say to Him, "Take away all iniquity and receive us graciously."*

God concluded His message to Israel by inviting her to return to Him. He declared at the beginning of His message that Israel was no longer His people, yet in His unending mercy, God relented and invited Israel to come back to Him (Hosea 1:9; 14:1).

His invitation came with a condition. He would allow her to return if she asked Him to take away all her iniquity. God did not tell Israel to take away her own sin; only He could remove it; all she had to do was ask.

Israel would come to realize that Assyria could not save her, and her idols could not save her. Only the LORD her God could save her. Not only would He save her, but He would turn His anger away from her, heal her, and love her (Hosea 14:3-4).

God extends the same invitation to you. He invites you to return to Him.

Pray Hosea 14:2a and 9 over yourself and those for whom you stand guard as a faithful, prayerful watchman (Isaiah 62:6-7).

> *"I take Your Words with me, and I return to You, LORD.*
> *Take away all of my iniquity and receive me graciously.*
> *LORD, make _____and me wise to understand these things.*
> *Make us discerning, so we can know them.*
> *LORD, Your ways are right;*
> *make us righteous, so we will walk in them.*
> *Do not let us be transgressors who stumble in Your ways.*
> *Because of Your name, Jesus~"*

Please read Psalm 1.

Meditate on verse 6.

> *For the LORD knows the way of the righteous,*
> *but the way of the wicked will perish.*

An amazing aspect of being in relationship with Jesus Christ is the intimacy that the Creator of the universe not only allows you to have with Him; intimacy is what He desires you to have with Him. When God talks about knowing you and you knowing Him, He uses the Hebrew and Greek words that are used for intimacy between a husband and wife. If Jesus is your life (Colossians 3:4), He intimately knows your way, the journey you are on, everything about you. Take comfort and joy in knowing these truths as you walk with Him, today.

Pray Psalm 1:1-3 over yourself and those for whom you stand guard as a faithful, prayerful watchman (Isaiah 62:6-7).

> *"LORD, do not let _____ and me*
> *walk in the counsel of the wicked,*
> *nor stand in the path of sinners,*
> *nor sit in the seat of scoffers,*
> *but let our delight be in Your Law,*
> *and let us meditate on it day and night.*
> *Let us be like a tree firmly planted by streams of water*
> *which yields its fruit in its season and its leaf does not wither.*
> *In whatever we do, let us prosper.*
> *In Your name, Jesus~"*

Please read Psalm 16.

Meditate on verse 8.

> *I have set the LORD continually before me;*
> *because He is at my right hand, I will not be shaken.*

Life can be hard. It is easy to be shaken by circumstances, struggles, and trials and lose sight of God who is sovereign. He is the only One who has supreme power and authority.

Refocus! Fix your eyes on Jesus (Hebrews 12:2). Turn your eyes away from other things and place them definitely and permanently on Christ.

Pray Psalm 16:1-2 and 5-11 over yourself and those for whom you stand guard as a faithful, prayerful watchman (Isaiah 62:6-7).

> *"Preserve _____ and me, O God.*
> *Let us take refuge in You. LORD, You are our Lord;*
> *we have no good besides You.*
> *You are the portion of our inheritance and our cup;*
> *You support our lot. Let the lines fall to us in pleasant places.*
> *Let our heritage be beautiful. I bless You, LORD.*
> *Please counsel _____ and me. Instruct our minds in the night.*
> *Let us set You continually before us; because you are at our*
> *right hand, do not allow us to be shaken.*
> *May our hearts be glad and our glory rejoice.*
> *Let our flesh also dwell securely,*
> *for You will not abandon our souls to Sheol.*
> *Make known to us the path of life.*
> *In Your presence is fullness of joy;*
> *in Your right hand there are pleasures forever.*
> *In Your name, Jesus~"*

OCTOBER 18

Please read Psalm 19.

Meditate on verse 14.

> *Let the words of my mouth*
> *and the meditation of my heart*
> *be acceptable in Your sight, O LORD,*
> *my Rock and my Redeemer.*

Do you ever regret something you said? I'm grieved when I leave a gathering of people or a conversation with my husband wishing I had not spoken certain things. I have learned the hard way to whisper this verse in prayer before interacting with others:

> *Set a guard, O LORD, over my mouth;*
> *keep watch over the door of my lips.*
> *Psalm 141:3*

Psalm 19:1-2 says the heavens are telling about the glory of God; they pour forth speech that declares the work of His hands. If a star is constantly talking about the LORD, how much more should the mouth of a person who has been saved by the Creator of the universe?

As you walk with Jesus, pray Psalm 19:13-14 over yourself and those for whom you stand guard as a faithful, prayerful watchman (Isaiah 62:6-7).

> *"LORD, keep _____ and me from presumptuous sins;*
> *let them not rule over us.*
> *Make us blameless and acquitted of great transgression.*
> *Let the words of our mouths*
> *and the meditation of our hearts*
> *be acceptable in Your sight, O LORD,*
> *our Rock and our Redeemer,*
> *Jesus Christ, in whose name I pray ~"*

OCTOBER 19

Please read Psalm 25.

Meditate on verse 14a.

The secret of the LORD is for those who fear Him.

The LORD confides in and reveals His secrets to those who fear Him. The Hebrew word for *secret* literally means intimacy, a couch, a cushion, a friendly conversation among friends. It is delightfully amazing that your God desires to couch with you and tell you His secrets.

If you are in relationship with God through Jesus Christ, you have the privilege of intimacy with Him. Incredible! Don't ever take it for granted and always take advantage of it.

Pray Psalm 25:7-15 over yourself and those for whom you stand guard as a faithful, prayerful watchman (Isaiah 62:6-7).

"LORD, do not remember the sins
of _____ and my youth or our transgressions;
according to Your lovingkindness, remember us.
You are good and upright, LORD; therefore, instruct
us in the way. Help us be humble, so You can lead us
in justice and teach us Your way. As we keep
Your covenant and testimonies, keep us on Your paths
of lovingkindness and truth. For Your name's sake, LORD,
pardon our iniquity, for it is great. Let us always fear
You, so You will instruct us in the way we should choose.
May our souls abide in prosperity and our descendants inherit
the land. LORD, as we fear You, reveal Your secrets to us
and make us know Your covenant. Keep our eyes continually
toward You and pluck our feet out of the net.
In Your name, Jesus~"

Please read Psalm 31.

Meditate on verse 16.

> *Make Your face to shine upon your servant;*
> *save me in Your lovingkindness.*

This is a beautiful prayer psalm. David acknowledged who God is: righteous, rock of strength, stronghold, fortress, his strength ... (Psalm 31:1-4). Then, David humbly yet unashamedly made requests of God because of who God is. "For Your name's sake You will lead me and guide me" (Psalm 31:3).

If you are born again into Christ Jesus, then you are a child of God, and you, like David, can come to the Father. Instead of simply reading Psalm 31, pray it now, humbly and unashamedly remembering who you are in Christ.

Pray Psalm 31:16 over yourself and those for whom you stand guard as a faithful, prayerful watchman (Isaiah 62:6-7).

> *"LORD, make Your face to shine upon _____ and me.*
> *Save us in Your lovingkindness.*
> *For the sake of Your name, Jesus~"*

October 21

Please read Psalm 34.

Meditate on verse 8.

O taste and see that the LORD is good;
how blessed is the man who takes refuge in Him!

As you walk this day with Christ, be intimately aware of everything He is doing in your midst. Notice the timing of events, conversations that are had, flowers that are blooming, provisions that are made... Take notice of the LORD like you would notice your favorite food prepared especially for you. And as you taste and see that He is good, say like David did, "LORD, You are intimately acquainted with all my ways" (Psalm 139:3).

Pray Psalm 34:1-2 and 13-14 over yourself and those for whom you stand guard as a faithful, prayerful watchman (Isaiah 62:6-7).

"LORD, I will bless You at all times;
Your praise shall continually be in my mouth.
My soul will make its boast in You, LORD;
the humble will hear it and rejoice.
Help ____ and me keep our tongue from evil
and our lips from speaking deceit.
Let us depart from evil and do good;
let us seek peace and pursue it.
In Your name, Jesus-"

Please read Psalm 37.

Meditate on verse 4.

Delight yourself in the LORD,
and He will give you the desire of your heart.

A mother shared about her baby who would light up with joy anytime she or her husband came into the child's presence. As soon as the baby's mama or daddy was in the room, the baby would no longer look at toys but would only have eyes for his parents. He delighted being in the presence of his parents.

Do you delight being in the presence of God? Do you stop whatever you are doing to spend time with Him? Do your eyes light up with joy as you notice Him in His Word and through His creation around you?

As you delight yourself in the LORD, as you enjoy Him, your heart's desires will become His desires. God will give you the desires of your heart because you will desire to do and be what pleases Him. Then as you commit your way to the LORD, He will establish your steps and delight in your way (Psalm 37:5, 23).

Pray Psalm 37:4-6 and 23 over yourself and those for whom you stand guard as a faithful, prayerful watchman (Isaiah 62:6-7).

"LORD, as _____ and I delight in You,
please give us the desires of our hearts.
We commit our way to You;
we also trust You, and know You will do it.
Bring forth our righteousness as the light
and our judgment as the noonday.
LORD, establish our steps and delight in our way.
In Your name, Jesus~"

Please read Psalm 39.

Meditate on verse 1a.

I said, "I will guard my ways
that I may not sin with my tongue."

Notice how David handled a situation where he wanted to say something so badly, but he knew if he spoke from a heart that was hot within him, he would be sinning. When he did speak, he talked to God. He recognized how short life is (is it too short to be this angry?). He asked deliverance from all of his transgressions (being in God's presence makes you aware of how sinful you really are; it's not just those "wicked" people [Psalm 39:1]), and he hoped in God.

Pray Psalm 39:1, 7-8, and 12a over yourself and those for whom you stand guard as a faithful, prayerful watchman (Isaiah 62:6-7).

"LORD, help _____ and me guard our ways;
do not let us sin with our tongues.
May we guard our mouths as with a muzzle
while the wicked are in our presence.
We wait for You, LORD;
our hope is in You.
Deliver us from all our transgressions.
Hear our prayer, O LORD, and give ear to our cry;
do not be silent at our tears.
For the sake of Your name, Jesus~"

Please read Psalm 57.

Meditate on verse 7.

> *My heart is steadfast, O God,*
> *my heart is steadfast;*
> *I will sing, yes, I will sing praises!*

David wrote this Psalm when things in his life were not going smoothly and as he had hoped. King Saul wanted David dead to ensure he not become king of Israel. A jealous Saul threatened to kill David for more than ten years of his life. Imagine David saying these words to God as he hid from Saul in the caves of the wilderness of Judah (1 Samuel 24).

The words of Psalm 57 can be your cry to God on days, weeks, months, even years when life is hard.

Pray Psalm 57:1-3 and 7 over yourself and those for whom you stand guard as a faithful, prayerful watchman (Isaiah 62:6-7).

> *"Be gracious to _____ and me, O God, be gracious to us,*
> *for our souls take refuge in You.*
> *In the shadow of Your wings we will take refuge*
> *until destruction passes by.*
> *We will cry to You, God Most High,*
> *who accomplishes all things for us.*
> *You will send from heaven and save us.*
> *Reproach him who tramples upon us.*
> *God, please send forth Your lovingkindness and Your truth.*
> *Our hearts are steadfast; O God, our hearts are steadfast.*
> *We will sing, yes, we will sing praises!*
> *In Your name, Jesus~"*

Please read Psalm 86.

Meditate on verse 11.

> *Teach me Your way, O LORD;*
> *I will walk in Your truth;*
> *unite my heart to fear Your name.*

A baby's heart starts beating around day 24 of pregnancy. Starting with the ninth week of a baby's life, their heart divides into four chambers. The week this was miraculously happening in one of our grandbabies, I prayed fervently for God to give that child and our other grandchildren undivided hearts. I asked God to let their hearts never be divided in their love, loyalty, and devotion to Jesus.

Examine your own heart. Better yet, allow the LORD to examine it. What do you really love? Do you love what God loves, or do you love what the world loves? What are your passions, desires, cravings? Are they the same as God's?

As a faithful, prayerful watchman (Isaiah 62:6-7), be honest with God and pray Psalm 86:11-12.

> *"Teach me Your way, O LORD;*
> *I will walk in Your truth;*
> *unite my heart to fear Your name.*
> *I will give thanks to You,*
> *O LORD my God, with all my heart,*
> *and I will glorify Your name forever.*
> *In Your name, Jesus~"*

Please read Psalm 100.

Meditate on verse 3.

> *Know that the LORD Himself is God;*
> *it is He who has made us,*
> *and not we ourselves;*
> *we are His people*
> *and the sheep of His pasture.*

It is easy to get full of yourself. Whether you suffer from thinking too highly of yourself or whether you experience low self-esteem, the root of the problem is pride and believing, "It's all about me."

Well, it is not all about you; it is all about God. Whether you choose to admit it or not or whether the world chooses to admit it or not, it is ALL about God! It has always been ALL about God; it will always be ALL about God. Be wise, take your eyes off of yourself, and fix your eyes on Jesus, today, for the rest of eternity.

Pray Psalm 100 over yourself and those for whom you stand guard as a faithful, prayerful watchman (Isaiah 62:6-7).

> *"May _____ and I shout joyfully to You, LORD.*
> *Let us serve You with gladness,*
> *and come before You with joyful singing.*
> *May we know that LORD, You are God.*
> *You made us and not we ourselves;*
> *We are Your people and the sheep of Your pasture.*
> *May we enter Your gates with thanksgiving*
> *and Your courts with praise.*
> *We give thanks to You and bless Your name.*
> *LORD, You are good;*
> *Your lovingkindness is everlasting,*
> *and Your faithfulness to all generations.*
> *In Your name, Jesus."*

Please read Psalm 101.

Meditate on verse 4.

A perverse heart shall depart from me;
I will know no evil.

In a world filled with perversity, this is a great psalm to pray for yourself and those you love. Psalm 101:3 is a good verse to write out and place on the corner of the television and computer screen.

I will set no worthless thing before my eyes;
I hate the work of those who fall away;
it shall not fasten its grip on me.

What have you allowed to fasten its grip on you that you know is displeasing to God? What worthless and vile things have a grip on members of your family? As a follower of Jesus Christ, what in your life do you need to cut off and cut out? If you have children that God has entrusted to your care, what do you need to do to ensure things of Satan are not destroying their minds and lives? Be obedient to what the Word of God and the Holy Spirit tell you to do; do not delay.

Pray Psalm 101:2-4 over yourself and those for whom you stand guard as a faithful, prayerful watchman (Isaiah 62:6-7).

"LORD, let _____ and me give heed to the blameless way.
May we walk within our house in the integrity of our heart.
Let us set no worthless thing before our eyes;
let us hate the work of those who fall away.
Do not let it fasten its grip on us.
Let a perverse heart depart from us;
may we know no evil.
In Your name, Jesus~"

Please read Psalm 138.

Meditate on verse 8.

> *The LORD will accomplish what concerns me;*
> *Your lovingkindness, O LORD, is everlasting.*
> *Do not forsake the works of Your hands.*

I love having Biblical truths tucked into my mind and heart that come to my remembrance the moment I need them. For example, when I feel weak: "I love You, O LORD, my strength" (Psalm 18:1). When I or someone I love feels anxious: "Let the peace of Christ rule in your hearts" (Colossians 3:15).

When I discovered Psalm 138:8, the LORD knew how much I needed it. There have been days I have repeated it literally hundreds of times. "The LORD will accomplish what concerns me." I have said it by faith when the circumstances around have screamed to the contrary. And, amazingly, but not surprisingly, the LORD has indeed accomplished what concerned me. As new concerns creep into my life, I will say it again, hundreds of times, knowing that God will always be true to His Word.

Pray Psalm 138:8 over yourself and those for whom you stand guard as a faithful, prayerful watchman (Isaiah 62:6-7).

> *"LORD, You will accomplish what concerns me.*
> *Your lovingkindness, O LORD, is everlasting.*
> *Do not forsake _____ and me, the works of Your hands.*
> *In Your name, Jesus-"*

October 29

Please read Habakkuk 1.

Meditate on verse 2.

> *How long, O LORD, will I call for help, and You will not hear?*
> *I cry out to You, "Violence!" yet You do not save.*

Have you felt like Habakkuk and cried out to God, "Why don't You hear me?"

God answered Habakkuk's question with, "Because I am doing something in your days. You would not believe if you were told" (Habakkuk 1:5).

Are you waiting for God to answer your prayers? Waiting can be grueling, yet waiting is the time God uses to grow your faith. A theme of Habakkuk is: "The righteous will live by his faith" (Habakkuk 2:4). As a follower of Jesus Christ, it must be a theme of your life as well (Romans 1:17; Galatians 3:11; Hebrews 10:38).

Reread Habakkuk 1. You will observe that Habakkuk questioned God about many things like, "Why are You silent when the wicked swallow up those more righteous than they?"

Ask God your questions. Tell Him your feelings and frustrations. These conversations with God will help you live by faith.

Pray Habakkuk 1:5 and 12 as you wait on the LORD as a faithful, prayerful watchman (Isaiah 62:6-7).

> *"LORD, I believe You are doing something in my days;*
> *if You were to tell me, I would not believe it. So because*
> *You are from everlasting, and You are the LORD, my God,*
> *my Holy One, I continue to believe _____ and I will not die.*
> *You have appointed this situation to judge us,*
> *and You have established it to correct us.*
> *You are our Rock, Jesus~"*

Please read Habakkuk 2.

Meditate on verses 2 and 3.

> *Then the LORD answered me and said,*
> *"Record the vision and inscribe it on tablets,*
> *that the one who reads it may run.*
> *For the vision is yet for the appointed time;*
> *it hastens toward the goal, and it will not fail.*
> *Though it tarries, wait for it;*
> *for it will certainly come, it will not delay."*

What is the vision God has given you for those you love? Are you praying for them to be established in the fruit of the Spirit (Galatians 5:22-23)? Do you repeatedly ask God to give them the characteristics of His wisdom from above (James 3:17-18)? Do you tirelessly pray for the LORD to grow them up in His love (1 Corinthians 13:4-11)?

Write out the vision God gives you for the people you are guarding with prayer. After you write it, run with it. Pray it to God everyday, reminding Him of the holiness that needs to be established in your loved ones. Wait by faith for God to bring them to the goal of Christlikeness.

Pray Habakkuk 2:4 and 14 over those for whom you stand guard as a faithful, prayerful watchman (Isaiah 62:6-7).

> *"LORD, _____ is a proud one;*
> *their soul is not right within them.*
> *Please make them righteous;*
> *may they live by faith.*
> *Let them be filled with the knowledge of the glory of You,*
> *LORD, as the waters cover the sea.*
> *For Your name's sake, Jesus~"*

Please read Habakkuk 3.

Meditate on verse 2.

> *LORD, I have heard the report about You, and I fear.*
> *LORD, revive Your work in the midst of the years.*
> *In the midst of the years, make it known;*
> *in wrath remember mercy.*

You may have somebody for whom you have been praying a long time. A man once told me his wife prayed for 16 years for him to come to know Christ. He is a follower of Jesus now and a wonderful example of God making His work known in a person. Thankfully, his wife did not grow weary in prayer. Cry out for God to revive His work in the midst of those you love. Ask God to make His work known in the lives of those you love. Beg Him to show them mercy even though they may be experiencing His wrath.

Pray Habakkuk 3:2 and 17-19 as a faithful, prayerful watchman over those you stand guard (Isaiah 62:6-7).

> *"LORD, revive Your work in the midst of _____ .*
> *In the midst of their years, make Your work known.*
> *In wrath remember mercy. Though it does not yet; I wait for the*
> *fig tree to blossom in their lives and for there to be fruit*
> *on their vines. Please do not let the yield of their olive tree fail.*
> *Let the fields of their lives produce food. Do not cut off their*
> *flock from the fold. May there be cattle in their stalls.*
> *As I wait, I will exult in You, LORD. I will rejoice in You,*
> *God of my salvation. LORD God, You are my strength.*
> *You have made my feet like hinds' feet,*
> *and You make me walk on the high places.*
> *Please do the same for _____ .*
> *In Your name, Jesus~"*

NOVEMBER

On your walls, O Jerusalem,
I have appointed watchmen;
All day and all night they
will never keep silent.
You who remind the LORD,
take no rest for yourselves;
And give Him no rest
until He establishes
And makes Jerusalem a
praise in the earth.
ISAIAH 62:6-7, NASB

Please read 1 Samuel 12.

Meditate on verse 23.

> *Moreover, as for me, far be it from me*
> *that I should sin against the LORD by ceasing to pray for you,*
> *but I will instruct you in the good and right way.*

Do you have someone in your life you feel like giving up on, someone who seems hopeless, like they will never change and do what pleases the LORD? Samuel was serving as pastor for a nation of people who fit that description. I love his resoluteness to not give up on the Israelites. Not only was he going to pray for them, he was going to teach them how to please God. He knew he would be sinning against God if he stopped praying for and teaching those who were so rebellious.

DO NOT give up on your child, your spouse, your friend, your co-worker, your loved one... God certainly hasn't, and He calls you to partner with Him in their journey to Christ, which God has allowed to be part of your journey into Christlikeness.

Pray 1 Samuel 12:24-25 over those for whom you stand guard as a faithful, prayerful watchman (Isaiah 62:6-7).

> *"LORD, let _____ fear You*
> *and serve You in truth with all their heart.*
> *Let them consider what great things You have done for them.*
> *May they stop doing wickedly, so they will not be swept away.*
> *For Your name's sake, Jesus~"*

NOVEMBER 2

Please read Deuteronomy 4.

Meditate on verse 39.

Know therefore today, and take it to your heart,
that the LORD, He is God in heaven above
and on the earth below; there is no other.

Moses wrote Deuteronomy to the children and grandchildren of the Israelites delivered from slavery in Egypt. Their fathers and grandfathers died during the 40 years of wandering in the wilderness (Numbers 14:28-32; Deuteronomy 2:14). Moses retold the Israelite's story and reiterated the commandments of God, so these children and grandchildren would know how to live pleasing to the LORD.

Thankfully, Moses penned God's Words, so you, your children, and grandchildren can know what pleases the LORD. Deuteronomy is full of treasure verses to live, teach, and pray. You will spend the next 8 days mining some of the chapters. If you have time, read the entire book of Deuteronomy.

Moses repeated a command in Deuteronomy 4 for the people to give heed and watch themselves diligently (vs. 9, 15, 23). God wants you to mightily guard and protect yourself from sin. You have His Words and His Holy Spirit, so you can hold fast to the LORD your God (v. 4).

Pray Deuteronomy 4:9 over yourself and those for whom you stand guard as a faithful, prayerful watchman (Isaiah 62:6-7).

"LORD, let _____ and me give heed to ourselves
and keep our souls diligently,
so we do not forget the things our eyes have seen from You.
Do not let Your truths depart from our
hearts all the days of our lives.
Let us make them known to our children and grandchildren.
In Your name, Jesus~"

Please read Deuteronomy 5.

Meditate on verse 29.

> *Oh that they had such a heart in them,*
> *that they would fear Me and keep all My commandments always,*
> *that it may be well with them and with their sons forever!*

Deuteronomy 5:29 is God Almighty crying for you! God the Father cries for you to have a heart for Him. Every thought, word, and command of God is from your heavenly Father who loves you and wants you to know Him intimately.

> *I will give them a heart to know Me, for I am the LORD,*
> *and they will be My people, and I will be their God,*
> *for they will return to Me with their whole heart.*
> —Jeremiah 24:7

Ask God to search your heart to see if there is any hurtful way in you (Psalm 139:23-24). Repent of the hurtful things He will show you. Ask Him to give you His heart to love, obey, and know Him.

Pray Deuteronomy 5:29 and 32-33 over yourself and those for whom you stand guard as a faithful, prayerful watchman (Isaiah 62:6-7).

> *"LORD, give _____ and me a heart to fear You*
> *and keep all Your commandments always,*
> *that it may be well with us and our children forever.*
> *Let us observe to do just as You command;*
> *do not let us turn to the right or to the left.*
> *Let us walk in all the way which you command,*
> *so we may live and it will be well with us.*
> *Prolong our days in the land You have given us.*
> *In Your name, Jesus~"*

Please read Deuteronomy 6.
Meditate on this phrase from verse 12.

*Watch yourself that you
do not forget the LORD.*

Deuteronomy 6 tells you how not to forget God. You are to have His Words on your heart, and you are to teach them diligently to your children; when you are sitting down, when you are moving, when you are lying down, and when you are getting up (Deuteronomy 6:7-8). In other words, there is never a time when you should not be talking about things of the LORD. Wow! Can you imagine what your family would be like if you were living these verses? You may already be living the blessings that come from obeying God's Word. I hope so!

Deuteronomy 6 is also one of those chapters filled with verses to pray over those for whom God has appointed you a prayerful watchman (Isaiah 62:6-7). Please reread Deuteronomy 6 praying it over those you love.

Pray Deuteronomy 6:12-14 over yourself and those for whom you stand guard as a faithful, prayerful watchman (Isaiah 62:6-7).

*"LORD, please help _____ and me
to watch ourselves so we do not forget You.
We want to fear only You,
worship only You,
and swear by Your name, God.
We will not follow other gods;
we will follow only You.
In Your name, Jesus~"*

NOVEMBER 5

Please read Deuteronomy 7.

Meditate on verses 6 and 8a.

> *For you are a holy people to the LORD your God;*
> *the LORD your God has chosen you to be*
> *a people for His own possession*
> *out of all the peoples who are on the face of the earth ...*
> *because the LORD loved you ...*

As a believer in Jesus Christ, you, like the Israelites, are holy to the LORD and are His own possession. Like Israel, God chose you because He loves you.

Read these truths about who you are in Christ:

> *Our great God and Savior, Christ Jesus,*
> *gave Himself for us to redeem us from every lawless deed*
> *and to purify for Himself a people for His own possession*
> *zealous for good deeds.*
> —Titus 2:13b-14

> *But you are a chosen race, a royal priesthood,*
> *a holy nation, a people for God's own possession,*
> *so that you may proclaim the excellencies of Him*
> *who has called you out of darkness into His marvelous light;*
> *for you once were not a people, but now you are the people of God.*
> —1 Peter 2:9-10a

As God's own possession, reread Deuteronomy 7 as if it were written personally to you. Ask God to show you His commands and promises for you and your family.

Pray Deuteronomy 7:9 and 11-12 over yourself and those for whom you stand guard as a faithful, prayerful watchman (Isaiah 62:6-7).

"LORD, You are my God. You are God the faithful God.
You keep Your covenant and lovingkindness
to a thousand generations
with those who love You and keep Your commandments.
Let _____ and me keep the commandment
and statutes and judgments
You are commanding us today to do.
Let it come about because we listen to Your
judgments and keep and do them
that You, LORD our God, will keep Your covenant
and Your lovingkindness with us.
Because of You, Jesus~"

Please read Deuteronomy 10.
Meditate on verses 17, 20, and 21.

> *For the LORD your God is the God of gods*
> *and the LORD of lords,*
> *the great, the mighty,*
> *and the awesome God*
> *who does not show partiality nor take a bribe.*
> *You shall fear the LORD your God;*
> *you shall serve Him and cling to Him,*
> *and you shall swear by His name.*
> *He is your praise, and He is your God,*
> *who has done these great and awesome things*
> *for you which your eyes have seen.*

Humbly meditate on God. There is none to compare to Him, and no one and no thing is His equal (Psalm 40:5; Isaiah 40:25). Pray the above verses back to Him by saying the words directly to Him like this:

> *"LORD, You are God. You are the God of gods*
> *and the LORD of lords.*
> *You are the great, the mighty,*
> *and the awesome God.*
> *You do not show partiality nor take a bribe.*
> *I will fear You, LORD my God.*
> *I will serve You and cling to You.*
> *I will swear by Your name.*
> *You are my praise, and You are my God.*
> *You have done these great and awesome things for me*
> *which my eyes have seen."*

God's Words are powerful! Enjoy using His Words to communicate with Him.

Continue talking to God and pray Deuteronomy 10:12 and 13 over yourself and those for whom you stand guard as a faithful, prayerful watchman (Isaiah 62:6-7).

"LORD my God, You have things
You require of _____ and me.
May we fear You, walk in all Your ways,
love You, and serve You, with all our heart and all our soul.
Let us keep Your commandments and statutes
which You are commanding us today for our good.
In Your name, Jesus~"

Please read Deuteronomy 12.

Notice the key repeated phrase, "… The place which the LORD your God will choose."

Meditate on verse 5.

> *But you shall seek the LORD at the place*
> *which the LORD your God will choose from all your tribes,*
> *to establish His name there for His dwelling,*
> *and there you shall come.*

God gave instructions to the Israelites for entering the Promised Land. He told them to completely destroy all the places where the previous occupants had worshipped idols. God commanded Israel to obliterate anything referring to idolatry, even the names of the gods because God was going to choose the place in the land for His name to dwell. The LORD's name would be established and worshipped in that place.

Notice that God always referred to the location He would choose as *the place*. He never gave a geographical location for *the place*. God did that on purpose because He had a very special place in mind for His name to dwell.

God knew the tabernacle would be erected in several locations: Gilgal, Shiloh, and Gibeon (Joshua 4:19; 18:1; 1 Chronicles 21:29). He knew that eventually a temple would be built in Jerusalem (2 Chronicles 3:1). But when God repeatedly said He would choose *the place* for His name to dwell in Deuteronomy 12, He had much more than a geographical location in mind. Every time He said *the place*, He was thinking about you!

> *Do you not know that you are a temple of God*
> *and that the Spirit of God dwells in you?*
> —1 Corinthians 3:16

God knew all along that His name would be established and dwell in you! He purposely called it *the place* because you are *the place* God chose for His name to dwell!

Reread Deuteronomy 12 asking God to reveal to you what He was thinking when He gave these words to Moses nearly 3500 years ago.

Pray Deuteronomy 12:2-3 and 11 over yourself and those for whom you stand guard as a faithful, prayerful watchman (Isaiah 62:6-7).

"LORD, help _____ and me utterly destroy, tear down, smash, burn, cut down, and obliterate everything in our lives that is an idol or god.
Thank You for choosing us as the place for Your name to dwell.
May we bring all of our lives to You as You command.
Because of Your name, Jesus~"

Please read Deuteronomy 28.

Meditate on verses 2 and 15.

All these blessings will come upon you
and overtake you if you obey the LORD your God.
But it shall come about, if you do not obey the LORD your God,
to observe to do all His commandments
and His statutes with which I charge you today,
that all these curses will come upon you and overtake you.

God carefully instructed the Israelites how to live and please Him. He told them exactly what would happen if they obeyed Him and what would happen if they disobeyed Him. If you are familiar with Israel's history, you know many times they chose not to obey God. They have experienced the curses of Deuteronomy 28.

It is important to know God well. There are things that make God happy, and there are things that make Him mad. There are behaviors that please God, and there are behaviors that He hates. You get to know God as you read His Word and as you spend your day talking to and listening to Him. The God of the universe who created you wants you to know His thoughts, words, attitudes, actions, and feelings. Your life will be overtaken with blessings as you live with your LORD.

Pray Deuteronomy 28:2,15, and 47 over yourself and those for whom you stand guard as a faithful, prayerful watchman (Isaiah 62:6-7).

"LORD, may _____ and I obey You.
Let Your blessings come upon us and overtake us.
Help us obey and keep Your commandments and statutes
so curses will not come upon us and overtake us.
May we serve You with joy and a glad heart
for the abundance of all things.
In Your name, Jesus~"

Please read Deuteronomy 30.

As you read, find treasures to pray over your family.

Meditate on verse 14.

> *But the Word is very near you,*
> *in your mouth and in your heart*
> *that you may observe it.*

I want God to bless my family. I want Him to prosper my husband, children, and grandchildren. I want the Word of God to be on the tip of their tongue and in their heart, so they will do His Word. As a prayerful watchman, I will remind the LORD of my heart's desires and will take no rest for myself and will give Him no rest until He establishes my family without blame in holiness (Isaiah 62:6-7; 1 Thessalonians 3:13).

I pray you have the same desire for your family and that you found powerful verses to pray over them from Deuteronomy 30.

Pray Deuteronomy 30:6-10 and 14 over yourself and those for whom you stand guard as a faithful, prayerful watchman (Isaiah 62:6-7).

> *"LORD, circumcise the heart of _____ and me*
> *and our descendants to love You with all our heart*
> *and with all our soul, so we may live.*
> *Let us obey You, LORD. Prosper us abundantly in all the work*
> *of our hand, in the offspring of our body, in the*
> *offspring of our cattle, and in the produce of our*
> *ground. LORD, rejoice over us for good,*
> *just as You have rejoiced over our fathers.*
> *Let us obey You, keep Your commands and statutes,*
> *and turn to You with all our heart and soul.*
> *Let us keep Your Word very near us,*
> *in our mouth and heart, that we may observe it.*
> *In Your name, Jesus~"*

Please read Deuteronomy 31.

Meditate on verse 6.

> *The LORD is the one who goes ahead of you;*
> *He will be with you. He will not fail you or forsake you.*
> *Do not fear or be dismayed.*

The Israelites were about to enter the Promised Land, but they would enter without their leader from the past 40 years (Exodus 7:7; Deuteronomy 31:2). Moses was about to die. He would not cross the Jordan River with the Israelites. The LORD would lead Israel into their Promised Land.

God's Words to Israel nearly 3,500 years ago are His Words to you today. Where are you going? What step are you about to take? Are you scared? Has the person you were depending on been taken out of the picture or perhaps is not as reliable as you had hoped?

The LORD is the One who goes ahead of you in the journey. He is the One who will always be with you.

God wanted the Israelites to depend on Him. The LORD took Moses to the top of Mount Nebo and showed him all the land Israel would possess. Moses died; God buried his body, and no one knows where that burial spot is (Deuteronomy 34:1-6).

The LORD wants you to depend on Him. Choose to trust Him today.

Pray Deuteronomy 31:6 over yourself and those for whom you stand guard as a faithful, prayerful watchman (Isaiah 62:6-7).

> *"LORD, help _____ and me be strong and courageous.*
> *Do not let us be afraid or tremble.*
> *LORD, our God, thank You that You go with us*
> *and will not fail us or forsake us.*
> *Because of Your name, Jesus–*

November 11

Please read Genesis 1.

Meditate on verse 1a.

In the beginning God...

The most important thing you will ever think
is what you think about God.
For what you think about God will determine
every other aspect of your life.
—Dr. D. Jeffrey Bingham

What you think about Genesis chapter one will determine how you think about every other page of God's Holy Word.

Please answer these questions:

- ❧ Who is the only eyewitness to creation?
- ❧ Whose account is Genesis 1?
- ❧ Who said six times, "There was evening and there was morning, one day" *(Genesis 1:5, 8, 13, 19, 23, 31)?*

The answer to all three questions is: God. God was the only one present at His creation of the world. He was the eyewitness to what took place 6000 years ago. He spoke the world into existence. He confirmed that truth in John 1:1-3; Colossians 1:15-17, and Hebrews 1:1-3, and He gave the added insight that Jesus is the Word of God who spoke. God is the definer of a day, and He told you six times exactly how long a day is.

Why would anyone dare question God's eyewitness account of what He alone did? What do you think of someone who questions or adds to a story you are telling when they weren't even at the event?

As a follower of the Creator of the universe, Jesus Christ, it is important to take His first recorded words literally. If you choose not to, you handle carelessly the rest of His Words, conveniently deciding which ones apply to your life and which ones do not.

Pray Genesis 1:2-3 over yourself and those for whom you stand guard as a faithful, prayerful watchman (Isaiah 62:6-7).

"God, apart from You, _____ and
I are formless and void,
and darkness is over us.
Spirit of God, move over our lives.
God, speak Light into us.
In Your name, Jesus~"

Please read Genesis 2.

Meditate on verse 4.

This is the account of the heavens and the earth
when they were created,
in the day that the LORD God made earth and heaven.

Genesis 2:1-3 completes the story of God's creation week. Genesis 2:4 begins with a phrase repeated throughout Genesis: "This is the account of ..." It is the Hebrew word *towledah*; and it literally means "these are the generations ..." This phrase is also in Genesis 5:1; 6:9; 10:1, 32; 11:10, 27; 25:12, 19; 36:1, 9, and 37:2.

Genesis 1-2 sets up an important pattern for the rest of the book. Genesis is organized by genealogies, followed by an elaboration on a section of the genealogy. Genesis 1 is the genealogy of creation. Genesis 2 gives more details focusing on the creation of man—part of the genealogy. The remainder of Genesis is written using this pattern: a genealogy will be given followed by a detailed story about one family from the genealogy.

Genesis is the story of God creating and establishing families. It is beautifully written by the One who perfectly created you and is currently writing your story. As you spend the rest of the year reading God's story about families, pray for His miraculous creative work in the families for whom you are praying.

Pray Genesis 2:20 and 24-25 over married couples for whom you stand guard as a faithful, prayerful watchman (Isaiah 62:6-7).

"LORD, make _____ a suitable helper for _____.
Let them leave their father and mother and be joined to each other.
May they become one flesh. Let them be naked
with each other and not ashamed.
In Your name, Jesus~"

Please read Genesis 3.

Meditate on this phrase from verse 1.

"Indeed, has God said ... ?"

These are the first recorded words of the serpent, who is also called the devil and Satan. Jesus called him a liar and the father of lies (Revelation 12:9; John 8:44).

The first thing Satan asked Adam and Eve was, "Did God really say that?" It is the same question the liar will ask you every time you are tempted to sin: "Did God really say not to do that?"

Then the father of lies will say to you, "What you are about to do isn't that big of a deal. Besides God really wants you to be happy."

Believing and submitting to the lies of the evil one brings separation and death, not happiness and contentment. When Adam and Eve submitted to the serpent, they were separated from God; they lost the privilege of walking with God in the cool of the day.

The rest of Scripture is about God restoring His relationship with people. It is the love story of God doing everything—even dying for you—so you can be in an intimate relationship with Him.

Do not let Satan tempt you to doubt God and His Word. Did God really say He died for you, so you can live for Him? Yes! Does Jesus really forgive your sins and remember them no more? Yes! Does God really want to walk and talk with you every moment of every day? Yes! Walk with God in truth and do not be deceived by the evil one.

Pray Genesis 3:8 over yourself and those for whom you stand guard as a faithful, prayerful watchman (Isaiah 62:6-7).

"LORD God, when _____ and I hear the sound of You
walking in the garden of our lives in the cool of the day,
may we come to You and never hide from You.
In Your name, Jesus~"

November 14

Please read Genesis 4.

Meditate on verse 7.

> *If you do well, will not your countenance be lifted up?*
> *And if you do not do well, sin is crouching at the door,*
> *and its desire is for you, but you must master it.*

This is an important passage of Scripture. In Genesis 4, God engaged Cain so he would not kill his brother Abel. Cain needed to hear God, subdue his anger, and find out why his sacrifice was not accepted by God. God was providing a way of escape for Cain from the temptation to kill Abel.

God provides you a way of escape with every temptation as well (1 Corinthians 10:13). God also gives you free will. He allows you to choose. You can obey God, or you can obey sin. The course your life takes is your choice. God will not force you to love and follow Him. You have the privilege of choosing.

Sin desires to control your life. Satan wants you to choose sin to be your master. God says when you master sin rather than allowing sin to master you, your countenance will be lifted up, you will be happy, and you will do well.

Remember the father of lies says sin will make you happy. God says mastering sin will make you happy. What will you choose? Do you choose to serve Satan and sin, or do you choose to serve God?

Pray Genesis 4:7 over yourself and those for whom you stand guard as a faithful, prayerful watchman (Isaiah 62:6-7).

> *"LORD, sin is crouching at the door of _____ and me.*
> *Its desire is for us. LORD, help us master it!*
> *Let us do well, so our countenance will be lifted up.*
> *In Your name, Jesus~"*

Please read Genesis 5.

Meditate on verse 24a.

Enoch walked with God...

Chapter 5 is the second recorded genealogy in Genesis. The first is in Genesis 1-2:3, the genealogy of creation. Readers of God's Word are often tempted to skip genealogy chapters; however, treasure verses are left undiscovered when they do.

Genesis 5:24 is the story of one of my favorite Bible heroes, Enoch. It contains the words I would like to be worthy of having inscribed on my tombstone: *She walked with God.*

Walked carries within it the idea of one's continual behavior and existence. Enoch walked with God. He lived life with God.

Enoch began walking with God when he was 65 years old, after he became the father of Methuselah (Genesis 5:21-22). From that point, walking with God was the beginning and the end of his story. No other detail was needed except the fact that Enoch so lived with God that his sentence in the genealogy does not end with "and he died" like every other man listed in the chapter. "Enoch walked with God; and he was not, for God took him" (Genesis 5:24).

It was as if God and Enoch were walking together, and the day came when God said, "You know, Enoch, today we really are closer to My house than yours; let's go spend the rest of eternity there."

Think about your life. How do people describe you? Would they describe you as walking with God?

Pray Genesis 5:24 over yourself and those for whom you stand guard as a faithful, prayerful watchman (Isaiah 62:6-7).

"God, let _____ and me walk with You!
In Your name, Jesus~"

Please read Genesis 6.

Meditate on verse 9b.

Noah walked with God.

Like Enoch in Genesis 5:21-24, Noah walked with God. God gives you details in Genesis 6 about those who walked with God and those who chose not to. Examine your life in light of these truths.

Noah was a righteous man, blameless, walking with God, and he found favor in the eyes of God (Genesis 6:8-9). Noah stood in direct contrast to the rest of mankind who grieved God and whom He described as having great wickedness, whose "every intent of the thoughts of their heart was only evil continually (Genesis 6:5-6)."

Which person are you?

Are you:

1. Righteous
2. Blameless
3. Walking with God

Or are you:

1. Wicked
2. The intentions of the thoughts of your heart are continually evil
3. You grieve God in His heart

Here is how to decide which list you are; you will not be both. Genesis 6:22 says, "Noah did according to all that God had commanded him, so he did."

Pray Genesis 6:8-9 and 22 over yourself and those for whom you stand guard as a faithful, prayerful watchman (Isaiah 62:6-7).

"God, _____ and I want to find favor with You.
Make us like Noah:
righteous, blameless, walking with You.
May we do according to all that You command us.
For the sake of Your name, Jesus-"

NOVEMBER 17

Please read Genesis 7.

Meditate on verse 5.

Noah did according to all that the LORD had commanded him.

The theme of obeying God runs throughout the book of Genesis. People's deliberate disobedience to God brought His righteous judgment on the earth. In the midst of judgment, one man, Noah, and his family were spared because Noah was righteous before God (Genesis 7:1).

Noah did according to all that God commanded him (Genesis 6:22). His obedience brought blessings to his entire family.

What about your family? Are the people in your life being blessed as you obediently follow Jesus Christ? Are they learning from your example how to live and walk every day with God?

Jesus Christ makes you righteous before God. Obedience to Christ draws others to want a righteous relationship with Him. Live for your Savior so the destroying flood of sin does not prevail over you and those you love. He wants to spare you and your family. Choose His righteousness.

Pray Genesis 7:1 and 5 over yourself and those for whom you stand guard as a faithful, prayerful watchman (Genesis 62:6-7).

"LORD, make me righteous before You for the sake of my family!
Let _____ and me do according to all that You command.
In Your name, Jesus~"

NOVEMBER 18

Please read Genesis 8.

Meditate on this phrase from verse 1.

But God remembered Noah…

God sent the prevailing, increasing, greatly increasing, prevailing more and more flood waters to blot out people whose every intent of the thoughts of their hearts was only evil continually (Genesis 6:5; 7:17-24). Noah was in the middle of those waters on the ark for one year and 17 days (Genesis 7:10-11; 8:14). I wonder if Noah ever thought God had forgotten him and his family during the course of that year. I wonder if he ever feared the prevailing floodwaters would blot out him and his family.

But God remembered Noah… What situation threatens to flood you and your family? What feels like it is about to blot you out? Come honestly before "the God and Father of your Lord Jesus Christ, the Father of mercies and God of all comfort" (2 Corinthians 1:3) and ask Him to remember you. Confess your sins and the sins of others and ask Him to remember you and yours with His mercy and comfort.

God remembered Noah, and the water decreased steadily (Genesis 8:1 and 5).

God remembers you, and He wants the floodwaters to decrease in your life. He waits for you to humbly ask Him to do it.

Pray Genesis 8:1 and 5 over yourself and those for whom you stand guard as a faithful, prayerful watchman (Isaiah 62:6-7).

"LORD, remember _____ and me.
Please let these waters decrease steadily.
For the sake of Your name, Jesus~"

NOVEMBER 19

Please read Genesis 9.

Meditate on verse 9.

> *Now behold, I Myself do establish My covenant*
> *with you and with your descendants after you.*

Before entering the ark, God promised to establish His covenant with Noah. Genesis 6:18 was the first time *covenant* was used in the Bible. The next time God used the word was in Genesis 9, after Noah and his family left the ark and offered sacrifices to God. A *covenant* is a contract between two individuals which is made official by signs, sacrifices, and vows. Seven times in Genesis 9 God said He would establish His everlasting covenant with Noah and his descendants after him for all successive generations to never again destroy the earth with a flood. The sign of His promise was His bow in the clouds (Genesis 9:13-14). This covenant set the pattern for the covenant God cut with Abram nearly 400 years later and the covenant He cut for you through Jesus Christ 2200 years after the Abrahamic covenant (Genesis 15; Hebrews 13:20).

God takes covenants very seriously. The next time you see a rainbow think about the fact that as you are looking at it, God is also looking at it and remembering His everlasting covenant with every living creature that is on the earth (Genesis 9:16). If you are a Christian, thank God for the everlasting Noahic covenant and for the everlasting covenant you have in Christ.

As a faithful, prayerful watchman (Isaiah 62:6-7), pray Genesis 9:16-17 over those who need to be in a covenant relationship with God.

> *"LORD, when You look upon _____ , please remember them.*
> *They need to be in an everlasting covenant with You.*
> *God, You establish covenant. Establish them in Christ.*
> *In Your name, Jesus~"*

Please read Genesis 10.

Meditate on verse 32.

> *These are the families of the son of Noah,*
> *according to their genealogies, by their nations;*
> *and out of these the nations were separated*
> *on the earth after the flood.*

From the three sons of Noah, the whole earth was populated (Genesis 9:19). The sons and grandsons of Japheth, Ham, and Shem are listed in Genesis 10. These are the men from whom all the nations on earth began.

God gave additional details about one man in this genealogy, like He did for Enoch in Adam's genealogy (Genesis 5:21-24). God wanted you to know more about Nimrod.

Nimrod was the founder and leader of Babel. According to Hebrew scholars, C.F. Keil and F. Delitzsch, *Nimrod* means "we will revolt." He may have hunted animals, but in the context of these verses, Nimrod was a hunter, a killer of humans. He walked in rebellion before God to make himself mighty on earth and to establish his kingdom.

God told you about Nimrod, so you would learn from Nimrod. Examine your life. Do you walk with God like Enoch did? Or do you rebelliously walk before God like Nimrod did?

Pray not to be Genesis 10:8-9 for yourself and those for whom you stand guard as a faithful, prayerful watchman (Isaiah 62:6-7).

> *"LORD, You are the Mighty One on the earth.*
> *Do not let _____and me try to become what only You can be.*
> *Do not let us do anything before You.*
> *Continue to make us like Enoch, walking with You (Genesis 5:24).*
> *In Your name, Jesus~"*

Please read Genesis 11.

Meditate on this phrase from verse 4.

Let us make for ourselves a name.

Moses recorded God's Words in Genesis in a distinct pattern. In Genesis, God listed five genealogies starting with the genealogy of the earth (Genesis 1). Immediately following each genealogy, God gave a closer look at one part of the genealogy. For example, Genesis 2 is a closer look at how God created man.

God followed His pattern in Genesis 10-11. Genesis 10 is the genealogy of the nations of the world beginning with Noah's three sons. Genesis 11 gives you a closer picture of Nimrod and his city, Babel, which were part of the genealogy in Genesis 10.

Nimrod's rebellion before God continued in Genesis 11. The people in Nimrod's city of Babel decided to make a name for themselves by building a city with a tower that reached into heaven. As they were saying, "Let us … let us … let us …," the LORD said, "Let Us go down there and confuse their language, so that they will not understand one another's speech" (Genesis 11:7).

God will not tolerate rebellion! When you try to make a name for yourself, you are in opposition to God, and He will come down into your business and confuse what you are doing until you choose to let God's name be glorified instead of your own.

Pray for God not to have to do Genesis 11:7 to you and those for whom you stand guard as a faithful, prayerful watchman (Isaiah 62:6-7).

"LORD, Your name is above every name in heaven and earth!
As _____ and I bow to You, I pray You do not have
to come down and cause confusion in our lives.
In Your name, Jesus~"

Please read Genesis 12.

Meditate on verses 1-3.

> *Now the LORD said to Abram,*
> *"Go forth from your country,*
> *and from your relatives,*
> *and from your father's house,*
> *to the land which I will show you;*
> *and I will make you a great nation,*
> *and I will bless you, and make your name great;*
> *and so you shall be a blessing;*
> *and I will bless those who bless you,*
> *and the one who curses you I will curse.*
> *And in you all the families of the earth will be blessed."*

You are about to start the Christian season many believers refer to as Advent. Advent begins four Sundays before Christmas day. It is a time for meditation and prayer in anticipation of celebrating the coming of Christ to earth as the perfect and acceptable sacrifice for the sins of the world.

Genesis 12 contains a prophecy from God to Abram about the Messiah. When God told Abram, "in you all the families of the earth will be blessed" (v. 3), God was prophesying that the Savior for the entire world would be a descendant of Abram.

As you continue reading Genesis for the rest of the year, look for Jesus. Genesis was part of the Scriptures Paul used to give evidence that Jesus is the Christ and to explain salvation through faith in Him (Acts 17:2-3). The New Testament was just beginning to be written when Peter, James, Paul, and the other New Testament preachers were teaching. The Scriptures the writers of the New Testament used are the same Scriptures used today known as the Old Testament.

Look for evidence that Jesus is the Messiah in Genesis. It is a great treasure hunt!

Pray Genesis 12:3b, 4, and 8 over yourself and those for whom you stand guard as a faithful, prayerful watchman (Isaiah 62:6-7).

"LORD, thank You for blessing _____ and me.
Help us go forth just as You command us to go.
Wherever we go, may we worship You
and call on Your name, LORD.
Because of You, Jesus~"

Please read Genesis 13.

Meditate on this phrase from verse 5.

Now Lot, who went with Abram …

There is a repeated phrase in Genesis 12-13: "Lot went with him" (Genesis 12:4; 13:1, 5). Lot was Abram's nephew, the adult son of Abram's deceased brother, Haran. Abram's father, Terah, assumed the responsibility of his grandson, Lot, after the death of Haran (Genesis 11:27-31).

God told Abram to go forth from his country and from his relatives and from his father's house to the land He would show him (Genesis 12:1). Well, Abram obeyed part of God's commands. He left his country and went to the land God showed him, but he took Lot with him.

Partial obedience to God is disobedience, and there are always consequences to disobeying God. Abram gave up the best of God's gift of land to selfish Lot in order to appease him and put an end to family strife. Abram finally obeyed God in Genesis 13:11, "thus they separated from each other." But by this point, the consequences remained, and you will continue to read about Lot in the days to come. In fact, to this day, the descendants of Lot occupy the land east of the Jordan River (Genesis 13:11), and there is still strife between the descendants of Lot (Jordan) and the descendants of Abram (Israel).

Does it matter whether you choose to completely obey God or not? The countries of Israel and Jordan live with the consequences of a relative who partially obeyed God over 4000 years ago.

Pray Genesis 13:18 over yourself and those for whom you stand guard as a faithful, prayerful watchman (Isaiah 62:6-7).

"LORD, help _____ and me to move
our tents as soon as You tell us,
to the place You tell us, and in the way You tell us.
Then and there we will build an altar and worship You, LORD.
Because of Your name, Jesus~"

Please read Genesis 14.

Meditate on verse 18.

And Melchizedek, king of Salem, brought out bread and wine;
now he was a priest of God Most High.

On the first day of the week, the day Christ arose from the dead, He met two men who were walking to Emmaus. Jesus started walking with them, asked them a few questions, then "beginning with Moses and with all the prophets, He explained to them the things concerning Himself in all the Scriptures" (Luke 24:27). (All the Scriptures means all of the Old Testament.) Genesis 14 was probably one of the passages Jesus explained to the two men because the writer of Hebrews recorded it in reference to Jesus Christ in Hebrews 7.

Abram won a battle against four kings who had taken his nephew Lot and other people captive. Abram rescued Lot and the others. As Abram returned home from the battle, the king of Sodom and the king of Salem came to greet Abram and thank him for his kind and courageous deed. The king of Salem was Melchizedek who was also a priest. He greeted Abram with bread and wine.

Why would God have Moses record this strange encounter between Melchizedek and Abram? God was giving a picture of Messiah. Jesus is King and Priest. He gave His disciples bread and wine to symbolize the covenant relationship He had with them. Melchizedek is not listed in any of the genealogies of Genesis; he has no date of birth or date of death. Hebrews 7:3 says God did that on purpose to show the Son of God has neither beginning of days nor end of life.

God's Word is amazing! Every Word is handcrafted by the Almighty to show you the Savior. Enjoy Him like you never have before this Christmas season.

Pray Genesis 14:14 and 16 in thanksgiving of what Christ has done for you.

"LORD, as soon as You heard I had been taken captive by sin,
You pursued me.
Thank You for bringing me back to You.
In Your name, Jesus~"

Please read Genesis 15.

Meditate on verses 17-18a.

> *It came about when the sun had set,*
> *that it was very dark,*
> *and behold, there appeared a smoking oven*
> *and a flaming torch which passed between these pieces.*
> *On that day the LORD made a covenant with Abram ...*

God reiterated His promises to Abram of land and descendants. God sealed the deal in Genesis 15 by making a covenant with Abram. When covenants were made in the Old Testament, they were literally cut. An animal was killed, cut in half, and the two people making covenant promises to each other would walk between the pieces of the sacrificed animal stating that if either person broke their covenant vows may what happened to the dead animal or worse happen to them.

Amazingly, God entered into a covenant relationship with Abram, but He did not require Abram to pass between the pieces of the sacrificed animals. Instead God caused a deep sleep to fall upon Abram, and while he slept, God appeared as a smoking oven and a flaming torch and passed between the pieces, cutting covenant with Abram.

Only God passed through the pieces (not Abram). By doing this God declared to Abram, "If I break this covenant, may what happened to the animal, or worse, happen to Me. And Abram, if you break the covenant, may what happened to the animal, or worse, happen to Me."

And it did—on the cross.

Pray Genesis 15:1 and 17-18a over yourself and those for whom you stand guard as a faithful, prayerful watchman (Isaiah 62:6-7).

Word of the LORD, You have come
to _____ and me.
Thank You that we do not have to fear.
You are our shield, our very great reward.
Jesus, You not only passed between
the pieces of the animal for us;
You were the sacrificed animal.
Thank You for making a covenant with us.
In Your name and blood, Jesus~"

Please read Genesis 16.

Meditate on verse 13.

> *Then she called the name of the LORD, who spoke to her,*
> *"You are a God who sees";*
> *for she said,*
> *"Have I even remained alive after seeing Him?"*

God reveals Himself by many names throughout the Bible. A few of them are:

- ᔆ God Most High – Genesis 14:18-20
- ᔆ The LORD Will Provide – Genesis 22:14
- ᔆ The LORD Who Heals – Exodus 15:26
- ᔆ The LORD Is Peace – Judges 6:24
- ᔆ The LORD Our Righteousness – Jeremiah 23:6

Almighty God allowed an Egyptian slave girl named Hagar to give Him one of His names, The God Who Sees. She was a despised and mistreated maid. Her jealous mistress, Sarai, treated Hagar harshly because she was pregnant by Sarai's husband, Abram. The whole affair happened because of a plan hatched by Sarai to hasten God's covenant plans. Oh, the messes we create when we think we know better than God! "LORD, forgive us!"

So, Hagar, who was with child, fled from her abusive mistress to the wilderness where God met her. Carefully reread Genesis 16:7-13. The angel of the LORD found Hagar. After He spoke to her, Hagar said, "The LORD spoke to me. You, God, see me! Have I even remained alive here after seeing Him?" (v. 13).

The "angel of the LORD" was God in physical form. Ponder this as one of your Jesus sightings in Genesis.

Ponder also the fact that God sees you. No matter your life situation, God sees you, hears you, and desires to speak to you. Call on the name of the LORD; call Him by the name You need to know Him as: God Who Heals, God Who Provides, etc.

Pray Genesis 16:11b and 13 over yourself and those for whom you stand guard as a faithful, prayerful watchman (Isaiah 62:6-7).

"LORD, please pay attention to _____ and my affliction!
You are the God Who Sees!
Thank You for seeing us.
In Your name, Jesus~"

Please read Genesis 17.

Meditate on verses 5 and 15.

> *"No longer shall your name be called Abram,*
> *but your name shall be Abraham;*
> *for I will make you the father of a multitude of nations."*
> *Then God said to Abraham,*
> *"As for Sarai your wife, you shall not call her name Sarai,*
> *but Sarah shall be her name."*

God continued establishing the covenant He made with Abram. God passed between the pieces of the sacrificed animals in Genesis 15 stating His promises to Abram. God introduced the name change aspect of covenant in Genesis 17. God's covenant relationship with Abram and Sarai changed their identity; so much so, God changed their names to Abraham and Sarah to signify they were in a relationship with Him.

God does the same thing to you when you enter into a covenant relationship with Him through Jesus Christ. Before Jesus, you were called child of wrath and son of disobedience (Ephesian 2:3; 5:6). Your father was the devil (John 8:44). After Christ became your life, you were called child of God and Christian (Colossians 3:4; 1 John 3:1-2; Acts 11:26).

God made everlasting promises to Abraham (Genesis 17:7-8, 13, 19). When He changed your name to child of God, it came with His promise to be your forever Father. What an amazing name change you received!

Pray Genesis 17:7 over those for whom you stand guard as a faithful, prayerful watchman (Isaiah 62:6-7) who need to be in an everlasting covenant relationship with God through Jesus Christ.

> *"LORD, establish Your covenant with _____ .*
> *Be their God! Be God to their descendants after them.*
> *Through Your name, Jesus~"*

NOVEMBER 28

Please read Genesis 18.

Meditate on verse 3.

> *My LORD, if now I have found favor in your sight,*
> *please do not pass your servant by.*

> *Genesis 18 begins with these words, "Now the LORD*
> *appeared to him by the oaks of Mamre … "*

Here is another situation where God showed Himself to people. The LORD appeared; Abraham lifted up his eyes and saw three men (Genesis 18:1-2). As soon as Abraham saw them, he knew he did not want these gentlemen to leave him! These were special guests, and Abraham wanted to fellowship with them; he wanted them to stay at his house, eat a meal with him, and talk to him.

How do you respond when the LORD intersects your life? Do you recognize Him throughout the day? Do you invite Him to share your meals with you? Jesus Himself said, "Behold, I stand at the door and knock; if anyone hears My voice and opens the door, I will come in to him and will dine with him, and he with Me" (Revelation 3:20).

It is incredible the Savior wants that kind of intimacy with you. Enjoy spending time with Him this Christmas.

Pray Genesis 18:3 over yourself and those for whom you stand guard as a faithful, prayerful watchman (Isaiah 62:6-7).

> *"My LORD, let _____ and me find favor in Your sight.*
> *Please do not pass us by!*
> *In Your name, Jesus~"*

Please read Genesis 19.

Meditate on this phrase from verse 29.

God remembered Abraham
and sent Lot out of the midst of the overflow.

Here are some facts about Lot:

- ❧ He selfishly chose the best of the land God gave to Abraham. (Genesis 13:10-11).

- ❧ He moved his tents to Sodom where the men were exceedingly wicked and sinners against the LORD (Genesis 13:12-13).

- ❧ Abraham went to war against five kings in order to save him. (Genesis 14:14-16).

- ❧ Abraham begged God not to destroy wicked Sodom where Lot lived (Genesis 18:23-33).

- ❧ Lot was willing to sacrifice his two virgin daughters to evil men to protect his two male guests (Genesis 19:4-8).

- ❧ His future sons-in-law did not respect him and thought he was a joke (Genesis 19:14).

- ❧ He hesitated when the LORD provided a way of escape (Genesis 19:16).

- ❧ He was afraid and argued with God about His place of provision for his family (Genesis 19:19-20).

- ❧ God showed Lot compassion and magnified lovingkindness (Genesis 19:16, 19).

Why? Why didn't God destroy Lot with the wicked people in Sodom? From his list of accomplishments, he certainly did not deserve to be saved. He was a mess!

God remembered Abraham. God had a covenant relationship with Abraham and because Lot had a relationship with Abraham, God saved Lot.

> *But God, being rich in mercy, because of His*
> *great love with which He loved us,*
> *even when we were dead in our transgressions,*
> *made us alive together with Christ (by grace you have been saved),*
> *and raised us up with Him, and seated us with Him*
> *in the heavenly places in Christ Jesus,*
> *so that in the ages to come He might show*
> *the surpassing riches of His grace in kindness*
> *toward us in Christ Jesus.*
> *For by grace you have been saved ...*
> *—Ephesians 2:4-8*

If you are a Christian, Lot's story is your story. You received lovingkindness magnified because you have a relationship with Jesus, and God always remembers Jesus and what He did for you on the cross. You are not destroyed because when God looks at you, He sees His Son. Throughout this Christmas season, thank God for saving you from the midst of your overflow of sin.

As a faithful, prayerful watchman (Isaiah 62:6-7), pray Genesis 19:16, 19, and 29 over those who are hesitating in their decision to follow Christ.

> *"LORD, _____ is hesitant.*
> *Please let your compassion be upon them.*
> *Seize them; bring them out of their sinful place.*
> *Let them find favor in Your sight.*
> *Magnify Your lovingkindness towards them.*
> *Please save their life!*
> *God, remember them*
> *and send them out of the midst of the overflow*
> *of the consequences of their sin.*
> *For Your name's sake, Jesus~"*

Please read Genesis 20.

Meditate on verse 6.

Then God said to him in the dream,
"Yes, I know that in the integrity of your heart you have done this,
and I also kept you from sinning against Me;
therefore I did not let you touch her.

Here is a prayer warrior's treasure verse! It is tucked in the middle of Abraham's story of trying to save himself at the cost of sacrificing his wife to King Abimelech. God's faithfulness to Abraham was unending, and He rescued Sarah from the king's harem.

Abimelech tried to justify himself before God by saying he had innocent hands and a heart of integrity. God quickly reminded the king He knew exactly what was in his heart, and He (God) had kept Abimelech from touching Sarah.

Do not be deceived! When the world tells you to "follow your heart," it is not advice from God. God says this about your heart in Jeremiah 17:9-10a: "The heart is more deceitful than all else and is desperately sick; who can understand it? I the LORD, search the heart; I test the mind ..."

God has the cure for your heart issues. In Christ, God promises this: "I will give them a heart to know Me, for I am the LORD, and they will be My people, and I will be their God, for they will return to Me with their whole heart" (Jeremiah 24:7).

Pray Genesis 20:6 over yourself and those for whom you stand guard as a faithful, prayerful watchman (Isaiah 62:6-7).

"LORD, You know _____and my heart.
Please keep us from sinning against You.
Do not let us touch what we should not.
In Your name, Jesus~"

On your walls, O Jerusalem,
I have appointed watchmen;
All day and all night they
will never keep silent.
You who remind the LORD,
take no rest for yourselves;
And give Him no rest
until He establishes
And makes Jerusalem a
praise in the earth.

ISAIAH 62:6-7, NASB

DECEMBER 1

Please read Genesis 21.

Meditate on verses 1-2.

> *Then the LORD took note of Sarah as He had said,*
> *and the LORD did for Sarah as He had promised.*
> *So Sarah conceived and bore a son to Abraham in his old age,*
> *at the appointed time of which God had spoken to him.*

God first promised Abraham descendants when he was 75 years old (Genesis 12:1-4). Abraham and Sarah took matters into their own hands to get the promised heir when Abraham was 86 years old (Genesis 16:16). The result was the birth of Ishmael.

When Abraham was 99 years old, God told him that Ishmael was not the child of the covenant promises. God promised to establish His covenant with the son yet to be conceived named Isaac (Genesis 17:21). Abraham was 100 years old when Isaac was finally born (Genesis 21:5).

God fulfilled His promise to Abraham at the appointed time. The appointed time was 25 years after the promise was first stated.

It can be long and difficult waiting on God. Remember His timing is perfect. Do not rush God's plans; wait for His promises. God cannot lie (Titus 1:2). He will keep His Word.

Pray Genesis 21:1-2 over someone for whom you stand guard as a faithful, prayerful watchman (Isaiah 62:6-7).

> *"LORD, please take note of _____.*
> *Do for them all You have promised*
> *at Your appointed time.*
> *In Your name, Jesus."*

DECEMBER 2

Please read Genesis 22.

Meditate on this phrase from verse 5.

We will worship.

God purposely uses the words *love, obey,* and *worship* for the first time in Genesis 22. They are used in the context of sacrifice. They are used in the context of a man not withholding from God what appeared to be most precious to him because God was most precious to Abraham, not Isaac.

Worship carries with it the idea of prostrating yourself or laying yourself down before God. What is God telling you to lay down before Him? What does He want you to give up because it is more precious to you than He is?

Abraham literally laid Isaac on the altar (Genesis 22:9). This was visual proof that Abraham *loved* God more than anybody or anything else. He would *obey* God no matter the cost. Abraham *worshipped* God. And God blessed Abraham (Genesis 22:17).

What do you need to stop withholding from God? Christmas is the season of giving. Use this time to give God everything out of obedience and love for Him, so you can live a life of true worship.

Pray Genesis 22:1 and 16-17 over yourself and those for whom you stand guard as a faithful, prayerful watchman (Isaiah 62:6-7).

"LORD, when You call,
let _____ and my response be, "Here I am."
Help us stop withholding _____ from You.
We want You to bless us!
In Your name, Jesus~"

DECEMBER 3

Please read Genesis 22.

Meditate on verse 8.

> *Abraham said, "God will provide for Himself the lamb*
> *for the burnt offering, my son."*
> *So the two of them walked on together.*

Genesis 22 is a rich chapter; you need at least two days to read and meditate on its treasures. Verse 8 is a beautiful verse of prophecy about Jesus. It can literally be translated as: "God will provide Himself as the lamb."

> *The next day he (John) saw Jesus coming to him and said,*
> *"Behold the Lamb of God who takes away the sin of the world!"*
> —John 1:29

Abraham and Isaac were led by God to a mountain in Moriah to worship Him. In obedience, they went taking nearly everything necessary for worshipping God: wood, fire, a knife, but they still needed a lamb for the sacrifice of worship to be made complete. When questioned by Isaac about the missing lamb, Abraham confidently answered that God would provide Himself the lamb.

God did provide an animal to replace Isaac on the altar that day, but it was a ram and not a lamb. God knew that 2000 years later on that same mountain in the land of Moriah, God Himself would be the sacrificial Lamb for the sins of the entire world.

> *Then Solomon began to build the house of the LORD*
> *in Jerusalem on Mount Moriah.*
> —2 Chronicles 3:1a

Mount Moriah is the place where God took His Son, His only Son, whom He loved and offered Him there for the sins of all mankind (Genesis 22:2). Let the wonder of God's revelation of Himself in this amazing chapter sink into your mind and heart today.

Pray Genesis 22:8 in thanksgiving to the Lamb of God for what He did for you. As a faithful watchman (Isaiah 62:6-7), pray for those who need to accept the sacrifice of the Lamb in their lives.

> *"LORD, You provided Yourself as the Lamb*
> *for the burnt offering I need to walk with You.*
> *Thank You, Jesus!*
> *Please let _____ accept Your provision, LORD.*
> *In Your name, Jesus~"*

Please read Genesis 23.

Meditate on verse 4.

I am a stranger and a sojourner among you;
give me a burial site among you
that I may bury my dead out of my sight.

Sarah was 127 years old and Abraham was 137 when Sarah died. Abraham had lived in the land of Canaan for 62 years; he was led there by God and promised the land when he was 75 years old (Genesis 12:4).

It is interesting that Abraham described himself as a stranger in the land given to him by God, the place where he had lived for 62 years. The writer of Hebrews gave insight into Abraham's sojourning attitude. Abraham desired a better country, that is, a heavenly one. Therefore God is not ashamed to be called his God for He has prepared a city for him (Hebrews 11:16).

As a child of God, you should have a sojourner's attitude. Your stay on earth is temporary. You are promised an unshakeable Kingdom (Hebrews 12:28). On earth, you do not have a lasting city; you should be seeking the city that is to come (Hebrews 13:14). Your citizenship is in heaven (Philippians 3:20).

Pray Genesis 23:4 over yourself and those for whom you stand guard as a faithful, prayerful watchman (Isaiah 62:6-7).

"LORD, as strangers on this earth,
let _____ and me sojourn with You.
Help us bury the dead in our lives out of our sight,
so we can live in You.
In Your name, Jesus~"

DECEMBER 5

Please read Genesis 24.

Meditate on verse 1.

> *Now Abraham was old, advanced in age;*
> *and the LORD had blessed Abraham in every way.*

Genesis 24 is another treasure chest for praying watchmen. It contains a faith filled prayer of a faithful servant, a worship prayer immediately following God's answer to a prayer, and a prayer of blessing from family members. Notice all three and keep them in your arsenal of weapons for praying over others.

Abraham sent his most trusted servant to find a wife for Isaac from among family, so Isaac would not marry an idolatrous Canaanite woman. The servant went, praying for God to grant him success and for God to show Abraham His lovingkindness. He asked God to give him a sign to know for certain which girl was to be Isaac's wife (Genesis 24:12-14).

Before the servant finished praying, God brought Rebekah to him and made it obvious she was the girl for Isaac. In front of Rebekah's family, the servant bowed low, worshipping and blessing God for not forsaking His lovingkindness and truth and for guiding him in the way he needed to go to find Rebekah (Genesis 24:26-27).

As Rebekah prepared to leave her family to marry Isaac, her mother and brother sent her off with a prayer of blessing for her descendants to become thousands and ten thousands and for them to possess the gate of those who hate them (Genesis 24:60). What an amazing prophetic prayer of blessing that you see God fulfilling still today in the nation of Israel!

Pray Genesis 24:1, 12-14, 27-28, and 60 over yourself and those for whom you stand guard as a faithful, prayerful watchman (Isaiah 62:6-7).

"LORD, bless _____ and me in every way!
O LORD, the God of my family,
please grant us success today
and show us lovingkindness.
As we seek Your will concerning _____,
please give us Your sign to know what to do.
We bow low and worship You.
We bless You, LORD, the God of our family.
You have not forsaken Your lovingkindness
and Your truth toward us.
You have guided us in Your Way.
Continue to bless us, God.
May we possess the gate of those who hate us.
For the sake of Your name, Jesus~"

Please read Genesis 25.

Meditate on these phrases from verses 8, 18, and 34.

Abraham died satisfied with life.
Ishmael settled in defiance of all his relatives.
Esau despised his birthright.

This is an interesting chapter filled with people and their choices. Abraham spent a lifetime believing God and walking in faith. He died at the good old age of 175 satisfied with life (Genesis 25:7-8).

It was prophesied that Ishmael would be a wild donkey of a man with his hand against everyone and everyone's hand against him (Genesis 16:12). The prophecy proved to be true; "he settled in defiance to all his relatives" (Genesis 25:18).

Esau chose to sell his birthright for a bowl of "red stuff" (Genesis 25:30). God said Esau "despised his birthright" (Genesis 25:34). In Malachi 1:3, God said He hated Esau because he despised something that was his God-given right, his birthright.

Every human has been given the right, the privilege by God, to become children of God, yet many choose to forfeit that right for the world's "red stuff." They deny God and His precious offer of salvation through Jesus Christ in pursuit of self and worldly desires.

Choose wisely and pray for others to do the same.

Pray Genesis 25:8, 18, and 30 over yourself and those for whom you stand guard as a faithful, prayerful watchman (Isaiah 62:6-7). Pray verse 34 over those who despise their birthright.

"LORD, let _____ and me die at a ripe old age,
satisfied with life, and gathered to You and our people.
Do not let us, or our relatives who love You, live in defiance of You.
Do not let us sell out for a bowl of "red stuff."
Please let _____ stop despising their birthright
of a relationship with You.
In Your name, Jesus~"

Please read Genesis 26.

Meditate on this sentence from verse 28.

We see plainly that the LORD has been with you.

Isaac probably learned from his father Abraham to call his wife his sister when he feared another man might hurt him because she was pretty (Genesis 12:11-20; 20:1-18; 26:6-11). Yet, despite generational sin and lack of good judgment, God chose to bless Isaac. God said Abraham obeyed Him and kept His charge, His commandments, His statutes, and His laws (Genesis 26:5). Thankfully God is merciful to iniquities and remembers sins no more (Hebrews 8:12). He obviously chose to forget Abraham and Isaac's sins.

The remainder of the chapter tells about Isaac getting richer and richer, of people being jealous of his prosperity and trying to sabotage him, and of God moving Isaac and caring for him and his family. God renewed the covenant promises He made to Isaac's father, Abraham. He promised to be with Isaac, to bless him, and multiply his descendants. God promised Isaac these things because of His love and commitment to Abraham (Genesis 26:24).

Does your walk with God reflect a life that brings blessings to your family? Are you passing down generational sin or generational blessing because of a faithful walk with Christ? Do people "see plainly that the LORD has been with you" (Genesis 26:28)?

Pray Genesis 26:4-5 and 28 over yourself and those for whom you stand guard as a faithful, prayerful watchman (Isaiah 62:6-7).

> *"LORD, help me to obey You and keep Your charge,*
> *commandments, statutes, and laws,*
> *so my descendants will be blessed.*
> *May people plainly see*
> *that You are with _____ and me.*
> *In Your name, Jesus"*

DECEMBER 8

Please read Genesis 27.

Meditate on verse 38.

> *Esau said to his father, "Do you have only one blessing, my father?*
> *Bless me, even me also, O my father."*
> *So Esau lifted his voice and wept.*

This is a chapter about blessings. The word is used 23 times in Genesis 27. Blessings were given; they were stolen; they were begged for.

After Jacob stole Esau's blessing, Esau cried and begged for his father, Isaac, to give him some sort of blessing. Hebrews 12:15-17 gives you more insight into what happened in Genesis 27. God had the writer of Hebrews describe Esau as immoral and godless because he sold his birthright for a single meal. (Remember the "red stuff" in Genesis 25?) The birthright was tied to the blessing. Esau was rejected from receiving the blessing because he did not have the birthright. After selling his birthright he did not repent. He cried because he did not receive a blessing. He had no tears of repentance; he was upset there would be no blessing in his life. He was not upset about the sin in his life that resulted in him having no blessing.

Analyze your life. Are you crying and begging God to bless you? Have you spent any time crying and begging God to forgive your sins? Esau's refusal to repent made him immoral and godless; learn from his life and make sure you do not come short of the grace of God.

Pray Genesis 27:28 over yourself and those for whom you stand guard as you come to God in brokenness and repentance as a faithful, prayerful watchman (Isaiah 62:6-7).

> *"LORD, let _____ and me repent and turn to you.*
> *When we do, please give us the dew of heaven,*
> *the fatness of the earth, and an abundance of grain and new wine.*
> *In Your name, Jesus~"*

Please read Genesis 28.

Meditate on verse 12.

He had a dream, and behold,
a ladder was set on the earth with its top reaching to heaven;
and behold, the angels of God were
ascending and descending on it.

In Genesis 11, the people tried to build a tower to reach into heaven. In Genesis 28, Jacob dreamed about a ladder coming down from heaven to earth. The LORD stood above the ladder; angels ascended and descended on it. God spoke to Jacob and blessed him.

God came down to man. There is no amount of human effort that can reach God. God reaches down to man. He walked with Adam and Eve in the Garden of Eden; He walked with Enoch; He walked with Noah; He walked with Abraham. God walks and talks with those who have a relationship with Him.

Every other world religion is man's attempt to reach God, vain efforts to accomplish what only Christ could do. Jesus Himself said in John 1:51, "Truly, truly, I say to you, you will see the heavens opened and the angels of God ascending and descending on the Son of Man."

Jesus is the ladder in Jacob's dream! He is the only way to God, the only way to heaven. He came to earth 2,000 years ago, so you can get to God! Praise Him today for being your Way, your Truth, and your Life (John 14:6).

Pray Genesis 28:13 and 15 over yourself and those for whom you stand guard as a faithful, prayerful watchman (Isaiah 62:6-7).

"You are the LORD, the God of my family!
Be with _____ and me and keep us wherever we go.
In Your name, Jesus~"

Please read Genesis 29.

Meditate on this phrase from verse 32.

The LORD has seen my affliction.

Jacob's mother, Rebekah, sent him to stay with her brother for a few days until Esau's anger over the loss of blessing subsided. Before Jacob left home, his father, Isaac, tasked him to find a wife from among his cousins (Genesis 27:43-45; 28:1-2).

Days turned into years because Uncle Laban said Jacob could marry one of his daughters after he worked seven years for her. Jacob agreed and worked to marry Laban's beautiful younger daughter, Rachel. On the honeymoon night, Laban substituted his older, not so pretty daughter, Leah. It must have been a lively wedding celebration because Jacob was unaware he had spent the night with Leah instead of Rachel until the next morning. When questioned by Jacob, Laban replied that it wasn't the custom for the youngest to marry first, and Jacob could work an additional seven years and be married to both Leah and Rachel. Jacob agreed.

Notice Leah in Genesis 29:31-35. She was unloved by Jacob. She knew it, and most importantly, God knew it. He saw her affliction, opened her womb, and let her have four sons, Reuben, Simeon, Levi, and Judah. Judah is the tribe from whom Christ would come. God let unloved Leah be the great, great, great ... grandmother of the Messiah. You will read tomorrow in Genesis 30 that Leah had two additional sons, Issachar and Zebulun and a daughter, Dinah. God gave unloved, unwanted Leah seven children because God loved her; He wanted her to be the mother of half of the tribes of Israel and the one from whom His Son would come.

No matter your circumstances, pain, or affliction, God sees you; He hears what is happening, and He notices you. Cry out to Him, and watch for what He is doing in your life.

Pray Genesis 29:31-33 and 35 over yourself and those for whom you stand guard as a faithful, prayerful watchman (Isaiah 62:6-7).

"LORD, You see what is happening to _____ and me.
You see our affliction; You have heard about it.
Because You know, I will praise You.
For the sake of Your name, Jesus~"

DECEMBER 11

Please read Genesis 30.

Meditate on verse 22.

Then God remembered Rachel,
and God gave heed to her and opened her womb.

If anyone tells you the Bible is boring, they have not read Genesis 30! It starts with two jealous sisters competing to have the most children by the same man. They even gave their maids to their shared husband in hopes of getting more children. (The writers of daytime television could only hope to have this kind of imagination!)

The chapter also described Jacob's method of livestock management. God blessed Jacob's selective breeding of his flocks and herds and made him exceedingly prosperous. God's favor on Jacob even brought blessings to Jacob's uncle who also happened to be his father-in-law.

Incredibly, the stories you are reading in God's Word are not the figment of someone's imagination. They are historical accounts of real people with real relationships with each other and with the real God of the universe. God recorded these events to give you hope as you walk with Him.

As you live with the LORD, take encouragement from Genesis 30:22: "Then God remembered Rachel, and God gave heed to her."

In the midst of your family circumstances, ask God to remember you and pay attention to you. Pray Genesis 30:22 over yourself and those for whom you stand guard as a faithful, prayerful watchman (Isaiah 62:6-7).

LORD, remember _____ and me.
God, give heed to us
and open up _____ for us.
In Your name, Jesus~"

Please read Genesis 31.

Meditate on verse 7b.

God did not allow him to hurt me.

Jacob worked a total of 20 years for his uncle, Laban. For his service, Jacob received two wives and flocks and herds of animals. God prospered and protected Jacob during this time despite the fact Laban often tricked and deceived him. After 20 years of living with Laban, the LORD told Jacob it was time to return home (Genesis 31:3).

Jacob relayed the message from God to return to Canaan to his wives, Leah and Rachel. They submissively responded to their upcoming move to another country by saying, "Do whatever God has said to you" (Genesis 31:16).

Husbands, do you seek God's favor and blessings for your family? Is the LORD your God?

Wives, how do you respond when your husband tells you God has given him direction for your family? Do you rebel against the direction God is leading or do you reply, "Let's do whatever God has told you"?

Pray Genesis 31:7 and 16 over yourself and those for whom you stand guard as a faithful, prayerful watchman (Isaiah 62:6-7).

"LORD, do not allow the enemy to harm _____and me.
As You tell us what to do, help us to do whatever You say, God.
For the sake of Your name, Jesus-"

DECEMBER 13

Please read Genesis 32.

Meditate on verse 7a.

> *Then Jacob was greatly afraid and distressed.*

God freed Jacob from Laban, and almost immediately forced him to face an old enemy, his brother Esau. Jacob had sent messengers to let Esau know he was coming home. The messengers returned telling Jacob his brother was coming to meet him with 400 men! Jacob assumed this welcoming party did not have good intentions (recall Jacob had tricked Esau out of a birthright and a blessing), and he quickly went into panic mode. He divided his family, the women and children, into two companies and surrounded himself with them, as if they were an army. He selected 580 of his animals, his blessings from God, to be given to Esau as a peace offering before having to face him. After his acts of desperation, Jacob put in a cry to God to deliver him.

Thankfully, in the midst of acts of faithlessness, God in His faithfulness will hear a cry for His help.

As the presents were being delivered and his wives and children were sent ahead to face the enemy, Jacob was left alone to face God. It wasn't a pleasant encounter because God wrestled with Jacob all night. But even wrestling matches with God are meant for good, so you can be thankful when they come. The match ended with God blessing Jacob and giving him a new name, Israel. He indeed would be the father of God's great nation as promised to his grandfather, Abraham (Genesis 12:2). The wrestling match also ended with Jacob being humbled by God; he walked the rest of his life with the limp God inflicted. That limp would always remind Jacob to fear God and not man.

Examine your life. What or who are you afraid of? What or who are you sacrificing to protect yourself? Are you giving away blessings from God because you are responding in fear to a situation?

STOP! Take a deep breath and pray Genesis 32:10-12 over yourself and those for whom you stand guard as a faithful, prayerful watchman (Isaiah 62:6-7).

"LORD, _____ and I are unworthy of
all the lovingkindness and of all the
faithfulness which You have shown us.
Deliver us, I pray, from the hand of _____,
for we fear them, that they will come out and attack us.
Help us to trust You and Your promises, LORD.
In Your name, Jesus~"

DECEMBER 14

Please read Genesis 33.

Meditate on verse 20.

Then he erected there an altar
and called it El-Elohe-Israel.

Wrestling with God changed Jacob; so much so, God changed his name to Israel. And even though he walked with a limp, he was no longer crippled by fear of man because like his grandfather, Abraham, now he feared God (Genesis 22:12).

Jacob divided his family into 3 companies in Genesis 33, and rather than using them as human shields, he walked in front of them and led his family to meet Esau. Miraculously the reunion was joyous, and after Jacob and Esau met, they went their separate ways without animosity between them.

Jacob traveled on to Canaan, to the city of Shechem. The last time Shechem had been mentioned in the Bible was when Abraham first arrived to the land of Canaan nearly 200 years earlier (Genesis 12:6-7). When he came to Shechem, God appeared to Abraham and promised him and his descendants the land. Abraham built an altar there to the LORD. It was the first altar Abraham built in the land promised to him by God.

Shechem was also the first city where Jacob stopped after returning to the land that would someday bear his new name, Israel. In Shechem, like his grandfather Abraham had done, Jacob built an altar to God and named it El-Elohe-Israel; God, the God of Israel.

Jacob, now named Israel, acknowledged that God was his God, not just the God of his ancestors, Abraham and Isaac. God was personally his God. God had sojourned with him and wrestled with him. He had blessed him and been with him in the midst of joys and fears. He was God, the God of Israel!

What about you? Is there a time and a place where you have spiritually built an altar, a place of sacrifice, where you died to yourself and acknowledged that God is your God? If not, let today be your Shechem. If you already have, thank God for the privilege of living with Him.

Pray Genesis 33:20 over yourself and your family for whom you stand guard as a faithful, prayerful watchman (Isaiah 62:6-7).

> *"LORD, You are El-Elohe-_____.*
> *You are God, the God of _____,*
> *   the God of me and my family.*
> *Because of Your name, Jesus~"*

Please read Genesis 34.

Meditate on this phrase from verse 5.

So Jacob kept silent.

Here is another chapter in God's Word that reads like a novel, yet it is fact not fiction. These words are eternally preserved to teach you about God and life and how to do better than those who have gone before.

Many of the families in the Bible are what would be described today as dysfunctional. The root of the dysfunction was often fathers who were not present, not speaking up, and not leading their families in the way of holiness.

When Jacob heard his daughter, Dinah, was raped by Shechem, he did nothing about it; he kept silent. His silence gave Hamor, Shechem's father, time to try to convince Jacob and his sons that their family should intermarry with his idolatrous family, settle down, buy land, and live happily ever after.

Observe this chapter carefully. Jacob did not say a word until the end of the chapter! His sons did all the talking! They deceived Hamor and Shechem, convincing them they would let the marriages begin after all the men in Shechem were circumcised. The men of Shechem agreed to the plan. After every male in the city was in pain from their circumcisions, Jacob's sons, Simeon and Levi, killed them all. They and their other brothers then took the women and children and pillaged their homes.

Jacob finally, selfishly spoke out, saying: "You have brought trouble on me by making me odious among the inhabitants of the land, among the Canaanites and the Perizzites; and my men being few in number, they will gather together against me and attack me, and I will be destroyed, I and my household" (Genesis 34:30).

Jacob's sons replied that their sister should not have been treated as a harlot! Since their dad refused to do anything, they handled the situation their way.

Husbands and fathers, this chapter is for you. Protect your family! Do not hesitate to speak up on their behalf. Do not hesitate to tell your children, no matter how old they are, that they cannot go visit the "pagans" of the land (Genesis 34:1). Your children do not need to attend godless parties, watch godless movies, and play godless games. You are the head of your home. Speak up!

As a faithful, prayerful watchman (Isaiah 62:6-7), use Genesis 34:5 as a reminder to pray for the men in your life to not be silent and to lead their families in Godliness.

> *"LORD, make _____ not keep silent about You.*
> *Help him lead and protect his family!*
> *In Your name, Jesus~"*

Please read Genesis 35.

Meditate on verse 2.

> *Put away the foreign gods which are among you,*
> *and purify yourselves and change your garments.*

After Jacob's sons massacred the men of Shechem, God told Jacob to move to Bethel. Jacob obeyed, instructing his family and everyone with him to get rid of the idols among them and purify themselves. They were moving to Bethel, the place where God revealed Himself to Jacob in a dream over 20 years earlier (Genesis 28:12-13).

Thankfully Jacob did not keep his "vow of silence" from Genesis 34 or hide in shame over past foolish decisions. Genesis 35 portrays a man who led his family, instructing them to purify themselves, and teaching them about God.

What an encouraging story! Satan's lie is that you have done such a poor job as a family member there is no hope for you or your family now or in the future. With God nothing is impossible; His mercies are new every morning (Mark 10:27; Lamentations 3:23)!

No matter what you did or did not do yesterday, take a stand for righteousness today! Speak about the faithfulness of God and be a Godly leader in your family.

Pray Genesis 35:2-3 over yourself and those for whom you stand guard as a faithful, prayerful watchman (Isaiah 62:6-7).

> *"LORD, may _____ and I put away the foreign gods*
> *which are among us. Purify us, LORD!*
> *Thank You for letting us exchange our garment of sin for your robe*
> *of righteousness. Let us arise and go to Bethel, to Your house, God.*
> *God, we will make an altar to You because You have*
> *answered us in our day of distress, and You have been*
> *with us wherever we have gone.*
> *In Your name, Jesus~"*

Please read Genesis 36.

Meditate on verse 2a.

Esau took his wives from the daughters of Canaan.

Esau married daughters of Canaan. The Canaanites were idol worshippers. In defiance to his parents, Isaac and Rebekah, Esau chose to marry women who did not worship the true God, Yahweh. Esau brought their idolatrous practices into his home, and God's Word describes his wives as bringing grief to Isaac and Rebekah (Genesis 26:34-35).

If you are not yet married, choose wisely. God does not want you to marry a "Canaanite," someone who does not love and worship the only true God, Jesus Christ. If you are already married to a "Canaanite," pray for God to bring them to faith in Christ. Rahab was a Canaanite who chose to become a follower of Yahweh. She is in the genealogy of Jesus Christ (Joshua 2; Matthew 1:5; Hebrews 11:31; James 2:25). There is hope for "Canaanites" because before you became a Christian, you, too, were one.

As a faithful, prayerful watchman (Isaiah 62:6-7), use Genesis 36:2 as a reminder of how to pray for those who will someday choose their husband or wife.

"LORD, please do not let _____marry a spiritual Canaanite.
Let them marry someone who loves You
more than they love themselves
because You hate every form of idolatry.
In Your name, Jesus~"

Please read Genesis 37.

Meditate on verse 31.

So they took Joseph's tunic,
and slaughtered a male goat
and dipped the tunic in the blood.

You are in the middle of Advent season, preparing yourself for the celebration of Christ's first coming to earth over 2,000 years ago. You have observed in Genesis "Jesus sightings," where an angel of the LORD appeared to people, and it became apparent from the conversations that the "angel" was actually the LORD (Genesis 16, 22). Now you come to the story of Joseph. For the next two weeks you will read the fascinating details of this man's life. While Joseph is not Jesus, his life has interesting parallels to the life of Christ. As you read, look for ways that Joseph's story was a foreshadowing of Messiah. Consider these parallels from Genesis 37:

- Joseph was loved by his father. Jesus is beloved by His Father (Mark 1:11).

- Joseph brought a bad report about his brothers to their father; they hated him for it. When Christ came to earth, He exposed sin; the world hated Him for it (John 15:22-24).

- Joseph's brothers thought they would never bow to him. They were wrong! People in the world think they will never bow to Christ. They are wrong! Someday every knee will bow to Jesus (Philippians 2:9-11).

- Joseph was mocked by his brothers. Jesus was mocked throughout His ministry and at His crucifixion (Matthew 27:29-31).

- Joseph's brothers plotted to kill him because of envy. The people plotted to kill Jesus because of envy (Matthew 27:17-18).

- Joseph was sold for 20 pieces of silver. Jesus was sold for 30 pieces of silver (Matthew 26:15).

- Joseph was stripped of his tunic. Jesus was stripped of His robe (Matthew 27:28).

- Joseph's tunic was dipped in blood. Jesus' robe is dipped in blood (Revelation 19:13).

- Joseph was sent to Egypt. Jesus went to Egypt (Matthew 2:13-15).

God's Word is fascinating! Just imagine what the two men on their way to Emmaus thought when Jesus explained this part of the Old Testament to them (Luke 24:13-36)! Be amazed by your Savior like never before this Christmas as you read about Him in the story of Joseph.

As a faithful, prayerful watchman, use Genesis 37:8 and 16 to pray for someone who needs to be found by the LORD and needs to submit to His rule over their life.

"LORD, like Joseph was looking for his brothers,
You are searching for _____ .
Please let them submit to Your reign and authority over them.
In Your name, Jesus-"

Please read Genesis 38.

Meditate on verse 7.

> *But Er, Judah's firstborn, was evil in the sight of the LORD,*
> *so the LORD took his life.*

Joseph's life story foreshadowed the coming of Jesus Christ. Why would God include such a scandalous story in the middle of it? Observe the chapter carefully, for it also contains the Christmas story.

Genesis 38 begins with God killing two men because they were evil and displeasing to Him (vs. 7, 10). The story continues with Tamar, the wife of the dead men, tricking Judah, her father-in-law, into having a physical relationship with her. He thought she was a prostitute, so he paid to have sex with her. Amazingly, God did not kill Judah and Tamar for their wickedness. In fact, God allowed Tamar to get pregnant by Judah. She gave birth to twins and named them Perez and Zerah.

> *The record of the genealogy of Jesus the Messiah …*
> *Judah was the father of Perez and Zerah by Tamar;*
> *Perez was the father of …*
> —Matthew 1:1, 3

Genesis 38 is the graphic story about people in the lineage of Jesus! It is a chapter that is usually left out of most Advent readings. Yet, it is the reason the world needs a Christmas story. Without Christ, everyone is Er and Onan, Judah's two sons who were struck dead by God because of their sin. All deserve to die because of their evil, displeasing acts against God and man. But God extends His love, grace, and mercy to everyone, even those who deserve it the least, just like He did to Judah and Tamar. The LORD redeemed their hopeless situation, and they became the great, great, great ... grandparents of Jesus Christ.

But God, being rich in mercy,
because of His great love with which He loved us,
even when we were dead in our transgressions,
made us alive together with Christ.
By grace you have been saved.
—Ephesians 2:4-5

Pray Genesis 38:7 and 26 over someone for whom you stand guard as a faithful, prayerful watchman who needs the righteousness of Jesus Christ.

"LORD, please give _____ more time on
earth to turn from evil to You.
Make them righteous and let them stop doing what displeases You.
In Your name, Jesus~'

Please read Genesis 39.

Meditate on verse 23b.

> *The LORD was with him,*
> *and whatever he did the LORD made to prosper.*

The LORD was with Joseph is repeated four times in Genesis 39. In the midst of being sold into slavery, God was with Joseph. When Joseph had favor with his bosses, God was with him. As Joseph faced false accusations, God was with him. When Joseph was confined to jail, God was with him.

> *Behold, the virgin shall be with child and shall bear a Son,*
> *and they shall call His name "Immanuel,"*
> *which translated means, "God with us."*
> —Matthew 1:23

Jesus came to earth because He is "God with us." As a Christian, you have the Spirit of Jesus filling you. When Jesus came into your life, He came with a promise: "I will never leave you, nor will I ever forsake you" (Hebrews 13:5b).

Joseph knew Immanuel. Throughout his life, the LORD proved to Joseph that He was with him, and He was not going to leave him. The LORD was with him in prosperous times, and the LORD was with him when it appeared Joseph had favor with no one.

Jesus is your Immanuel. He is with you when times are good and when times are really bad. Your Savior is always with you; get to know Him even better this Christmas.

Pray Genesis 39:2-5 over yourself and those for whom you stand guard as a faithful, prayerful watchman (Isaiah 62:6-7).

"LORD, be with _____ and me.
As You are with us, make us successful where You have put us.
Cause everything we do to prosper.
Give us favor in the sight of our bosses;
bless them and their homes as well.
In Your name, Immanuel~

DECEMBER 21

Please read Genesis 40.

Meditate on verse 23.

> *Yet the chief cupbearer did not remember Joseph,*
> *but forgot him.*

Notice the time phrases in Genesis 40. "Then it came about after these things … (v.1)" "When Joseph came to them in the morning … (v. 6)." "Thus it came about on the third day … (v. 20)."

"Timing is everything" is certainly true in Genesis 40. The cupbearer and baker had to offend Pharaoh after Joseph was put in jail, so Joseph could be in jail with them the morning after they had disturbing dreams, so he could interpret their dreams, so three days later they could—forget about Joseph!

Does God's timing ever make you want to scream? The cupbearer forgot Joseph! How was that even possible? It happened because it was not time for the cupbearer to remember Joseph. God had much bigger plans for Joseph's life than just whisking him out of prison and back home to daddy. In God's timing, Joseph will …

Well, you will get to read another time phrase tomorrow. Until then, ponder this:

> *While they were there,*
> *the days were completed for her to give birth.*
> —Luke 2:6

Approximately 730,000 days were completed from the time of God's first promise to Abraham of Messiah (Genesis 12:3) until Jesus was born. The Old Testament faithful believed God would keep His promise of Messiah (Hebrews 11). God kept His promise; Jesus was born when God's fullness of time came (Galatians 4:4).

Do you feel forgotten? Have you felt forgotten for quite some time now? Be encouraged by God's planning and God's timing. Joseph had to be in prison at the perfect time for a certain number of days for God's plan to work. Jesus had to come to earth in the full, completed timing of God for God's plan to work.

As a faithful, prayerful watchman use Genesis 40:23 to pray over those who feel forgotten.

> *"LORD, _____ feels forgotten.*
> *They think no one remembers them.*
> *Let them know that You and I remember them.*
> *In Your name, Jesus~"*

Call that person today and tell them you are praying for them. If possible, spend time with them this Christmas.

Please read Genesis 41.

Meditate on verses 16b, 25b, 32b, and 39.

It is not in me; God will give Pharaoh a favorable answer.
God has told to Pharaoh what He is about to do.
The matter is determined by God, and
God will quickly bring it about.
So Pharoah said to Joseph, "Since God has informed you of all this,
there is no one so discerning and wise as you are.

Now it happened at the end of two full years
that Pharaoh had a dream …
—Genesis 41:1

Joseph, forgotten by Pharaoh's cupbearer, remained in prison for two more full years. He was enslaved and in jail for a total of 13 years (Genesis 37:2; 41:46).

Joseph was betrayed by his brothers, falsely accused by others, and forgotten by those who should have remembered. Yet Joseph never forgot God, and God remembered Joseph. God vindicated him when the time was perfect.

The cupbearer finally remembered to tell Pharaoh about Joseph. He was hurriedly brought out of the dungeon to meet the most powerful man in the world. Imagine Joseph being able to shave himself and change his clothes after being in a dungeon! Joseph answered Pharaoh with clarity of mind that God would give the answer to Pharaoh's puzzling dreams. He did not self-promote (Genesis 41:9-16)!

Throughout the chapter, Joseph continued to give God glory, which caused Pharaoh to give God glory, which pleased God. God then caused Pharaoh to put Joseph in charge of the entire land of Egypt

(Genesis 41:39-43). After waiting on God for 13 years, in one day Joseph went from a dungeon to being in control of the most powerful country in the world!

Be encouraged by the Word of God. Glorify God no matter what is happening to you.

Do not let bitterness or depression control you; it will blind you to God's work in your life. God determines the matters of your life, and He will quickly bring them about (Genesis 41:32). Be ready!

Pray Genesis 41:32 and 39 over yourself and those for whom you stand guard as a faithful, prayerful watchman (Isaiah 62:6-7).

> *"LORD, please determine this*
> *matter for _____ and me.*
> *Quickly bring it about. Inform us, God.*
> *Make us wise and discerning.*
> *For the glory of Your name, Jesus~"*

Please read Genesis 42.

Meditate on this phrase from verse 19.

Confined in your prison ...

The last time Joseph's brothers saw and heard him was over 20 years ago. They had thrown him into a pit then sat down to eat a meal. Their dinner music that day was a young Joseph crying and pleading in his distress (Genesis 37:23-25; 42:21).

They spent the next 20 years living a lie. They told their father, Jacob, a wild animal killed Joseph. The truth was they sold him to some Ishmaelites (Genesis 37:28). The truth had never been told, and Jacob still mourned for his beloved son.

Now more than 20 years later, they saw and heard Joseph, the boy they had been seeing and hearing in their memories every time they looked into their grieving father's eyes. They did not recognize him yet as Joseph their brother.

They lived in an emotional prison; now Joseph also put them in a physical one. After three days, he released all but Simeon and sent the remaining nine to go home and bring the young brother they had spoken of back to Joseph. (Benjamin is described as a little child and a lad in Genesis 44:20-22. Genesis 42 is probably the first time Joseph knew he had a younger brother.)

They returned to Canaan and told their father what happened in Egypt. After hearing their story, Jacob made a statement revealing he had known all along these older brothers were behind Joseph's disappearance, "You have bereaved me of my children; Joseph is no more, and Simeon is no more, and you would take Benjamin ..." (Genesis 42:36).

Think about your life and the lives of those you influence. Are you in a spiritual prison? Have you put others into spiritual and emotional prisons? Are you in a prison of unforgiveness and bitterness? Does your anger, selfishness, or jealousy put those around you into prisons of fear and insecurity? Are lies keeping all of you in prisons of mistrust and deception?

The best present you could give this Christmas is freedom from the prisons created by past sins. Ask God for forgiveness, ask others to forgive you, and forgive others like Jesus forgives you.

Pray Genesis 42:19 over yourself and those for whom you stand guard as a faithful, prayerful watchman (Isaiah 62:6-7).

> *"LORD, _____ and I are confined in our prisons.*
> *Help us go and carry grain for the spiritual*
> *famine that has been in our households.*
> *In Your name, Jesus~"*

Please read Genesis 43.

Meditate on these verses.

> *When Joseph came home,*
> *they brought into the house to him the present*
> *which was in their hand and bowed to the ground before him.*
> —Genesis 43:26

> *After coming into the house they saw the*
> *Child with Mary His mother;*
> *and they fell to the ground and worshipped Him.*
> *Then opening their treasure,*
> *they presented to Him gifts of gold, frankincense, and myrrh.*
> —Matthew 2:11

Cleopas and his friend on the road to Emmaus with Jesus must have smiled when Christ explained this part of Genesis to them (Luke 24:18, 27). The brothers bringing presents and bowing to Joseph foreshadowed the wise men coming to worship Christ.

Every part of the Bible is perfectly written by God Himself in order to reveal Himself as Jesus Christ, the only Way, the only Truth, and the only Life. Jesus explained Himself as revealed in ALL the Old Testament Scriptures (Luke 24:27). Philip began with the Old Testament passage the Ethiopian was reading and preached Jesus (Acts 8:35). Paul reasoned with people from the Old Testament Scriptures explaining and giving evidence that Jesus is the Messiah (Acts 17:2-3).

If you are not already a studier of the Bible, the entire Bible, I hope this year long treasure hunt of God's Word has given you a hunger to dig deeper and know God's Word better. Knowing Jesus through the revelation of Himself on every page of the Bible will make you a wise person. In that God-given wisdom, you, too, will bow before your Savior giving Him the gift of your life.

Merry Christmas! Worship your Immanuel, God with us!

Pray Genesis 43:26 over yourself and those for whom you stand guard as a faithful, prayerful watchman.

"LORD, I give You everything I am holding in my hand.
Please let _____ do the same.
I bow before You, Jesus, today and for the rest of eternity.
Because of Your name, Jesus~"

Please read Genesis 44.

Meditate on verse 16.

> *So Judah said, "What can we say to my lord?*
> *What can we speak? And how can we justify ourselves?*
> *God has found out the iniquity of your servants;*
> *behold, we are my lord's slaves,*
> *both we and the one in whose possession the cup has been found."*

Recall Judah devised the plan to sell Joseph into slavery and lie that an animal killed him (Genesis 37:26). Judah slept with his daughter-in-law, Tamar, thinking she was a prostitute. She and Judah became the parents of twin sons (Genesis 38). Time changed Judah and over the course of twenty-two years, Judah became a different man. He promised his father to protect Benjamin with his life when Benjamin went to Egypt (Genesis 43:8-9). When Joseph's silver cup was discovered in Benjamin's sack of grain, Judah begged Joseph to let him take the punishment for Benjamin's apparent crime. Judah was willing to give his life for his brother.

This sacrificial act on the part of Judah, brought the Joseph story to its climax, (Joseph revealed his true identity in Genesis 45:1), and it sealed Judah's place in history for the coming of Messiah. The Judah of Genesis 44 is a picture of Jesus Christ. He was willing to be the substitutionary sacrifice for the life of Benjamin. He was the lion protecting his little brother. He is the father of the tribe from which King David and Jesus descended (Luke 2:1-7; 3:31-33).

> *Behold, the Lion that is from the tribe of Judah,*
> *the Root of David, has overcome so as to*
> *open the book and its seven seals.*

And I saw between the throne (with the four
living creatures) and the elders
a Lamb standing, as if slain ...
—Revelation 5:5-6

The baby you celebrate today is the Lion of Judah, the Lamb of God who takes away the sin of the world (John 1:29)!

As a faithful, prayerful watchman (Isaiah 62:6-7), pray Genesis 44:16 as a prayer of confession to your LORD.

"What can I say, my LORD? What can I
speak? How can I justify myself?
You know my iniquities. Behold, I am Your bond-slave.
You give me Your cup of salvation.
Thank You, Lion of Judah, Lamb of God.
In Your name, Jesus-"

Please read Genesis 45.

Meditate on this phrase from verse 8.

It was not you who sent me here, but God ...

Joseph saw life from God's perspective. God used the evil done by his brothers to get Joseph where He needed him. Joseph chose not to be jaded by 22 years of family separation. He saw clearly and stated with confidence, "God sent me before you to preserve life" (Genesis 45:5).

Joseph's forgiving response of "do not be grieved or angry with yourselves" (Genesis 45:5) foreshadowed the forgiveness Christ extends to you. God sent Christ to the cross to preserve your life. With His forgiveness comes His provision and promise to be near you and take care of you (Genesis 45:10-11).

What a glorious gift from God! With God's forgiveness, provision, and protection, comes the ability for you to have a Joseph perspective on life. No matter where you are or how you got there, God wants you to see with His eyes. God put you where you are, and He has a purpose for you being there. God has sent you to preserve life. As you choose to live for Jesus Christ and others, ask God how you can preserve and protect the people God has given you.

As a faithful, prayerful watchman (Isaiah 62:6-7), you are protecting those God wants you to guard. Pray Genesis 45:7 over them.

"LORD, make _____ to be a remnant in the earth for You.
Keep them alive by Your great deliverance.
For the sake of Your name, Jesus~"

Please read Genesis 46.

Meditate on verse 1.

> *So Israel set out with all that he had, and came to Beersheba,*
> *and offered sacrifices to the God of his father Isaac.*

Israel (Jacob) had not seen his beloved Joseph for 22 years. Jacob thought he was dead, but miraculously, after 22 years, Jacob was told Joseph was alive. He would see his precious son. As he traveled to be reunited with Joseph, Jacob made a stop. When he came to Beersheba, the place where his grandfather Abraham had called on the name of the LORD, the Everlasting God, and where Jacob had grown up, he stopped and offered sacrifices to God (Genesis 21:33; 28:10).

Jacob worshipped God first! Following the pattern of his grandfather Abraham, worshipping God took precedence over his son (Genesis 22). God honored Jacob's sacrifice of time, and He spoke these words to him:

> *"I am God, the God of your father; do not*
> *be afraid to go down to Egypt,*
> *for I will make you a great nation there.*
> *I will go down with you to Egypt, and I*
> *will also surely bring you up again;*
> *and Joseph will close your eyes."*
> —Genesis 46:3-4

These were words from the Everlasting God to an old man taking a long journey with his family of 66 people to a land that was not theirs. The words of the prophecy made to his grandfather 213 years earlier must have been in the back of his mind:

Know for certain that your descendants will be
strangers in a land that is not theirs,
where they will be enslaved and oppressed four hundred years.
—Genesis 15:13

Would this journey be the beginning of the fulfillment of that prophecy? Jacob needed to spend time with his God. God knew his fears; His were the words Jacob needed to hear.

Where are you about to journey? Whether it is to the other side of the world or to your place of work, stop and worship God. Hear the words He wants to whisper into your ears today.

Pray Genesis 46:2 in response to God as you hear Him call your name.

"LORD, I hear you calling me.
' _____ , _____ . '
Here I am, LORD."

Please read Genesis 47.

Meditate on verse 31b.

> *Then Israel bowed in worship at the head of the bed.*

Genesis 46 records Israel (Jacob) worshipping God before he journeyed to Egypt to be with Joseph. By the end of Genesis 47, Jacob was seventeen years older and about to die. The chapter ends with Jacob bowed in worship. Jacob described his 130 years of life as unpleasant (v. 9). Yet, despite the unpleasantness, Jacob worshipped God.

Genesis 47 also portrays a respectful son. Joseph was the second most powerful man in the world. His wisdom and management skills saved the people from death during the famine and amassed all the money, livestock, and land in Egypt and Canaan for Pharaoh (vs. 13-20). Yet when an old man called for him, Joseph went to his father and swore to do everything as he said.

God's command to honor your father and mother does not come with an age clause, but it does come with a promise: "that your days may be prolonged in the land which the LORD your God gives you" (Exodus 20:12).

No matter how young or old you are, God commands you to honor your parents. If you have children, they are learning how to treat you by the way they see you treat their grandparents. Learn from God's Word how to honor your parents.

Pray Genesis 47:29-31 over yourself and those for whom you stand guard as a faithful, prayerful watchman (Isaiah 62:6-7).

> *"LORD, may _____ and I deal with our*
> *parents in kindness and faithfulness.*
> *Let us honor their requests, even in respect*
> *to where they will be buried.*
> *May we find favor in Your sight, LORD,*
> *as we bow in worship of You by the way we treat our parents.*
> *In Your name, Jesus-"*

DECEMBER 29

Please read Genesis 48.

Meditate on verse 15b.

The God who has been my Shepherd all my life to this day ...

Israel (Jacob) was about to die. He called for Joseph to come to his deathbed and bring his sons, Ephraim and Manasseh with him. Joseph, came at his father's bidding and humbly bowed before him. Israel adopted these two sons of Joseph and gave them an inheritance in the land of Israel, along with Joseph's brothers; thus, giving Joseph a double portion of Israel's inheritance (Genesis 48:5, 22).

As Israel blessed Joseph and his sons, he gave his testimony: God Almighty appeared to him and blessed him and had been his Shepherd all of his life (Genesis 48:3, 15).

Recall some of the events of Israel's life. He fled to another country because his mother was afraid his brother would kill him (Genesis 27:41-45). He worked 20 years for a deceptive uncle (Genesis 29-31). His favorite son, Joseph, was sold into slavery, and for 22 years Israel thought he was dead (Genesis 37). Jacob's beloved wife, Rachel, died in childbirth (Genesis 36:16-20).

Jacob's faith in God Almighty caused him to be able to say God was the Shepherd of his life in the good times and the bad.

Is that your testimony? Pray Genesis 48:3 and 15 over yourself and those for whom you stand guard as a faithful, prayerful watchman (Isaiah 62:6-7).

"God Almighty, appear to _____ and me and bless us.
Let us walk with You. You have been our
Shepherd all of our lives to this day.
Because of Your name, Jesus~"

Please read Genesis 49.

Meditate on verse 28b.

He blessed them,
every one with the blessing appropriate to him.

Before Jacob died, he called his twelve sons to him to give them individual blessings. Five of the brothers' blessings are noteworthy.

Reuben, the firstborn, should have received the greatest blessings. He forfeited those blessings because of immorality (Genesis 35:22).

Simeon and Levi were cursed rather than blessed because of their violence, self-will, anger, and wrath (Genesis 34:25-30).

Judah was blessed. He was described as a lion, and the scepter would never be taken from his family. Jesus Christ, the Lion of Judah, is descended from this son of Israel (Revelation 5:5). Despite Judah's immoral, violent, and self-willed past, he was blessed because he repented and became a man of God (Genesis 37-38; 44).

Joseph was blessed with abundant, surpassing blessings from God Almighty because in the midst of attacks and affliction, he bore the fruit of righteousness. He entrusted himself to the hands of the Mighty One (Genesis 37-48). In the middle of Jacob pronouncing blessing on Joseph, he prophesied Jesus' coming: "From the hands of the Mighty One of Jacob (from there is the Shepherd, the Stone of Israel)" (Genesis 49:24b).

Which son are you? Have you robbed yourself and your family of God's blessings because of sin in your life? Is your life marked by immorality, violence, self-will, anger, and wrath? If so, do not let your story end as a Reuben, Simeon, or Levi. Become a Judah! Repent and become a person of God! Act like Joseph! No matter the circumstances, entrust yourself to the hands of the Mighty One. Live a fruitful life for the LORD.

Pray Genesis 49:22 and 24-25 over yourself and those for whom you stand guard as a faithful, prayerful watchman (Isaiah 62:6-7).

"God Almighty, help and bless _____ and me.
Bless us with the blessings of heaven above
and the deep that lies beneath.
Make us a fruitful bough, a fruitful bough by a spring;
let our branches run over a wall.
In Your name Shepherd, the Stone of
Israel, Jesus Christ our LORD~"

Please read Genesis 50.

Meditate on this sentence from verse 17.

> *Please forgive, I beg you,*
> *the transgression of your brothers and their*
> *sin, for they did you wrong.*
> *And now, please forgive the transgression of*
> *the servants of the God of your father.*

After their father Jacob died, Joseph's brothers feared retaliation from Joseph. They sent a message to him saying their father asked, before he died, for Joseph to forgive them their sins. The message was delivered; then the brothers themselves asked Joseph to forgive them. Interestingly, Genesis 50:17 is the first time God recorded the brothers actually asking Joseph for forgiveness. The brothers sold Joseph into slavery 39 years before this act of contrition; they had lived with Joseph in Egypt for the past 17 years. Joseph cried when his brothers asked him to forgive them.

Joseph forgave his brothers. He reminded them God had used their evil for good. He told them not to be afraid; he would provide for them and their little ones. "He comforted them and spoke kindly to them" (Genesis 50:21).

Today you celebrate the end of a year and the start of something new. Spend this day asking God to forgive you of sins from this past year. Perhaps you even have sins from 39 years ago that you need to confess. Is there somebody you need to call or go see and ask their forgiveness? Is there somebody who needs you to forgive them and who needs you to stop withholding comfort and kindness to them? End this year humbly before your God ready to receive His blessings for the new year.

Pray Genesis 50:17 and 20-21 over yourself and those for whom you stand guard as a faithful, prayerful watchman (Isaiah 62:6-7).

"God, my Father, please forgive my transgressions.
Help me to forgive the transgression
and sin of _____ ;
even though they did me wrong.
God, use for good what was meant for evil.
Let them not be afraid of me.
Help me provide for them and their little ones.
Help me comfort them and speak kindly to them.
In Your name, Jesus~"

H

Holiness

3-Jan
10-Jan
26-Feb
29 Feb
12-Mar
20-Apr
12-May
8-Jun
9-Jul
13-Jul
14-Jul
1-Aug
10-Aug
17-Aug
18-Aug
24-Aug
25-Aug
15-Sep
21-Sep
25-Sep
11-Oct
21-Oct
16-Dec

Humility

16-Jan
19-Jan
25-Feb
4-Mar
27-Mar
2-Apr
27-May
20-Apr
29-Apr
13-Sep

I

Integrity

1-Feb	7-Aug
19-Feb	16-Aug
19-May	8-Sep
23-May	22-Sep
22-Jun	9-Oct
25-Jun	16-Oct
3-Jul	18-Oct
8-Jul	27-Oct
20-Jul	
28-Jul	

L

Love

24-Jun
29-Jun
2-Jul
12-Aug
27-Aug
18-Sep
4-Oct

M

Marriage

5-May
31-May
9-Aug
25-Aug
4-Oct
12-Nov
17-Dec

O

Obedience

7-Jan	20-Aug
8-Jan	21-Aug
9-Jan	23-Aug
4-Feb	10-Sep
6-Feb	28-Sep
11-Feb	8-Nov
24-Mar	9-Nov
16-Jun	2-Dec
6-Jul	7-Dec

P

Parenting

22-May
25-Aug
29-Sep
2-Nov
3-Nov
17-Nov
15-Dec

Protection

10-Mar
14-Mar
1-Apr
27-Sep
17-Oct
24-Oct
30-Nov
9-Dec
10-Dec
12-Dec

Peace

2-Jan
17-May
14-Jun
15-Jul
4-Aug

Praise/Worship

6-Mar
6-Apr
28-Aug
26-Oct

R

Repentance

5-Jan
29-Jan
3-Feb
9-Mar
25-Mar
2-Jun
21-Jun
5-Sep
22-Sep
1-Oct
6-Oct
7-Oct
13-Oct
8-Dec

Salvation

4-Jan
21-Jan
9-Feb
10-Feb
13-Feb
14-Feb
21-Feb
3-Mar
19-Mar
28-Mar
29-Mar
8-Apr
10-Apr
23-Apr
28-Apr
1-Jun
4-Jun
10-Jun
13-Jun
16-Jul
18-Jul
19-Jul
15-Aug
3-Sep
14-Sep
8-Oct
12-Oct
14-Oct
30-Oct
19-Nov
29-Nov
19-Dec

Spiritual Growth

11-Jan
2-Feb
23-Mar
26-Mar
9-Apr
13-Apr
5-Jun
17-Jun
19-Jun
27-Jun
30-Jun
25-Jul
31-Jul
31-Aug
1-Sep
16-Sep
20-Sep
24-Sep
26-Sep
4-Dec

MEET DR. RON HARVELL

D r. Ron Harvell is a colonel serving in the United States Air Force where he is responsible for ministry to all Air Force personnel stationed in the Middle East.

A Senior Ministry Professional, Ron is successful at building and leading high-performance ministry teams in extremely diverse and demanding environments. He is an award-winning church growth pastor in both civilian and military organizations and a visionary leader serving God in His transformation of individuals, communities, and institutions.

Ron places a high value on training and education and has devoted himself to the disciplines of study, earning a BA from Hardin-Simmons University, a Master of Divinity from Southwestern Baptist Theological Seminary, and a Doctor of Ministry from Asia Graduate School of Theology with a focus in Transformational Leadership for the Global City. He also has a Master of Science in National Security Strategy from the National Defense University and a Master of Arts in Organizational Management from George Washington University. Above all, Ron values the study of God's Word.

Ron felt called to ministry when he was 17 years old. After being licensed to the Gospel Ministry by Circle Drive Baptist Church in

Colorado Springs, he attended college where he met and married Marsha (1984). In June of 1985, he was ordained by Friendship Baptist Church in Weatherford, Texas. Following seminary, he pastored Northside Baptist Church in Kermit, Texas. Since 1991, Marsha and Ron have lived in 12 locations around the world serving as commissioned missionaries by the North American Mission Board to the Air Force Active Duty Chaplain Corps.

Ron and Marsha have been married over thirty years and have two grown children, Stephanie (married to Jonathan) and Steven (married to Rachel), who also serve the LORD. They have three grandchildren: Nathan, Adilynn, and Kik.

LEARN MORE

To learn more about Ron and Marsha or to access their FREE daily devotional for how to pray Scripture for your family, visit:

WWW.GODSGREATERGRACE.COM

Meet Marsha Harvell

Marsha Harvell has a passion for the LORD and treasures His Word. She has led more than 100 Bible studies and is an international trainer for Precept Ministries, teaching people how to study the Bible and lead Bible studies. She has dedicated her life to helping others discover the promises found in Scripture. This commitment to know the riches of God's Word and activate the power available to believers when they pray Scripture over themselves and their loved ones, led her to create a devotional from her daily practice.

With a Bachelors in Education from Hardin-Simmons University and a Masters in Gifted and Talented Education from Texas Women's University, Marsha Harvell is an accomplished woman who has taught in both public and private schools. She has helped plant churches, served as a worship leader, and even as a women's ministry director.

Currently she serves in the Middle East with her husband, Ron (married in 1984), as a missionary to the military as a chaplain's wife, appointed by the North American Mission Board (1991).

A gifted conference speaker, some of her favorite topics include: The Covenant Maker, Godly Relationships, Being a Godly Wife and Mother, Hearing and Heeding God, Being Complete in Christ, Knowing God, and more.

She is the author of *The Covenant Maker: Knowing God and His Promises for Salvation and Marriage* and co-author of *The Watchman: on the Wall: Daily Devotions for Praying God's Word Over Those You Love.*

Marsha and Ron have been married over thirty years and have two grown children, Stephanie (married to Jonathan) and Steven (married to Rachel), who also serve the LORD. They have three grandchildren: Nathan, Adilynn, and Kik.

INVITE MARSHA

To book Marsha Harvell to speak at your conference or retreat, send an email to: *marsha@marshaharvell.com*

LEARN MORE

To learn more about Marsha or to access her FREE daily devotional for how to pray Scripture for your family, like her on Facebook or visit:

WWW.MARSHAHARVELL.COM

or

WWW.GODSGREATERGRACE.COM